Developing Teaching Skills in the Primary School

Jane Johnston, John Halocha and Mark Chater

Open University Press

Open University Press
McGraw-Hill Education
McGraw-Hill House
Shoppenhangers Road
Maidenhead
Berkshire
England
SL6 2QL

email: enquiries@openup.co.uk
world wide web: www.openup.co.uk

and Two Penn Plaza, New York, NY 1012–2289, USA

First published 2007

A catalogue record of this book is available from the British Library

ISBN-13: 978 0335 22096 0 (pb)   978 0-335 22095 3 (hb)
ISBN-10: 0 335 22096 7 (pb)   0 335 22095 9 (hb)

Library of Congress Cataloging-in-Publication Data
CIP data has been applied for

Typeset by BookEns Ltd, Royston, Herts.
Printed and bound in Poland by OZGraf. S.A.
www.polskabook.pl

The McGraw·Hill Companies

Contents

Figures and Pictures

Figures

Pictures

Acknowledgements

The authors would like to acknowledge the contributions made to this book by all the teachers, student teachers, academics and children with whom we have worked. In particular we would like to thank the following who have made specific contributions in the chapters and responded in such a positive way to our badgering:

Kate Adams, Bishop Grosseteste University College Lincoln
Ashley Compton, Bishop Grosseteste University College Lincoln
Jane Cox, Early Years Teacher, Lincolnshire
Helen Fielding, Bishop Grosseteste University College Lincoln
Denise Gudgin, Bishop Grosseteste University College Lincoln
Karen Harding, SENCO and class teacher, St. David's Primary, Moreton-in-Marsh, Gloucestershire.
Chris Johnston, St Mary Magdalene Primary School, Sutton-in Ashfield, Nottinghamshire
Catherine Maynard Clark, Bishop Grosseteste University College Lincoln
Vanessa Richards, Primary Music Consultant in Lincolnshire and Leicestershire
Bia Sena, Foundation Stage Coordinator, The British School, Rio de Janeiro
Claire Taylor, Bishop Grosseteste University College Lincoln
Niki Whitburn, Bishop Grosseteste University College Lincoln
Richard Woolley, Bishop Grosseteste University College Lincoln

Abbreviations

AfL	assessment for learning
CPD	continuing professional development
DES	Department of Education and Science
DfEE	Department for Education and Employment
DfES	Department for Education and Skills
DT	design and technology
EYP	early years professional
IBP	individual behaviour plan
ICT	information and communication technology
IEP	Individual Education Plan
ISP	Intensifying Support Programme
LA	local authority
NCSL	National College of School Leadership
Ofsted	Office for Standards in Education
PCK	pedagogical content knowledge
PPA	planning, preparation and assessment
PSHE	personal, social and health education
QCA	Qualifications and Curriculum Authority
QTS	qualified teacher status
SAT	standard assessment task
SENCO	special educational needs coordinator
SIP	School Improvement Plan
TA	teaching assistant
zpd	zone of proximal development

1

Developing Teaching
Skills in the Primary
School

Jane Johnston

Introduction

Teaching is a skill that is best developed over time. Like all skills, teaching should be developed through practice underpinned by theory, research and reflection, which is why teacher training (or 'education' as I prefer), is very specific about the need for both trainees and practising teachers to reflect on and practise their developing skills. There are three components to teaching, identified in the skills tests for qualified teacher status (QTS) and professional standards:

- Content knowledge, or the knowledge of different subjects taught in primary school, both the core and foundation subjects and other subjects and issues, such as religious education (RE) and citizenship (see Johnston *et al.* 2002).
- Pedagogical knowledge or the knowledge and skills about teaching.
- Pedagogical content knowledge (PCK) (Shulman 1987) or the knowledge and skills of teaching specific to a subject such as knowledge of strategies, ways of representing the subject, common pupil conceptions and learning difficulties.

Pedagogical knowledge and skills

This book is concerned with the second of these, pedagogical knowledge and skills, although examples in the chapters aim to highlight commonalities, such as differentiation, planning and assessment as well as PCK differences within subjects, such as different questioning or assessment techniques and the development of investigative and thinking skills. Teaching is a complex process which involves the development and utilization of knowledge, skills and attitudes. There has been much emphasis in recent years on developing teachers' knowledge and skills, particularly through the development of national standards (DfEE 1998; TTA 2002; TDA 2007), although the description of these and how they can be developed is vague, and how they can impact on the learning of pupils is not clearly identified. Further, the subtle differences in pedagogy in different subject areas is not well documented, thus causing confusion for primary student teachers and teachers who are attempting to support learning in a number of subject areas. However, all subjects and phases require teachers who are reflective practitioners (see Chapter 14, Developing as a Reflective Practitioner), and who operate in a professional manner, communicating and working together in a reflective way (see Chapter 13, Professional Communication). Reflective practitioners plan creative activities for individual learners (see particularly Chapter 2, Planning for Creative Teaching), teach to support individual learning (see particularly Chapter 7, Differentiation) and review both teaching and learning to enable them to plan the next stage of learning for the children in their care (see particularly Chapter 11, Assessment for Learning). This plan–do–review format is reflected in the structure of the book, which is divided into three parts:

- **Part 1**, Planning, contains chapters on creative planning skills, such as planning for organization, citizenship and behaviour management.
- **Part 2**, Doing, contains chapters on the practical skills of teaching, such as questioning, differentiating, using ICT in teaching, recording children's work and supporting investigations.
- **Part 3**, Reviewing, contains support for the reflective practitioner on assessment for learning, target setting, professional communication and how reflective practice develops.

Contemporary issues in primary education

There are a number of contemporary issues or new ideas and initiatives to support teaching and learning, and reflective practitioners take these into consideration when teaching. For example, over the past 20 years there has been research into constructivist learning, where children develop understandings and thinking skills through social interaction and experience, constructing their own meaning, including alternative conceptions, from experiences and learning. Learning is viewed as an active and continuous process whereby children construct links with their prior knowledge, generating new ideas, checking and restructuring old ideas or hypotheses. As a result, teaching is more about facilitating this learning through the skills of planning, questioning, differentiating, assessing and all the pedagogical skills this book explores. Constructivist teaching builds on the work of Piaget (1929) and Vygotsky (1978) and underpins cognitive acceleration (Shayer and Adey 2002). There is no common agreement about what cognitive acceleration is, with some believing it is about:

- supporting cognition by removing artificial obstacles in the development of gifted and talented children;
- advancing cognition through practices, such as meditation and brain gym (Dennison and Dennison 1994);
- accelerating and supporting the cognition of all.

What we do know is that cognitive acceleration does seem to support teaching and learning probably because children are being stimulated and involved in their own learning and developing their thinking skills (see Chapter 10, Developing Investigative Work / Enquiry).

Recently, creativity has been another theme in primary education and it is advocated by both government (DfES 2003a; QCA 2003) and educators (Beetlestone 1998; Craft 2002; Wilson 2005). Like cognitive acceleration the definition of creativity is vague, has different meaning to different groups or individuals and means different things in different subjects. In Chapter 2, Planning for Creative Teaching, we propose a definition of creativity (Compton 2005), which is all-encompassing (see Figure 2.1 in Chapter 2, Compton's continuum of creativity) and aims to support teachers in becoming creative. After all, creativity is an essential element of a developing society, and creative adults develop from creative children and creative children require creative teachers. One aspect of creative teaching is the popular idea of differentiating teaching to accommodate different learners and their different styles of learning (see Chapter 7, Differentiation). Differentiated learning requires child-centred teaching (see Chapter 12, Target Setting) and assessing (see Chapter 11, Assessment for Learning). Both learning theories and assessment for learning are popular themes in education and form the basis of much discussion. Learning theories often divide learners into three groups (visual, auditory and kinaesthetic learning; Dryden and Vos 1999), although some (Johnston 1996) identify four ways in which learners process information, and others multiple abilities or intelligences (Gardner 1983). Again there is no common agreement about what learning styles are and little research evidence of their impact on learning (Coffield *et al*. 2004). In particular we know that primary children learn best through enquiry (see Chapter 10, Developing Investigative Work / Enquiry), but there is little understanding of what kinaesthetic learning is and how we should use it (see Chapter 7, Differentiation).

Child-centred education is once again facing a re-emergence, with the publication of *Every Child Matters* (DfES 2003b) which identifies five outcomes for every child:

- to be healthy
- to stay safe
- to enjoy and achieve
- to make a positive contribution
- to achieve economic well-being.

This balances the focus of education, which for many years has been on the cognitive but now recognizes the importance of social and emotional development and the health of children. Children's cognitive development is affected by their physical, social and emotional development, and this fact is recognized by the introduction of Sure Start, early excellence centres, extended school, wrap-around care, healthy school meals and physical exercise. Multi-agency settings are providing breakfast, after-school care, and educational (nurseries, speech therapy), social services (social workers, behaviour therapists) and health facilities (doctors, dentists, physiotherapy). Generally these initiatives are welcomed, but there is a tension between teachers who have educational targets to meet and do not understand how to implement the initiatives and the government, which advocates the underpinning philosophy but has no evidence that the initiatives will work.

The book and how to use it

The book has been designed to support those teaching from their initial teacher training through to their leadership and support teachers in their schools and settings. It does this by:

- developing deeper understanding of the entire range of skills of teaching;
- supporting the analysis of pedagogical skills in primary education, focusing particularly on generic teaching skills;
- supporting the development of pedagogical skills and professional reflectiveness in teachers;
- supporting teachers in the effective delivery of the curriculum.

The book contains easily accessible yet rigorous support for the development of pedagogical knowledge and skills, through critical analysis of issues, practice and problems. Most importantly, it emphasizes the child as a partner in the learning process and the importance of teaching for child-centred learning which gives ownership and responsibility for learning with the child.

The authors and contributors to the book come from a range of educational backgrounds (schools, consultancies and higher education) and are at different stages of their careers (students, teachers, headteachers, consultants and education-alists). As such, the book is a collaboration between educators and practitioners with a wealth of experience and expertise in teaching, and builds upon the strengths of all. The chapters identify what are the skills of teaching and how they can be developed. Research, cameos and case study examples are provided which show how teaching skills can be utilized in practice and how they can be modified for different contexts and subjects. In each chapter there are also reflective and practical tasks which aim to support training and practising teachers as well as teacher-researchers looking more deeply into teaching and learning. Each task is at three levels. Level 1 is for the student teacher or beginner practitioner; Level 2 is aimed at the classroom teacher; and Level 3 at experienced or lead practitioners. When undertaking these tasks, readers should choose a level that is appropriate to their stage of development and experience. In this way the book will, it is hoped, support analysis of pedagogical practice in schools through the reflective and analytical tasks and through examples of practice / cameos which link theory and practice.

References

Beetlestone, F. (1998) *Creative Children, Imaginative Teaching.* Buckingham: Open University Press.

Coffield, F., Moseley, D., Hall, E. and Ecclestone, K. (2004) *Should we be using Learning Styles? What Research has to say to Practice.* London: Learning and Skills Development Agency.

Compton, A. (2005) What is creativity? Unpublished EdD thesis, University of Leicester.

Craft, A. (2002) *Creativity and Early Years Education: A Lifeworld Foundation.* London: Continuum.

Dennison, P. and Dennison, G. (1994) *Brain Gym.* Ventura, CA: Educational Kinesiology Foundation.

DfEE (1998) *Teaching: High Status, High Standards.* Circular 4/98. London: DfEE.

DfES (2003a) *Excellence and Enjoyment: A Strategy for Primary Schools.* London: DfES.

DfES (2003b) *Every Child Matters.* London: DfES.

Dryden, G. and Vos, J. (1999) *The Learning Revolution: To Change the Way the World Learns.* Auckland: The Learning Web.

Gardner, H. (1983) *Frames of Mind: The Theory of Multiple Intelligences.* London: Heinemann.

Johnston, C. (1996) *Unlocking the Will to Learn.* California: Corwin Press.

Johnston, J, Chater, M. and Bell, D. (eds) (2002) *Teaching the Primary Curriculum.* Buckingham: Open University Press.

Piaget, J. (1929) *The Child's Conception of the World.* New York: Harcourt.

QCA (2003) *Creativity: Find it, Promote it.* London: QCA / DfEE.

Shayer, M. and Adey, P. (eds) (2002) *Learning Intelligence: Cognitive Acceleration Across the Curriculum from 5 to 15 Years.* Buckingham: Open University Press.

Shulman, L. S. (1987) Knowledge and teaching: foundations of the new reform, *Harvard Educational Review,* 57: 1–22.

TDA (Training and Development Agency) (2007) *Draft Revised Professional Standards for Teachers in England.* Available at www.tda.gov.uk/upload /resources /pdf/d/draft_revised_standards_ framework_jan_2007.pdf

TTA (Teacher Training Agency) (2002) *Qualifying to Teach: Professional Standards for Qualified Teacher Status.* London: TTA.

Vygotsky, L. (1978) *Mind in Society: The Development of Higher Psychological Processes,* eds M. Cole *et al.* Cambridge, MA: Harvard University Press.

Wilson, A. (2005) *Creativity in Primary Education.* London: Learning Matters.

Part 1

Planning

2
Planning for Creative Teaching

Jane Johnston and John Halocha

Introduction

This chapter will consider a number of questions connected to creativity and planning in education. Firstly, it will consider what creativity is and provide a working definition for the rest of the chapter and indeed the book. We will then try to apply this definition to identify what creative teaching and learning look like and how you can plan for creative teaching and learning. It may be that creativity is not a term you normally associate with education and teaching. It may be that you cannot see how you can be creative in planning. Hopefully, by the end of the chapter you will see how you can become a more creative practitioner.

What is creativity?

Creativity is acknowledged as an important construct in education (Kneller 1965; de Bono 1992; Gardner 1993; Beetlestone 1998; Costello 2000; Craft *et al.* 2001; DfES 2003; QCA 2003), although there does not appear to be a consensus about what creativity is or even why it is important. There is even a school of thought (for example, Duffy 1998) that posits that to define creativity is to limit it.

The increasingly extensive literature on creativity in education (for example, Beetlestone 1998; Sternberg 1999; Craft *et al.* 2001; DfES 2003; QCA 2003; Wilson 2003) identify certain features of creativity, which together make up a coherent definition:

- Originality: new ideas, new designs, new styles; termed big C creativity by Csikszentmihalyi (1997).
- Innovation.
- Encompassing both arts and sciences (Prentice 2000) and making links between different aspects of the curriculum (Duffy 1998; DfES 2003).
- Problem solving (de Bono 1992).

Practical and reflective task

Brainstorm words that will help you to define creativity. Try to link these in a mind or concept map. A concept map links ideas and explains the rationale behind the links. Begin your concept map with the question 'What is creativity?' in the middle of a page and then link your brainstormed words to that question, explaining what the link is along the link line.

Level 1:
Think of a creative experience you have had recently. With this experience in mind, look at your concept map to help you to identify the creative features of this experience.

Level 2:
Think of a creative teaching experience you have had recently with children. With this experience in mind, look at your concept map to help you to identify the creative features of this experience. Reflect on the experience from both your perspective and the children's perspective and consider similarities and differences.

Level 3:
Think of a creative experience you have observed in your school. This may be a lesson, in-service, parents or staff meeting, community liaison etc. With this experience in mind, look at your concept map to help you to identify the creative features of this experience. Reflect on the experience from both different perspectives (children, teachers, parents, community etc.) and consider similarities and differences.

- Thinking skills, including lateral and divergent thinking (de Bono 1992; Gardner 1993; Costello 2000), termed little c creativity (Craft 2001).
- A characteristic of everyone, and one that can be developed (Medawar 1969), although some believe it is not a characteristic of young children (Shapiro 1976; Pickard 1979).
- Involves a well-defined sense of self and self-discipline (Shallcross 1981).

Ashley Compton (2005) has skilfully combined these different definitions into a model identifying a continuum of creativity (see Figure 2.1). In this model the first stage or level of creativity involves observation, in its widest sense; noticing things and being interested enough to find out more or observe more. The next level involves taking this interest further by making connections between ideas, observations, developing an individual style, solving problems, exercising judgement, maybe as the result of evaluating. The third level involves using skills, knowledge and imagination to make something new and valuable to others, and the final level involves making something new to society as a whole and / or working at the pinnacle of a field in skills, knowledge, understanding and vision.

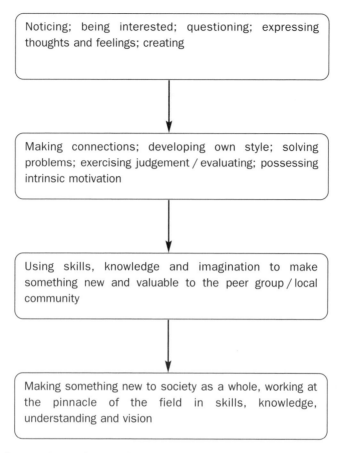

Figure 2.1 Compton's continuum of creativity (with considerable indebtedness to Beetlestone 1998)

What is creative teaching and learning?

Compton's (2005) model identifies the importance of motivation in creativity. Johnston (2005a) considers the motivation of children in the classroom a challenge because of difficulties of competing with stimulation in the outside world (media, computer games and sophisticated toys) which involves a child in being passively entertained rather than being actively engaged. This is a theme taken up by a large number of prominent academics, writers, educationalists and others in a letter to the *Daily Telegraph* (2006) which expresses concern about a childhood characterized by a poverty of food, practical experiences including play, adult interaction, coupled with an early start to formal education. The concern about children's psychological well-being is endorsed by the Archbishop of Canterbury, Dr Rowan Williams, who, in an interview with the BBC, says that a new generation of young parents fail to offer the right example to their children who, in turn, are becoming 'infant adults'

(BBC 2006). The childhood described by the letter to both the *Daily Telegraph* and Rowan Williams is felt to be 'stifling the natural creativity of many youngsters' (BBC 2006: 1).

The formal curriculum (DfEE 1999b; DfES 2007), national strategies in literacy (DfEE 1998), numeracy (DfEE 1999a) and schemes of work have changed the nature of teaching and learning (Cullingford 1996) and increasingly made creative teaching and learning difficult. The primary strategy (DfES 2003) emphasizes the importance of creativity by teachers who 'incorporate the features of effective creative practice, but maintain the rigour and focus on key objectives for development and learning' (Johnston 2005a: 129). Creative teachers are ones who:

- are able to provide original and creative activities;
- make a real impact on the children they teach;
- have good subject and pedagogical knowledge and pedagogical skills;
- have an infectious enthusiasm that motivates children;
- provide learning environments which meet children's individual needs;
- involve children as active participants in their own learning.

Creative teaching is recognized by national awards for teaching and chartered teaching awards (for example, Chartered Geography and Science Teachers awarded by subject association with a Royal Charter bestowed by the Privy Council). Creative teaching approaches can be said to fall along two continua: constructivist / positivist and traditionalist / post-modernist (Longbottom 1999; Johnston 2005b) as seen in Figure 2.2. They include:

- teacher-led explorations, where the teacher sets up and structures explorations and investigations to enable pupils to construct their own scientific conceptions and develop skills, which can be found in the traditionalist / constructivist sector;
- exploration and discovery where teachers guide pupils and support the construction of understandings through scientific challenge and discourse, which can be found in the constructivist / postmodernist sector;
- discussion and argumentation which can be found in the positivist / post-modernist sector.

The least creative teaching involves imparting knowledge or demonstrating concepts or instructing children and can be found in the traditionalist / positivist sector.

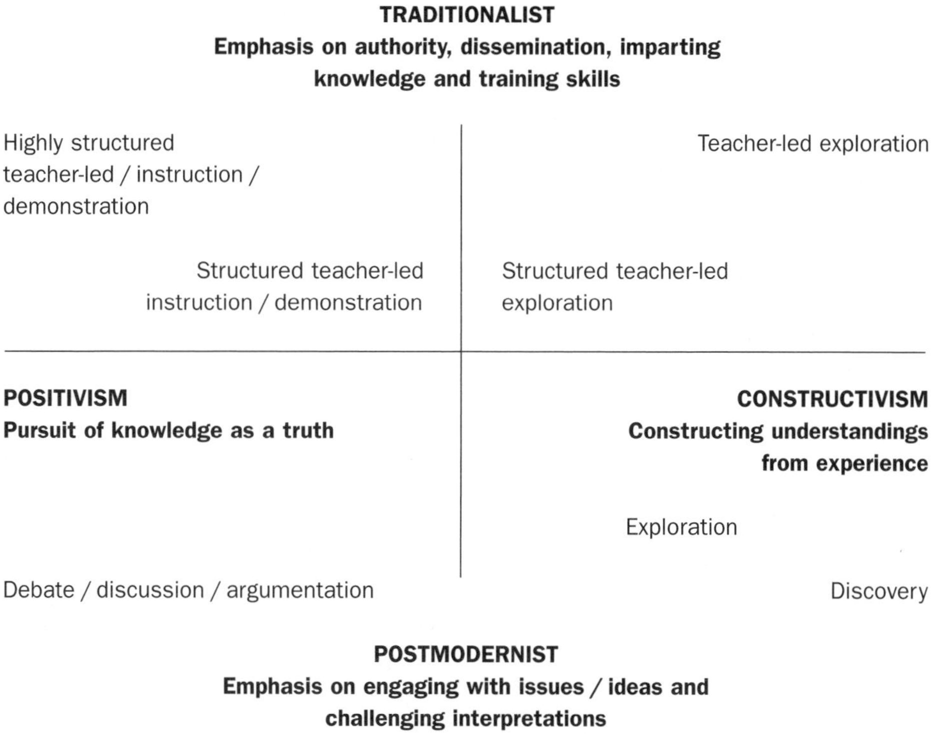

TRADITIONALIST
Emphasis on authority, dissemination, imparting
knowledge and training skills

Highly structured   Teacher-led exploration
teacher-led / instruction /
demonstration

                Structured teacher-led   Structured teacher-led
                instruction / demonstration   exploration

POSITIVISM   **CONSTRUCTIVISM**
Pursuit of knowledge as a truth   **Constructing understandings**
                                                      from experience

                                                      Exploration

Debate / discussion / argumentation   Discovery

POSTMODERNIST
Emphasis on engaging with issues / ideas and
challenging interpretations

Figure 2.2   Creative teaching approaches (Johnston 2005b, adapted from Longbottom 1999)

Reflective tasks

Level 1
Consider some recent teaching you have observed, taught or been involved in. Identify what teaching approach (see Figure 2.2) was used. How could the teaching be modified to make it more creative?

Level 2
Consider some recent teaching in your class. Identify what teaching approach (see Figure 2.2) was used. How could the teaching be modified to make it more creative?

Level 3
Look at your medium- or long-term planning and consider how the teaching relates to the approaches in Figure 2.2. How could the teaching be modified to make it more creative?

It is not only different teaching approaches, but different subject areas that are considered creative. In a recent study, student teachers in England and Finland were questioned about their attitudes towards teaching their mother tongue (English or Finnish), mathematics, science and physics (Johnston and Ahtee 2006). The attitudes were ascertained using a previously validated semantic differential questionnaire with twenty bipolar adjective pairs (Ahtee and Rikkinen 1995; Ahtee and Tella 1995), grouped in four broad categories with five pairs in each:

- *Level of difficulty* (easy / difficult, self-evident / abstract, commonplace / mystical, simple / complicated, productive / trivial);
- *Level of interest and involvement* (interesting / boring, gripping / undesirable, active / passive, social / individual, practical / theoretical);
- *Perceived nature* (free / compulsory, open / closed, creative / non-creative, cheerful / sad, broadening / constricting);
- *Perceived value* (valuable / worthless, profound / superficial, wise / foolish, selfish / unselfish, sublime / ridiculous).

Creativity located in the responses in the third category of perceived nature. The results, as seen in Figure 2.3, show that there are differences in the Finnish and English students, with Finnish student teachers ranking science as the most creative subject, followed by their mother tongue (Finnish), mathematics, and lastly physics as the least creative subject. English student teachers considered their mother tongue (English) as the most creative subject, with science, physics, and finally mathematics (in order) as least creative.

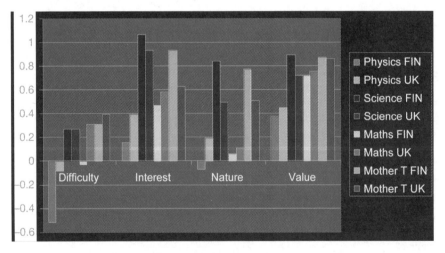

Figure 2.3 The mean values from the Finnish and English student teachers' ratings for teaching of physics activities, science, mathematics and mother tongue in the four categories: level of difficulty, level of interest and involvement, perceived nature and perceived value (adapted from Johnston and Ahtee 2006: 8)

Reflective tasks

Consider the different subjects in the primary curriculum (mathematics, English, science, design and technology, art, ICT, geography, history, PE) and rank in order of your perception of creativity.

Level 1
Pick on the lowest-ranking subject in your list and consider how you could plan a creative lesson in this area.

Level 2
Look at your planning for the next term in the subject that ranks lowest in your list. How can you modify your planning to make the subject more creative?

Level 3
Look at your school's long-term planning (scheme of work) in the subject that ranks lowest in your list. How can you modify the planning to make the teaching of the subject more creative?

Reflective tasks – Is music always creative?
by Ashley Compton, Bishop Grosseteste University College Lincoln

Creativity is often associated with the arts, although many creativity researchers believe that creativity has a much greater scope (for example, Sefton-Green and Sinker 2000; Craft 2001, Cropley 2001). This link between creativity and the arts is reinforced in the *Curriculum Guidance for the Foundation Stage* (QCA 2000) in which creative development refers specifically to art, music, dance and drama. An important question is whether these arts are always creative.

Example 1
Give a group of children chime bars tuned to C D E G and A. The musical 'score' for this piece is a 100 square. The children are each assigned a different number (for example, C = 2, D = 3, E = 5, G = 7 and A = 11). The conductor points to each number on the 100 square in turn and the children play only when the number is a multiple of the number they were assigned. The result is very soothing and satisfying and provokes an image of Buddhist monks. The performers and audience are pleased with the outcome, but is it creative?

The definition for creativity in *All Our Futures* and used by QCA in *Creativity: Find it, Promote it* (2003) is 'imaginative activity fashioned so as to produce outcomes that are both original and of value' (NACCCE 1999: 30). In the above example the outcome is of value but the imaginative activity has been the sole domain of the teacher who devised the activity. In order to extend the creativity the children should be given choices. Useful questions are: How are you going to play? How could you change the original rules to make a more interesting performance?   *cont.*

Example 2

At the other extreme the children are given a collection of instruments and instructed to play. Some start immediately whereas others spend a short time listening and thinking. The result is loud but not particularly satisfying for the performers or audience. The outcome was definitely original but was not valued. In order to extend the creativity the children should be encouraged to evaluate their work. Useful questions include: What did you like about your performance? What do you think would improve it? What atmosphere would you like to create? How could you do that effectively?

Music in the national curriculum is divided into performing, composing, listening and appraising. Is it possible to be creative in all of these areas?

Example 3

Most people would agree that composing is a creative activity. You are making decisions about choosing and organizing the sounds for a purpose. The resulting music is your creation. What about performing? No two performances, even by the same performer, are identical, which means that the performer must be bringing something individual to the performance. Does this make it creative? If you have performed, whether as a dancer, musician, actor or even teacher, you will be aware that the reaction of the audience can influence your performance. A particularly responsive audience can draw out great performances. Does this mean that the listeners and appraisers are creative because they are changing the performance? Is it possible to not be creative while engaging in a performance or is it merely a question of degree? (See also Compton 2002.)

Planning

In preparing for battle I have always found that plans are useless, but planning is indispensable.

D. Eisenhower (1890–1969)

Planning can be divided into long-term, medium-term and short-term. Long-term planning identifies the bare bones of planning and has two levels:

1 Curriculum plans or the long-term planned programme of work in all subjects for the whole school and which reflects the school context and ethos, aims and priorities.
2 Long-term plans (sometimes known as schemes of work), which identify the bare bones of planning in one subject, over the course of a school or key stage (DfES 2006). These long-term plans identify the learning objectives in the subject and map the timing of delivery within units of work. The QCA (www.qca.org.uk) has schemes of work in every subject in the primary curriculum and these can be

used as a baseline for more creative planning to motivate learners and facilitate learning. They should also take into account new advice and guidelines which come from a number of sources, such as the DfES, Primary National Strategy and QCA. As a result, these plans need to be reviewed at regular intervals and modified to meet new initiatives and after reflection from within the school. It is important that schools do not use any long-term plans / schemes of work without adapting them for their children and their context. The DfES (2006) standards website identifies key points to help planning:

- successful planning enables teachers to provide a coherent, relevant and engaging curriculum that promotes continuity in pupils' learning;
- effective plans take many forms, but show clear objectives and how these will be achieved;
- adapting existing plans and using high-quality published resources as starting points can save on planning time and support schools' ongoing review of the curriculum;
- using ICT can make it much easier to share, re-use, copy and amend plans.

Medium-term plans provide more flesh to the bare bones of long-term planning. Medium-term plans are also sequences of work and detail the teaching and learning for one or more subjects for a half term or term, or number of weeks or lessons. Medium-term plans identify the learning objectives and outcomes over the period of time and outline the activities to achieve these objectives / outcomes. The detail may include a sequence of activities showing progression and coherence, with cross-curricular links made between medium-term plans in different subjects. Many teachers download these plans from internet sites such as the QCA website, but care needs to be taken to ensure that they are modified appropriately for the individuality of the class and teacher.

Short-term planning adds more detail to the flesh and bones of the long- and medium-term plans. They can be details of activities over a period of a week, as with literacy (DfEE 1998) or numeracy (DfEE 1999a) planning, or planning in the Early Years Foundation Stage (DfES 2007). They may detail work over the period of a day or one lesson. Short-term planning acts as an aide-mémoire and should help teachers to meet the planned objectives. As such, it should have certain features, such as:

- clear learning objectives or learning outcomes and how they relate to the medium- and long-term planning or national curricula (DfEE 1999b; DfES 2007);
- the activities to achieve the learning objectives / outcomes;
- differentiation by task, outcome, questioning or support to help achieve individual children achieve the learning objectives / outcomes (see Chapter 7, Differentiation, for more help with understanding differentiation);
- key questions which will help to focus on the learning objectives / outcomes (see also Chapter 6, Questioning);
- detail of resources needed in the activities;

- detail of assessment focus and strategy (see also Chapter 11, Assessment for Learning).

Although many experienced teachers do not always provide the detail and may even work from medium-term plans, I (JJ) find that even after thirty years of teaching I provide this level of detail. This is because it ensures I am focused on the learning, rather than the organization, and enables me to meet the learning objectives for all children more effectively. It also enables me to evaluate my teaching and assess children's learning against pre-identified criteria. Figure 2.4 shows an example of my own planning with a class of Reception children, with typical attention to detail that I find useful. While planning in this detail may seem onerous, it will take less time as you become more experienced and, of course, the use of ICT and saved plans makes the task much easier.

Title of Session Jim and the Beanstalk	**Year Group** Reception
Date of session	
Length of session 1 hour	**Method** Whole class introduction and individual/group sorting, making and problem solving
Key Learning Objectives	
Body Mapping	**Make a Climbing Jim**
Knowledge and understanding of the world	Knowledge and understanding of the world
The human body: similarities and differences between children	Making and evaluating a climbing Jim
Language and literacy: describing using their own words	Exploring the forces involved in a climbing Jim
Emotional development	Problem solving
Enthusiasm	Emotional development
	Enthusiasm
Build a Body	**Story – Jim and the Beanstalk**
Knowledge and understanding of the world	Knowledge and understanding of the world
The human body	The human body: similarities and differences between people
Problem solving, reasoning and numeracy	Language and literacy
Number recognition	Reading
Language and literacy	Emotional development
Speaking and listening	Enthusiasm, cooperation
Social development	
Cooperation	
Social development	
Cooperation	*cont.*

Key Teaching Points

- There are many similarities and differences between us.

Activities

Whole-class introduction

Story of Jim and the Beanstalk. Identification of similarities and differences between Jim and the Giant and us.

Follow-up activities

Body mapping. Children identify the main external parts of the body and label them on a large outline. They then attempt to place the main organs of the body into the outline and identify their names.

Build a body game. This is a game where each child has a character / body made up of separate body parts. The body of a character is made up by throwing a die and collecting body parts, which have numbers on the front and numbers / words / shapes on the back. Children can play the build a body games (1 mathematical and 1 language) and collect the body parts if they can read the word on the back or identify the number on the back. Children who cannot read the word or recognize the number will put the body part back, once the word or number is read out for them. This encourages them to identify the number/word next time.

Story – Jim and the Beanstalk. Children can retell the story of Jim and the Beanstalk, using characters.

Make a climbing Jim. Children make a climbing man using a pre-made one as a template. They can be encouraged to identify how Jim can be made to climb down the beanstalk as well as up.

Differentiation

By support. Teachers will provide appropriate support for the less able children.

By questioning. Questions will be varied to support the less able and extend the more able, e.g. How is Jim different from the giant? Where does the brain go in the body? How can you get the man to climb down the string?

By outcome. Individual children will achieve the learning objectives at different levels (see assessment below).

Assessment

High achievers:

- **Language and science:** Be able to describe the similarities and differences between us in own words, using a number of criteria such as height, hair colour, gender.

- **Science and technology:** Be able to explain how they think the climbing man works in their own words but using some scientific language such as push, pull, force.

Middle achievers:

- **Language:** Be able to describe the similarities and differences between us in own words.

- **Science and technology:** Be able to explain how they think the climbing man works in their own words.

cont.

Low achievers:

- **Language:** Be able to describe the similarities and differences between us, with support and prompting from an adult.
- **Science and technology:** Be able to explain how they think the climbing man works in their own words, with some support from an adult.

Resources

Body Mapping	Make a Climbing Jim
Large sheets of paper – poster size	Outlines
Large felt-tip pens	Ball of string
Body mapping parts	20 plastic straws
	2 packs of plasticine
	Scissors
	Felt-tip pens
	Crayons
	Sellotape
Build a Body	**Story – Jim and the Beanstalk**
Build a Body game and die	Big book Jim and the Beanstalk
	Story bag

Figure 2.4   Example of a short-term plan / lesson plan for Reception children

Picture 2.1   Retelling the story of *Jim and the Beanstalk* (Briggs 1970)

Planning for creativity and developing a range of thinking skills

Education is not the filling of a pail but the lighting of a fire.

W. B. Yeats (1865–1939)

Creative planning was given a boost, by the endorsement of the DfES, who identified that 'excellent teaching gives children the life chances they deserve ... enjoyment is the birthright of every child. But the most powerful mix is the one that brings the two together' (DfES 2003: foreword). Creative planning will have a number of the features of creativity, as identified at the beginning of the chapter. It will:

- have an element of originality, presenting old ideas in new ways or new ideas in original contexts;
- make links across the curriculum;
- involve an element of problem solving, developing thinking skills, discussion and debate.

Creative planning is important for a number of reasons. Firstly, creative planning aids motivation and helps children to be actively involved in their learning and makes achievement of the learning objectives more likely. Secondly, creative planning is likely to be cross-curricular, making links across the curriculum in creative ways, and this will help to make the learning relevant to children. Thirdly, creative planning will help to develop higher-level thinking skills through problem solving and enquiry (see Chapter 10, Developing Investigative Work / Enquiry).

In planning for creative learning, teachers need to have good subject knowledge and pedagogical knowledge. They also need to plan for:

- the children's creative learning (including the development of skills and attitudes, as well as knowledge and understanding);
- your role in the learning;
- a creative learning context;
- continuity, differentiation and progression (including different learning styles);
- creative organization.

Reflective task

Level 1

Reflect on a recent lesson you have taught.
- What creative features are in your planning?
- How could you modify this plan to make it more creative?
- What do you think prevents you from being more creative?
- How can you overcome the constraints that prevent you from being more creative in your planning?

Level 2

Take one piece of future planning and try and make it more creative by including some of the features of creative planning. Try out your plans and reflect on their success.
- How successful was your teaching and the children's learning?
- What part was played by creativity in the success of your plans?
- What do you think prevents you from being more creative?
- How can you overcome the constraints that prevent you from being more creative in your planning?

Level 3

Look at your school's long-term planning with your staff and plan how to make it more creative by including some of the features of creative planning. Try out your plans and reflect on their success.
- How did the children and staff respond to the changes?
- What do you think prevents your school from being more creative?
- How can you overcome the constraints that prevent your school from being more creative in your planning?

Planning for effective learning in science
by Niki Whitburn, Bishop Grosseteste University College Lincoln

Many teachers find it hard to cover all areas of the science curriculum owing to pressure on their time. Science is often the poor relation of the core subjects, with most schools allocating between one and two hours per week. One way to ensure full coverage, or even to enhance and add to the science curriculum, is to approach the subject in a cross-curricular way. Many areas of science, such as measuring skills, movement and sound, lend themselves to being taught in conjunction with other subjects. Literacy and numeracy are two that may seem rather obvious but are not always integrated with science as much as they might be. Non-fiction big books, as well as being read together with various forms of writing such as lists and non-story texts, can be used to enhance a science topic. A literacy lesson can be completely based around a current science topic, thus enhancing both subjects – science

cont.

becoming part of the everyday work and literacy given a broader perspective. The same can be done within numeracy as science often involves measuring and recording results. Foundation subjects can enhance science and their own area by looking at similar phenomena at the same time. Link work on rivers in geography with rocks and soils in science; electricity with design and technology (DT) by adding circuits to models; chemical changes with cooking within DT; many history topics include food, which can be linked to nutrition and health.

So whether your school works on a subject- or topic-based approach, think laterally in order to include more science. Careful medium-term planning can enable you to cover more areas within the same timescale.

Planning for effective learning in music
by Catherine Maynard Clark, Bishop Grosseteste University College Lincoln

Careful and imaginative planning is crucial in order to ensure that teachers and pupils explore fully the interrelationships between performing, composing, listening and appraising through an exciting, collaborative investigation of sound.

Be confident to expect the ideal. Remember that it is our entitlement as teachers and learners to access high quality experience in music.

Effective planning will take into consideration strengths and will support areas for development. Time must be made to address music in the following ways:

- Discrete subject knowledge is essential, where thorough skills auditing and staff development programmes ensure that children are in receipt of well-paced, progressive subject-specific knowledge and skills. This can be implemented through shared planning with the music coordinator, specialist teacher or external agency, inclusive of *all* staff. Consequently, it need not depend on the individual teacher's musical skills or taste but on the shared rationale resulting in collaborative planning appropriate for the needs of the staff team and school as a whole.

- Music's place within a cross-curricular context should be incorporated into planning, where skills are further developed through any other subject area, topic-based scheme or personal, social and health education (PSHE) programme, enhancing experience of different curriculum areas. Often this is an ideal way to encourage the generalist teacher to develop skills and confidence in teaching music through another subject in which they have expertise and experience. It may provide valuable opportunities for team teaching where the skills development of staff can also be addressed.

Links are too numerous to list but consider including music with language / literacy through singing and listening, play / imagination through musical improvisation and composition; movement and dance through composition, listening, responding to music; sense of number through songs and instrumental performance; art through exploring colour / mood / textures in sound; history and geography through listening, performing and composing. *cont.*

The combination and careful balance of these two approaches in planning for music will encourage children to begin to build a bank of learning strategies, enabling them to listen, discuss, perform, create and reflect upon their own and others' work, building confidence in their ability to make judgements based on sound knowledge and where *creativity* remains at the centre of the teaching and learning process and facilitating the innate musicianship in all of us.

Planning effective music will go on to address significant issues of inclusion, special needs, behavioural management, gifted and talented, and many others. Additional music activities will further enhance staff and pupil experience through, for example, instrumental ensembles, choral groups, technology clubs etc. Collaborative music making provides social and musical opportunities for shared endeavour and achievement for teachers and pupils as musicians in school and makes a valuable contribution to their community beyond.

Planning for effective learning in mathematics
by Helen Fielding, Bishop Grosseteste University College Lincoln

Since the introduction of the National Numeracy Strategy (DfEE 1999a), the planning of mathematics in primary schools in England has changed considerably. The recommendation of a three-part lesson has been widely adopted and teachers have sought to plan for these effectively, aiming to meet the needs of their class as well as the recommendations of National Numeracy Strategy. There is now considerable support for teachers' numeracy planning in the form of unit plans, commercially produced schemes and worksheets and websites created by local authorities, schools and individuals.

Effective teachers of numeracy are able to make appropriate connections at the planning stage. Firstly, they are able to adapt their planning to match what the children already know and adjust the length of their mathematics topics and balance and level of activities to accommodate this (Ofsted 2005). They are able to make explicit the connections between the different areas of mathematics and how these support each other (Thompson 1999). The hierarchical nature of mathematics is recognized so that the prerequisite skills are considered in order for the planning of the next step to be successful; for example, when trying to compare equivalent fractions, a good understanding of multiplication tables and division is essential before the comparison can be attempted and understood. Related to this is an appreciation of the connections between different types of representations, aiming to include a range of models to clarify the mathematics taught. It is important to put mathematics, where possible, in a real-life context so the purpose and value of the mathematics being undertaken is understood and appreciated by the learner.

The careful planning of a plenary is a vital part of an effective numeracy lesson. The plenary serves a variety of purposes. An effective plenary aims to bring the lesson to a conclusion with a positive emphasis on the learning objective. The plenary

cont.

ideally should focus on activity with the participation of all children, rather than reporting back from independent groups, so that the main ideas and vocabulary can be reinforced and assessed.

There are many generic issues which also contribute to the planning of an effective numeracy lesson. However an equally important issue, which is reinforced by a recent Ofsted report (2005), suggests that in successful lessons teachers are not afraid to depart from their planned lesson, if appropriate, in order to extend their pupils' thinking and address any emerging misconceptions.

Case study
Creative science
by Jane Cox, early years teacher, Lincolnshire

As a means of reflecting upon the importance of planning time for exploratory play in Key Stage 1 science and whether it can lead to self-differentiation, I focused on the responses of two children (Sam and Jon) during an investigative science lesson.

This involved an activity in which the children could make a 'fish' from weighted straws, which could be made to float or sink inside a lemonade bottle by half filling the bottle with water and squeezing the sides. Each child was supplied with a bowl of water, straws of different widths and plasticine. Time was planned for the children to explore these materials before we made our 'fish', simply stating that we would eventually be using the plasticine to make the straws float upright.

I found that the children were very involved. They explored the floating and sinking abilities of the straws and the effects of adding plasticine to the ends. However, one particular question from Jon led to an impromptu investigation:

'When I sink my straws, bubbles come out. Do bigger straws have more bubbles in?'

We discussed different ways in which this could be investigated and eventually the children agreed that we would count the number of bubbles that came out of the ends of the different width tubes.

We carried out the investigation the children had suggested and then made the 'fish'. I found that when we tried the fish in the lemonade bottles the children's observations and comments suggested a good understanding that the straws were full of air and needed to be sealed at both ends to stop the bubbles getting out.

I had noticed Sam on a previous occasion during an activity in which children made observations on the ability of different substances to mix with water. A recognized kinaesthetic learner, he had been interested in the materials but impetuous in his approach and had been unable to make any observations, even when prompted. In this exploratory play, however, although still very enthusiastic I found him far more focused. He was able to demonstrate observation skills, agreeing with the comments of his peers and offering his own. Alongside most of the other children he was able to make the conceptual link between his observations of air bubbles escaping from a

cont.

weighted straw and its inability to float and therefore the importance of sealing the air in. When his own floating fish was made to sink by placing it in a lemonade bottle and squeezing, he was able to offer his own reasons for and interpretations of this phenomenon. For this child I felt that the exploratory approach had proved successful.

Jon has in the past stated that Science is his favourite lesson and comes to the classroom with science-based knowledge gained from reading at home. His learning style would appear to be different from that of Sam, so would exploratory play prove to be as relevant? Jon's question led to the group investigating if a greater number of air bubbles came from a wide straw as opposed to a narrow one. He was also able to interpret his results: 'About the same number of bubbles but the ones from the wide straw are a bit bigger, that's because there's more air in the wide straw.' Through exploratory play Jon was able (with guidance) to carry out an investigation based on a question he had himself raised.

The outcomes for Sam and Jon were different, even though they were involved in the same learning activity. From his verbal responses Sam developed his observation skills and both children progressed their conceptual knowledge of floating and sinking. Additionally, Jon showed a noticeable progression in his understanding of the need to carry out a fair test.

Ovens (2004: 19) describes the approach of creative science teaching: 'Our role is to *Stimulate* (encourage and challenge enquiry thinking) and elicit *Authentic curiosity*'. Ovens describes how broad SC1 objectives from the national curriculum would be planned but detailed learning objectives would be emergent, from negotiation with the children, and not pre-specified. By anticipating a range of lines of enquiry the appropriate learning objectives could be prepared. 'The precise objectives will emerge, *differentially and accurately related to* where the children are' (p. 20).

References

Ahtee, M. and Rikkinen, H. (1995) Luokanopettajaksi opiskelevien mielikuvia fysiikasta, kemiasta, biologiasta ja maantieteestä (Primary student teachers' images about physics, chemistry, biology and geography), *Dimensio*, 59: 54–8.

Ahtee, M. and Tella, S. (1995) Future class teachers' images of their school-time teachers of physics, mathematics and foreign languages, in S. Tella (ed.) *Juuret ja arvot: Etnisyys ja eettisyys – aineen opettaminen monikultturisessa oppimisympäristössä (Roots and Values: Ethnicity and Ethics – Teaching a Subject in a Multi-cultural Learning Environment)*. Proceedings of a subject-didactic symposium held at the Department of Teacher Education, University of Helsinki. Research Report 150, pp. 180–200.

BBC (2006) Archbishop warns of child crisis. http://news.bbc.co.uk/go/pr/fr/-/1/hi/uk/5354998.stm (posted 18 September 2006).

Beetlestone, F. (1998) *Creative Children, Imaginative Teaching*. Buckingham: Open University Press.

Briggs, R. (1970) *Jim and the Beanstalk*. London: Penguin (Picture Puffin).

Compton, A. (2002) Creative music, in J. Johnston, M. Chater and D. Bell (eds) *Teaching the Primary Curriculum*. Buckingham: Open University Press.

Compton, A. (2005) What is creativity? Unpublished EdD thesis, University of Leicester.

Costello, P. J. M. (2000) *Thinking Skills and Early Childhood Education*. London: David Fulton.

Craft, A. (2001) Little c creativity, in A. Craft, B. Jeffrey and M. Leibling *Creativity in Education*. London: Continuum.

Craft, A., Jeffrey, B. and Leibling, M. (2001) *Creativity in Education*. London: Continuum.

Cropley, A. (2001) *Creativity in Education and Learning*. London: Kogan Page.

Csikszentmihalyi, M. (1997) *Creativity*. New York: HarperPerennial.

Cullingford, C. (1996) *The Politics of Primary Education*. Buckingham: Open University Press.

Daily Telegraph (2006) Modern life leads to more depression amongst children. Letter to the editor, 12 September.

de Bono, E. (1992) *Serious Creativity*. London: HarperCollins.

DfEE (1998) *The National Literacy Strategy*. London: DfEE.

DfEE (1999a) *The National Numeracy Strategy*. London: DfEE.

DfEE (1999b) *The National Curriculum: Handbook for Teachers in England*. London: DfEE / QCA.

DfES (2003) *Excellence and Enjoyment: A Strategy for Primary Schools*. London: DfES.

DfES (2006) DfES standards website www.standards.dfes.gov.uk/primary

DfES (2007) Statutory Framework for the Early Years Fundation State; Setting the Standards for Learning, Development and Care for children from birth to five. *Every Child Matters*, Change for Children. London: DfES

Duffy, B. (1998) *Supporting Creativity and Imagination in the Early Years*, Buckingham: Open University Press.

Gardner, H. (1993) *Creating Minds*. New York: HarperCollins.

Johnston, J. (2005a) *Early Explorations in Science Second Edition*. Buckingham: Open University Press.

Johnston, J. (2005b) What is creativity in science education?, in A. Wilson (ed.) *Creativity in Primary Education*. Exeter: Learning Matters, pp. 88–101.

Johnston, J. and Ahtee, M. (2006) What are primary student teachers' attitudes, subject knowledge and pedagogical content knowledge needs in a physics topic?, *Teaching and Teacher Education*, 22(4): 1–10.

Kneller, G. (1965) *The Art and Science of Creativity*. San Francisco: Holt, Rinehart & Winston.

Longbottom, J. (1999) Science education for democracy: dilemmas, decisions, autonomy and anarchy. Paper presented to the European Science Education Research Association Second International Conference, Kiel, Germany,

Medawar, P. B. (1969) *Induction and Intuition in Scientific Thought. Memoirs of the American Philosophical Society. Jayne Lectures 1968*. London: Methuen.

NACCCE (National Advisory Committee on Creativity and Cultural Education) (1999) *All Our Futures*. Available at http://www.dfes. gov.uk/naccce/index1.shtml

Ofsted (2005) *Annual Report of Her Majesty's Chief Inspector of Schools 2004/05.* Annesley, Notts: The Stationery Office.

Ovens, P. (2004) A 'sane' way to encourage creativity, *Primary Science Review*, 17–20.

Pickard, E. (1979) *The Development of Creative Ability.* Windsor: NFER.

Prentice, R. (2000) Creativity: a reaffirmation of its place in early childhood education, *The Curriculum Journal*, 11(2): 145–58.

QCA (2003) *Creativity: Find it, Promote it.* London: QCA/DfEE.

Sefton-Green, J. and Sinker, R. (2000) *Evaluating Creativity: Making and Learning by Young People,* London: Routledge.

Shallcross, D. (1981) *Teaching Creative Behaviour.* Englewood Cliffs, NJ: Prentice Hall.

Shapiro, E. (1976) Toward a developmental perspective on the creative process, in C. Winsor (ed.) *The Creative Process: A Symposium.* New York: Bank Street College of Education.

Sternberg, R. (ed.) (1999) *Handbook of Creativity.* Cambridge: Cambridge University Press.

Thompson, I. (ed.) (1999) *Issues in Teaching Numeracy in Primary Schools.* Buckingham: Open University Press.

Wilson, A. (2003) *Creativity in Primary Education.* Exeter: Learning Matters.

3
Classroom Organization
John Halocha

Introduction

Primary school classrooms are fascinating and complex environments. The purpose of this chapter is to help you examine your own classroom organization through reflective practice. Human beings are very good at getting used to a particular place and getting on with their lives and accepting what is around them. Just think of your journey to visit a friend: you know the way and probably travel there on personal autopilot. In how much detail can you actually recall what you see and pass on the way? It's very much the same with workspaces. Once we arrive in them, we are mainly concerned with getting on with the job that we do there.

You may still be training to become a teacher, in which case you are probably 'borrowing' a classroom and its organizational structures from a qualified teacher. Alternatively, you could be in your first year of teaching and just beginning to realize what a task it is to effectively organize your own classroom for the first time. Hopefully, you are also enjoying the freedom to create your own learning environment, which is one of the privileges of being a primary school teacher in England. You could also be an experienced teacher who may well have had to organize many classrooms during your career. This chapter offers a range of ways to look afresh at your classroom organization through asking some key questions and challenging what you see, hear and do.

Before looking at your own practice, we need to place classrooms in a broader context. Unless you are in a brand new school, you have probably inherited your classroom from another teacher within a whole-school setting. There may be some things that you cannot easily change. For example, staff may have agreed a whole-school policy on how classrooms should be set out for literacy lessons. Each classroom may be fitted with fixed storage cupboards around some of the walls which could restrict how you distribute teaching resources. Your school may have been built in the early 1970s when open-plan designs were popular with some local authorities. This is clearly going to affect how you currently operate and ideas you may have for the future. The interactive tasks offered in this chapter aim to help you critically reflect on how you may take these starting points in order to develop classroom organization to support you in effective teaching and learning. There is no one definition of effective classroom organization: the tasks are designed to help you create the most effective learning environment through a combination of various features that make up how your classroom is organized.

The physical environment

Being involved in teacher education, I have visited many classrooms around the country. One of the main impressions gained is the extent to which teachers take classroom organization for granted. Sometimes it is suggested to a student that a piece of furniture could be moved to improve ease of movement around the room. Students may be anxious about asking their teacher whether they can do this. However, the teacher's reply is often that they had never really thought about why the furniture was there and of course the student can move it. Sometimes the teachers themselves then see how the rearrangement has improved the learning environment. This section encourages you to ask those questions yourself and to consider how you can adapt the physical environment to support teaching and learning.

Maslow (1968) argues that basic physical needs must be met before effective learning can take place (see Figure 3.1). A basic starting point therefore is space, heat, light and sound. Look carefully at the space in your classroom.

- Do pupils have sufficient space in which to carry out a particular activity?
- How easy is it for you to move around and monitor progress and behaviour?
- Do you adapt the spaces depending on the activity in progress.

For example, a large-scale art construction may be best approached by removing chairs and putting tables together. This may seem obvious but there are many times during the teaching day when small changes to the physical space can improve learning because the children are both comfortable and best positioned to carry out an activity.

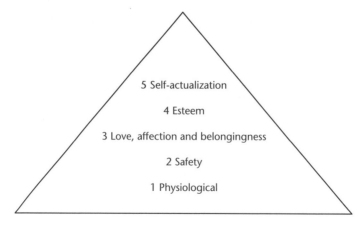

Figure 3.1 Maslow's (1968) theory of hierarchical needs

Managing space can also support behaviour, a simple example being to ensure ease of movement around the room to prevent pupils disturbing each other. Although a carpeted sitting area is very useful in a primary classroom, have a look at the percentage of your classroom that is used for sitting on the floor. Does it take up too much space when you consider the length of time it is actually in use? If the classroom is small, perhaps allow some pupils to sit on chairs near the carpet as a special privilege.

Look carefully at heat, light and sound. Do some pupils spend their day in the glare of constant sunlight and heat, making for an uncomfortable working environment? Do computer screens reflect the glare from windows making them hard to use? Do you allow a high level of noise most of the day, preventing those pupils whose preferred learning environment is quiet, from progressing? Equally, these questions can take an environmental focus, raising questions about the hidden messages you are giving children. Do you need lights on during a sunny day? Why are the windows open when the heating is on? These are just a few examples which, if you look closely at the learning environment you create, may help you analyse how comfortable your pupils are in order to maximize their learning. It can sometimes be worth asking yourself whether you would be able to work in that physical environment.

Health and safety factors also need to be considered. Are chairs and tables so close together that children can hurt themselves and each other when they move about? Are children placed so that classroom assistants risk hitting their heads on the storage units when they are working with particular children? Are electrical cables positioned so that people cannot trip over them? Many aspects of health and safety in your school will be considered by management, but it is occasionally well worth taking the time to re-evaluate such physical issues, not least because we often take our working environment for granted.

Room layout is also an important consideration in classroom organization. How much space do children and groups have in order to do a particular activity? In addition, what is the quality of that physical environment? For example, if you are expecting children to produce accurate drawn work on a large piece of paper, is this activity hampered by the fact that the working surface is not flat enough? Have you placed a distracting activity right alongside a group of children who are expected to work quietly on a task? Often, considering these organizational factors can go a long way to managing behaviour in the classroom. Room layout is also important when considering access to resources for both adults and children. Layout also gives messages about you. Is there a particular place from which you tend to operate? Do people in your classroom talk about it having a 'front'? Think about how this message is created and the extent to which it is helpful for everyone to have a common understanding of the function of this place.

Although it can take a little time, it may be worth moving furniture around more often in order to establish effective classroom organization. Try to plan ahead to minimize disruption. Hastings and Chantrey-Wood (2002) analysed the layout of primary classroom and argue that careful and flexible use of space can have positive effects on learning and teaching. Also, have a look at where resources are positioned

Picture 3.1   A typical primary classroom

in relation to each other. Is a stimulus display positioned on a board where maximum use and visibility are obtained? Are resources and materials for a particular activity placed so children have easy access without disturbing others? Can a mobile display board be used to partition the room to help children concentrate on a particular activity? As with many aspects discussed in this chapter, it can be valuable to regularly step back in your classroom and ask just why something is where it is, and is that part of classroom organization doing all it can for learning and teaching?

Another factor relating to layout is the nature of personal and group space within your classroom. As you get to know your children you will observe how best they work both individually and in groups. If a child works best alone in mathematics, try to provide a suitable personal space for them. If you have children grouped in a particular way, does this arrangement always stay the same? Are there some subjects where the ethos of whole-class learning may be most beneficial? For example, displaying images on an interactive whiteboard and using them within geographical enquiry may help to create a shared approach to learning from each other. Also think about the extent to which you give ownership of space to individuals and groups. This can also support the management of the classroom where various people take responsibility for space and resources. Lucas (1990) discusses ways in which teachers can adapt the physical space in a classroom to support individuals and groups.

The layout of your classroom can also give numerous messages to children. Taking the time over lunch to change the layout from a morning literacy lesson to an afternoon of historical investigation can subconsciously say to the class that there will be a different way of working and thinking in the afternoon. At this point it may also be worth considering how national initiatives affect classroom organization. Literacy and numeracy hours have been present for a number of years. Going into many classrooms one often sees the daily layout of the room dominated by the need for various parts of these, often morning, initiatives. Many schools are now looking afresh at how they are interpreted and it may be worth considering how new classroom layouts can support revised thinking in how English and mathematics are best taught in the primary school.

Resources need to be well organized in the classroom. By this we would include books, subject-specific equipment, ICT facilities, consumables, artefacts, children's property and the teacher's own personal resources. Here are some key questions for you to ask about your classroom:

- Are resources stored in the most suitable location?
- How easy is it for children and adults to access these?
- Does everyone understand the rules in place for managing resources?
- Are resources in good condition?
- Is there sufficient of everything for their purpose?
- Do the resources help to convey the types of learning you are expecting?
- Do you make the most of opportunities for children to learn transferable skills through using classroom resources?
- To what extent do you provide a role model for the use of classroom resources?

Display plays an important part in the organization of primary classrooms. This section is not about display techniques but about the role and purpose of display. Try the following activity in your classroom.

Reflective task

Level 1

Consider a recent school experience and display(s) you provided or contributed to. What categories were the displays in, for example celebratory, information-giving, enquiry-setting, instructional?

- How balanced is the range of displays you have contributed to?
- Is there a dominance of one type?
- How could you make a display cross-curricular and interactive?

Level 2

Look around your classroom and perhaps also any associated display areas beyond, for example in a corridor. Looking at each display, try to put it into a category, for example celebratory, information-giving, enquiry-setting, instructional.

- How balanced is the range of display you currently have?
- Is there a dominance of one type?
- Might you try to introduce more of another type, such as cross-curricular?

cont.

- How many displays allow children to interact with them in various ways?
- Is there a balance of subjects represented at any one time?
- How does this balance change during a term or a school year?
- What is the proportion of teacher- or child-generated display?

When you have completed this activity, set yourself two or three targets for ways of making your displays an even more dynamic part of how you organize your classroom.

Level 3

Look around your school with your staff and consider what categories the displays fall into, for example, celebratory, information-giving, enquiry-setting, instructional.

- How balanced is the range of display you currently have?
- Is there a dominance of one type?
- Might you try to introduce more of another type, such as cross-curricular?
- How many displays allow children to interact with them in various ways?
- Is there a balance of subjects represented at any one time?
- How does this balance change during a term or a school year?
- What is the proportion of teacher- or child-generated display?

When you have completed this activity, set yourselves two or three targets for ways of making your displays an even more dynamic part of how you organize your school environment.

When we decorate our lounge at home or remodel the bathroom, we are often looking to create a particular ambience, such as relaxing, country-style or minimalist. Ambience is just as important in your classroom. Perhaps the easiest way in which to appreciate this is not to look at your classroom but to walk around the school and visit others, especially if there are some you have not been into recently. What is the immediate impression as you walk in? Try to do this both when the school day is in progress and when the room is empty. Now try to imagine how other people – children especially – perceive the physical ambience of your classroom. Is there an emphasis on celebrating children's work? Does it feel exciting and challenging? Do elements feel muddled and unclear? Is it relaxing and purposeful? This activity should help you to assess the extent to which your design of the physical learning environment affects the quality of teaching and learning that takes place.

Classroom ethos

Walk into any classroom and you immediately gain an impression of what sort of place it is at that particular moment in time. But what might we mean by classroom ethos? It is not just the physical ambience discussed in the previous section. Is it, to you, perhaps the accumulation of physical, social, emotional, educational and ethical features that can be identified? Does one feature predominate? This can manifest itself in many ways. I recall a student who had created a positive, safe and challenging ethos through her unrelenting use of constructive and encouraging language that she used for giving instructions, explaining, asking questions, responding to pupils and generally orchestrating what happened in her classroom. So, how can we begin to get under the surface of what we might mean by classroom ethos?

Reflective task

This task is designed to help you create a personal construct for how you assess classroom ethos.

We normally define the ethos of classroom organization from our impressions of what we think may be happening and the language we use to describe it. The first stage is to look beneath the surface of how we ourselves evaluate classrooms. Choose one of the tasks appropriate to the current stage of your career and try to reflect on what you really mean by the words you will be using.

Level 1

Think back to the school placements you have already experienced. Choose a lesson that you think was particularly 'successful' because of the ethos you had created. Before you go on, note down what you mean by successful. Now, imagine your class teacher or tutor coming into your classroom. What words might they use to describe the ethos of how you organized your classroom for learning? Make a list of these. The next stage is to write down the opposite word you could have used. So, if you wrote 'exciting', you might put 'dull' or 'unimaginative' beside it. Look at the combination of words you used to describe the ethos of your lesson. Is it the same combination for all your lessons? Are some more apparent in some subjects than others? Consider whether this may be a further way in which to evaluate future lessons.

Level 2

Hopefully, you are receiving regular support from a range of people during this stage in your career. You are getting to know your class and establishing ways of working with them. Think back over a range of lessons that you have taught recently, trying to cover as many subjects as possible. For each lesson, try to write no more than three words to describe the ethos you consider prevailed. For example, for a lesson preparing pupils for a SATs test the ethos might be described as 'pressured, focused or mechanistic'. When you have completed lists for all the lessons, make a list of words to describe an ethos that you wish you could have written down. How might you aim to achieve these in future lessons? Do some subjects lend themselves more readily than others? What support might you need in achieving these?

cont.

Level 3

You have probably developed very effective skills in judging how pupils respond to the various ways in which you create an ethos within your school. Choose three subjects that complement each other, such as mathematics, geography and PE. Write a list of five words that you think pupils might use to describe the ethos you create for each of the subjects. Try to do this with your staff and then discuss why you think pupils might describe the ethos of your lessons that way. Do individual members of staff feel they have complete control over why they do this or are there factors beyond their control? Although this is not easy, discuss together the overall impression of ethos that your pupils gain by spending long periods of time with you in your classroom.

Much of what you will have written in the preceding task could also be considered a part of the organizational ethos you use to shape how your pupils learn. This is expanded further in Chapter 10 where the focus is on investigative work and enquiry.

A prime concern of many teachers is to create an ethos that encourages effective behaviour as a key foundation for learning. But just how has that particular ethos become established in your classroom? It is likely that it is based upon a broader framework of school policy and rules governing behaviour. Another aspect to consider may be the extent to which pupils actually have ownership of the ethos behind the rules for organizing your classroom. There can often be hidden agendas here which help to reinforce the whole organizational structure. A teacher was observed in a school with a strong environmental policy which underpinned many aspects of classroom organization. One rule was that the waste from morning break fruit was placed in the recycling tub. Each day two children were allowed to put the contents of the tub on the school compost heap. They knew exactly why they were doing this because they were using the contents of composted heaps on their own class garden. This occurred every day and the head firmly believed that many pupils might take this aspect of classroom ethos into organizing their own lives beyond the school. Regular observations showed that very little teacher direction was required and, indeed, the ethos flowed over into paper recycling and the use of electricity in the classroom.

Classroom ethos may also be developed and reinforced through whole-school initiatives. The Lincolnshire 'Golden Boot Challenge' encourages classes to compete for a weekly award by recording how pupils travel to and from school each day, with the most points awarded for those who walk all the way from home. Such activities also help to establish continuity of ethos along with a practical introduction to active citizenship which children can begin to understand operates in the real world at a variety of scales.

The ethos in some primary classrooms is established through a particular skill or interest of the teachers themselves. The teachers bring part of their own lives into the classroom to share with pupils in order to reinforce an ethos that helps maintain the organization of the classroom. A teacher with a keen interest in keeping ferrets has been seen to create a magical classroom ethos in which class rules, a caring approach to living creatures and a clear pupil understanding of 'how their classroom operates'. At a time when standardization and uniformity are creeping into state education, this human level of approach may have much to commend itself, especially with pupils experiencing an increasingly isolated and fragmented society beyond school.

It may also be worth considering that the ways in which you use language in your classroom helps to create a particular atmosphere. This can be looked at from both the teacher's and the children's point of view. What you say as a teacher is not just about how effective your questions are or how you ensure you use the correct vocabulary in a particular subject. It is also about the way in which you speak and how you use language.

Reflective task

Level 1

Think of a recent learning experience for you (a lecture, seminar, lesson, placement day in school). On the left-hand side of a sheet of paper note down what language was used during the experience. For example, you might put down giving instructions, asking questions, motivating an individual or explaining a task. Then, on the right-hand side of the paper, note down how you as a listener perceived the use of language.

- Was time given to you as an individual?
- Was too much time spent using instructional language?
- Were too many questions asked?
- Were the questions closed or open-ended (see Chapter 6, Questioning)?
- Was time given to consider a range of possible answers in a supportive and enquiring ethos?

Now reflect on your answers to these questions and how you use language in your interactions with children.

Level 2

Think back to a recent day in your classroom. On the left-hand side of a sheet of paper note down what you used language for. For example, you might put down giving instructions, asking questions, motivating an individual child or explaining a task to a classroom assistant. Then, on the right-hand side of the paper, note down how you think the listeners may have perceived your use of language.

- Did the individual child perhaps appreciate the time you gave to them?
- Did you spend too much time using instructional language?

The final stage is to try to imagine all these uses of language blended together from the perspective of any listener in your classroom.

cont.

- Do children have an overall impression of you asking too many questions and, perhaps even more important, do those questions tend to be sharp and factual in nature?
- Or, do you include a blend of more open-ended questions and give the children time to consider a range of possible answers in a more supportive and enquiring ethos?

Level 3

In a staff meeting consider a recent day in your school. Get each teacher to write down on the left-hand side of a sheet of paper how they used language in their classroom: giving instructions, asking questions, motivating an individual child or explaining a task to a classroom assistant. On the right-hand side of the paper, they should note down how they think the listeners may have perceived their use of language. Get small groups of two or three staff to compare their lists. It can be particularly useful to group colleagues who work closely together, as this will provide differing perspectives of the same experience. Discuss the questions below.

- Did the individual child perhaps appreciate the time you gave to them?
- Did you spend too much time using instructional language?
  The final stage is to try to imagine all these uses of language blended together from the perspective of any listener in your classroom.
- Do children have an overall impression of you asking too many questions and, perhaps even more important, do those questions tend to be sharp and factual in nature?
- Or, do you include a blend of more open-ended questions and give the children time to consider a range of possible answers in a more supportive and enquiring ethos?

How does the way in which you use language in your classroom create a particular organizational ethos? Are too many instructions given at the last minute? Might your intonation, in combination with your body language, be giving the impression that you are not totally in control of a situation? Once you have started to consider these more subtle and hidden uses of language, you may be better able to explain how other people in your classroom perceive your organization of the learning environment.

We organize classrooms in various ways to support learning and teaching, often trying to develop children's ability to enquire about the world, whether it be in mathematics, geography or in other areas of the curriculum. But do you also organize the classroom to demonstrate how you are also a part of that community of enquiry? Doing so can be an effective way of modelling ways in which you wish your children to work. For example, if the class is investigating a distant place in geography, do you also set yourself some geographical enquiry and then share it with the pupils? It can change children's perceptions of a teacher and sometimes raise in their own minds the value of what they are expected to do. This can also be achieved in physical actions: when mounting a piece of work, do you ensure that you adopt the same high standards that you expect from the children?

Social organization

Primary classrooms offer many opportunities for people to interact in a variety of ways. This section is designed to help you reflect on how your classroom organization can be used to manage social organization to enhance teaching and learning. The broader issues of physical layout have already been discussed. We now consider the social mechanisms that work within them.

Within a given period of time you will probably group your children as individuals, in groups or work as a whole class. Subsets of this can also exist. While half of the class are working as a large group, perhaps the rest are working as individuals. When you are planning, consider the whole variety of ways to organize children. On top of this, also consider the ways in which adult support, including yourself, can best be used within these various social groupings. You may decide that pupils working individually should be given a block of time where adult interaction is minimal and others in the class are getting more support. So often in primary classrooms one observes the same patterns of child / adult organization at a given time of day. There may often be good reasons for these, but it can be worth asking whether alternative models may provide learning environments where children can experience various levels of autonomy and support. In planning such types of classroom organization, it may be worth mentally tracking the experience that children will have in, say, a day, a week or a term.

Another layer of organization may now be laid over this way of planning. Look at the range of subjects being taught and decide how to bring a variety of social groupings to them. This is not simply for the sake of variety: it can help children maximize their learning within a given subject. Look carefully at the particular activities you want them to undertake and adapt the social groups accordingly. For example, if you work in a small village school and your class has a wide age range, how might you best group children within a music lesson in which they are exploring an aspect of composition? Should each group include the whole age range or might it be better to group the children according to musical ability?

The models of organization suggested by the Literacy and Numeracy strategies still play a major part in any primary school day. If it is your school's policy to adopt particular methods of social and ability groupings for what is often at least 50 per cent of the school day, think about how you will organize the class for the rest of the day. This is not only for reasons of variety. It can provide opportunities for children from different backgrounds and abilities to work together and share ideas. It can also be a way of developing the children's own self-image. Although we often try as teachers not to emphasize children's ability or lack of it in a particular subject, most children are very aware of where they sit within various hierarchies in the classroom. With careful planning, it is quite possible, for example, for children who know they are in lower-ability groups for literacy or numeracy, to be given an opportunity to shine in other subjects, not simply because they are good at them but also because you have designed the groups to help them achieve this.

As teachers, we often socially organize classes in order to achieve certain teaching and learning objectives. There may, however, be some opportunities where your prime motivation is in developing children's social interaction. There are a number of factors that you could consider: boy–girl, age differences, personal interests and abilities which may not be directly related to the curriculum, personal backgrounds perhaps valuable in schools where children come from a wide and varied catchment area. Citizenship is not statutory in primary schools and teachers' understanding of the concept is often confused or unclear. Taking some of the above factors into account, you could argue a case that your planning and organization are providing children with opportunities to develop skills in citizenship through interacting with a variety of peers who offer alternative views of life and experiences. The key issue here is to encourage diversity not only of experience but also of how children are encouraged to think about people both near and far and how they can be celebrated as human beings living together on one planet.

A further important parameter in this social organization is the mix of ethnic and religious groups within your class. We live at a time of globalization, when it is crucial for children to develop an understanding of and respect for people with histories, beliefs, traditions and cultures that are different from what they experience in everyday life. The way in which you manage this in your classroom will clearly depend on the cultural mix that is present. Perhaps the most important thing to consider here is the extent to which all the other factors discussed in this chapter may produce types of organization which do not allow children to make the most of opportunities to learn from each other's backgrounds. For example, if you set across classes for literacy, this may group children together for part of the day where they do not benefit from working within a culturally diverse group.

Another factor to consider in how you organize groups within a classroom is your knowledge of children's preferred learning styles within any particular subject. It may be possible not only to place children in environments that encourage learning, but also to expose them to ways in which other children learn and think. An example of this might be when you draw on the vast range of teaching methods advocated through the various thinking skills materials that are now available for primary schools. These methods allow children opportunities to think about and express their own thinking, normally referred to as metacognition. The ideas suggested by the 'Thinking on the Edge' resources (Rowley and Lewis 2003) would provide excellent starting points to these social experiences. Subjects such as geography and history naturally provide enquiry opportunities in which children can engage in problem solving, justifying ideas and analysing information.

Adults play an increasingly important role in primary classrooms. Look carefully at the way in which you plan for adults to interact with children at any given time or session. Do certain classroom assistants always work with the same children? How might some children benefit from working with particular parent volunteers? What do you actually ask adults to do when they work with children? Layered over these considerations is the extent to which those adults are able to manage children and allow their personality to shine through. For example, a parent with a strong sense of humour and sensitivity might be just the person to help you draw out a more reserved child, especially if you think they have more developed skills than you in this area.

Organizing children into groups for specific tasks is a further way of developing social interaction while also creating challenging learning environments. De Bono

(1982) suggests that the use of thinking hats can enable a class of children to analyse an issue or enquiry from various perspectives. The use of 'expert groups' can also be a way of using groups to make an in-depth study of a topic. For example, a class may be working on a science / geography project on 'energy'. They reach a point where the development of wind farms is discussed. The class could be divided into expert groups who research their focus in depth and then report back to the whole class. One group will collect relevant facts. Another group will investigate a case study of an existing wind farm. A further group will collect the arguments for and against. A final group might research the emotive and subjective issues raised through debates on wind farms. After reports from each expert group, children can be encouraged to come to their own conclusions on the range and quality of evidence available.

ICT resources provide numerous ways in which to support your organization of the classroom. The range of resources is beyond the scope of this chapter but is discussed in more depth in Chapter 8. However, there are some underlying principles that may be applied across the curriculum when organizing ICT within the classroom.

ICT should be viewed as a tool for solving problems and providing facilities for children to use, rather than simply an end in itself. Whatever piece of equipment you choose to use, think carefully about why it is fit for purpose and how it can help you provide effective learning environments. For example, if you video a science experiment in which a bridge construction is tested to destruction, children can then replay the video or DVD recording at leisure to study exactly what happened and offer scientific explanations. Photographs of distant places can be projected onto an interactive whiteboard and a whole class can ask questions and offer perspectives on their analysis of the images. A set of wireless laptops can be distributed around a classroom in order for very small groups to investigate selected websites offering materials of use in an historical investigation, leading to posters being produced for display in the classroom. Also see opportunities for other forms of social interaction through ICT. Can children be grouped in order that technical skills can be shared? Put children in groups where they can learn the skills of sharing equipment and taking turns. Provide opportunities for individuals and groups to be responsible for managing the use of ICT equipment, for example caring for a digital camera on an out-of-classroom activity.

Beyond the classroom

Although this chapter is about classroom organization, it is also important to consider organization beyond the classroom. The central argument here is that working with children beyond the bounds of the classroom may provide opportunities to extend the range of organizational styles experienced by your children.

Spencer and Blades (2006) argue that many modern children have more restricted experiences of the wider environment and fewer opportunities to learn how to survive in new and challenging situations. When you are planning out-of-classroom activities, look for opportunities to develop these skills. For example, on a river walk, instigate a buddy system to add a further layer of safety to those already provided by adults. This will enable children to take more responsibility both for themselves and for others. Use field visits to put children into groups that may seem unusual in the classroom: this can enable new social skills to be learnt in situations where the rules are not taken for granted. Use outdoor activities to let children see aspects of yourself as a person they may not be able to see in the classroom. For example, join in the canoeing activities while on a residential adventure week, rather than just leaving it to the instructors.

Picture 3.2 Working beyond the classroom

Use out-of-classroom activities to develop skills that may not be so easy to achieve in the classroom. For example, physical problem-solving challenges such as bridge building over imaginary rivers helps develop team skills while solving large physical challenges that could not be experienced in the classroom. New experiences can also be developed: environmental enquiries can be made much more concrete outdoors: tree hugging requires not only team skills and trust, but also greatly extended use of the senses. Finally, when out of the classroom, organize time for children to sit, look and ponder. You may be providing them with one of the few opportunities they get to look beyond home and school into the wider world.

References

de Bono, E. (1982) *De Bono's Thinking Course.* London: BBC Books.

Hastings, N. and Chantrey-Wood, K. (2002) *Re-organising Primary Classroom Learning.* Milton Keynes: Open University Press.

Lucas, D. (1990) Systems at work in the primary classroom – a retrospective study of classroom layout, in N. Frederickson (ed.) *Soft Systems Methodology: Practical Applications in Work with Schools.* London: Educational Psychology Publishing.

Maslow, A. H. (1968) *Towards a Psychology of Being.* New York: Van Nostrand Co.

Spencer, C. and Blades, M. (2006) *Children and their Environments: Learning, Using and Designing Spaces.* Cambridge: Cambridge University Press.

Rowley, C. and Lewis, L. (2003) *Thinking on the Edge: Thinking Activities to Develop Citizenship and Environmental Awareness around Morecambe Bay.* London: Living Earth.

4

Planning for Citizenship

John Halocha

Introduction

The purpose of this chapter is to help you plan for elements of citizenship using the broader learning environment, such as the family, home and wider community. The content is designed to help you develop a personal construct of what you believe citizenship to be and why it may be an important part of the whole curriculum in primary schools.

Background

During the late 1980s politicians were becoming concerned about a number of trends in British society. Young people were becoming less interested in the whole political process including their democratic right to vote. They were becoming alienated from the rest of society and a trend towards more violence was being observed: The most recent example of this is the apparent increase in knife violence. Relationships within communities and families were breaking down and there was a growing sense that networks of people at many levels were becoming less effective in supporting both individuals and shared needs. Citizenship was not brought into the educational debate simply to make young people 'good' citizens and inform them of the mechanics of society such as local politics or how court processes work. It was much deeper than that.

> Citizenship education stands at the confluence of the political, moral and social developments of our time. It is not bending language too much to refer to this as the 'crisis – the crossing point – of citizenship'. The crisis of citizenship calls for a holistic vision, shared values and a political framework capable of promoting these at every level.
>
> (Potter 2002: 38)

Potter's argument is that if future citizens are to participate in society and be responsible for their actions, some of their experiences at school need to prepare them for this. The Crick Report (1998) provided the framework and key concepts that are central in much of what we do in schools today. The philosophy behind the report clearly promotes the idea that young people need to develop a sense of social and moral responsibility, become involved in communities and a range of levels and finally, to develop a political literacy.

Social and moral responsibility

This strand is designed to help young people learn to become self-confident and to develop a sense of personal and shared responsibility both for their own actions and for those of larger groups.

Community involvement

The key to this is how schools can provide experiences through which young people begin to understand the power of working together as a community. Ideally this would happen at a range of scales, for example knowing how they can make a difference ny taking care of a pet. At a larger scale it might help them understand how communities need shared values in order to survive, by for example living within a set of classroom 'rules'.

Political literacy

This involves children becoming aware of how they can become effective in public life again at a range of levels from the local to the global. For example, will learn how conflict resolution and decision making take place in society.

The Crick Report (1998) also made clear that Citizenship is a unique subject in three ways:

- It is linked with other subjects.
- It is a way of life.
- It involves active participation by young people.

Citizenship is non-statutory in primary schools and the then Secretary of State for Education, David Blunkett, made it clear that it was a light touch Order in the sense that the three strands provided the framework for what pupils should learn, but the content and learning experiences should firmly be placed in the hands of teachers in order to make it relevant to their pupils and communities. The rest of this chapter examines how this may be done in practice.

Values underpinning a modern, participating democracy

In order to be clear about what you are planning and why you are doing it, the values listed in the Crick Report (1998) need noting in order to help you decide when and how these may be integrated into your planning for citizenship experiences.

- concern for the common good;
- belief in human dignity and equality;
- practice of tolerance;
- courage to defend a point of view;
- determination to act justly;
- commitment to equal opportunities and gender equalities;
- commitment to active citizenship and voluntary service;
- concern for human rights and the environment.

You are now probably becoming very aware of how important it is for Citizenship to be planned and at whole school level, based on a shared understanding by all involved of the key concepts. It is therefore assumed in this chapter that you will not be working alone and isolated in your classroom, but that your pupils will see their time with you as part of a greater inter-related whole. For example, there is little point in you being the only teacher whose pupils actively create, operate and amend a set of class rules. There is little point in you being the only teacher who has practical means for pupils to become involved in re-cycling. On the other hand you may disagree with this statement and say that if you find yourself doing something alone in a school, then someone has to start somewhere. However, a collaborative approach really does underpin the importance of a whole-school approach and commitment to active citizenship.

Practical and reflective task

Make a list of what you think it means to be an 'ideal citizen'. Date this list and try to look back to it in the coming months and amend it as you evolve your thinking based on practical experience.

Level 1
List what you think you may already be doing in your own life to promote the three strands identified by the Crick Report (1998). Put a date on this list and try to re-read it in the coming months to see if you can find other practical examples of the things you are doing. The reason for doing this is to help you see how far citizenship is rooted within your everyday life.

Level 2
List what you think you may already be doing in your classroom to promote the three strands identified by the Crick Report (1998). Put a date on this list and try to re-read it in the coming months to see if you can find other practical examples of the things your pupils' experience. The reason for doing this is to help you see how far citizenship is rooted within the everyday life of your class community.   *cont.*

> **Level 3**
>
> List what you think you may already be doing in your school to promote the three strands identified by the Crick Report (1998). Put a date on this list and try to re-read it in the coming months to see if you can find other practical examples of the things your whole school experience. The reason for doing this is to help you see how far citizenship is rooted within the everyday life of your school community.

But how do the values outlined in Crick (1998) become a real experience for pupils? It may be helpful to think about how pupils will experience citizenship. One may be at a very personal level, for example a friend helping them to sort out an argument with another child. Another may be at a school level where all pupils agree on one charity that as a school they will support for a year. I have seen this done very successfully in an Oxfordshire school where pupils invite adult representatives from a number of charities to give a presentation on their work. The whole school then votes to choose one charity and pupils develop relevant ideas to support the charity for a year. At another level, is the extent to which pupils develop their understanding of citizenship at a European or global scale. For example, a design technology project may involve them in choosing appropriate materials having researched their sources and any impacts their work might have on the environment and people both near and far away.

Planning for effective and active citizenship needs to consider how it may be built into lessons in many subjects. It also needs to take into account how it might interact with the broader life of the school. The above example showed how this could happen. One year the pupils chose a local hedgehog hospital charity. Science lessons examined what living things need to survive and be healthy. This linked in well with the school's healthy eating project, so pupils could begin to see how the individual and their community are inter-related and supportive of each other. This was reinforced by visits to a vet's surgery and a local medical practice to see the types of jobs people to there. Some interesting geography arose from a visit to an ambulance station to consider the best routes to reach patients and get them to hospital. It also raised issues about the level of medical facilities they had in their community. The key to successful planning is to think creatively about how pupils may experience citizenship in action through the broader whole school curriculum and the wider society in which they live.

> It is a move to involve young people consciously and positively in playing their part amongst the profound changes and fundamental disagreements and frustrations that make up today's society.
>
> (Potter 2002: 44)

At this point it may be helpful to reflect on the issues raised in the chapter on enquiry. The fundamental concept in that chapter was the extent to which pupils were actively responsible for asking questions to help their developing understanding of the world. In order to be successful, we need to consider the real messages of citizenship the school transmits to pupils. If all rules are created by adults, all enquiries set by teachers and narrow social conditions of learning such as working alone are commonplace, then perhaps there is little opportunity for pupils to develop much notion of citizenship apart from being compliant. This may lead to apathy and eventual withdrawal from any active approaches to citizenship. Indeed, this was the thinking behind the political initiatives leading up to the citizenship Orders. At the current time, the Assessment for Learning strategies and the extensive developments in the curriculum at Key Stage 3 may be seen as mechanisms whereby more traditional approaches to education are changing.

> Educational debate needs to move up a gear. Instead of tinkering around with the cosmetic changes to this or that bit of an antiquated curriculum, we need the breadth of vision to challenge the whole notion of curriculum, in the light of the kind of society we want to be.
>
> (Griffith 2000: 215)

Griffith (2000) reports on extensive research in primary and secondary schools into just what type of curriculum pupils experience and the messages it gives about what it is to be a citizen. He also draws on theoretical perspectives from other writers such as Jones (1990) and Giddens (1991). He suggests that independent learning is the key to pupils being able to gradually become active citizens through the process of education. He (Griffith 2000: 18–19) offers twelve factors that support the development of practical independent learning in school and wider contexts. They are listed below in order to help you develop a range of tools to help you plan citizenship into the curriculum. Clearly, they would not all appear in every learning experience. The key to effective planning is to apply these factors in the most appropriate situations and to ensure that pupils have a broad and balanced experience of them. Each one gives an example from the history study unit idea in order to see how it may work in practice while taking full account of the current legal requirements of the national curriculum.

Picture 4.1   Collaboration in building a sea defence

1 *Collaborative groupwork.* This would involve a small group of self- selected boys and girls developing an enquiry they have chosen themselves. For example, they could research into the lives of child evacuees in the Second World War or build a sea-defence.

2 *Cooperative groupwork.* This is where groups of pupils engaged in collaborative groupwork share ideas and information to move all their research forward. One group may find an especially useful book on children in the war and pass to another group.

3 *Individual responsibility.* Groups are taught to provide individuals with responsibility within their group. This might mean one pupil agreeing to do some research outside school and promise to report back the next day. For example, the group may decide that a local building may have some clues to help their history enquiry.

4 *Pupil-designed tasks.* Within the current legal requirements, pupils decide what each collaborative group want to research and their expected outcomes. For example, they may produce a life-size collage display of an evacuee which presents their findings.

5 *Pupil-designed assessment.* Each collaborative group is responsible for stating what should be assessed, the criteria and who is involved. To some extent, the 'Assessment for Learning' initiative goes some way to putting this into practice. In the history example, pupils might try to measure their increased understanding of what it was like to be an evacuee.

6 *Pupil-negotiated deadlines.* Griffiths (2000) argues that pupils should have the opportunity to decide how long an enquiry may take. This sounds rather idealistic in the current educational climate, but he would argue that if pupils are never given this experience, they may find it harder in life to manage personal and group time effectively. This is something for you also to reflect upon.

7 *Pupil-initiated research.* This is where pupils do not only use traditional sources such as books to develop their enquiries. The teacher's role is one of supporting their learning by providing IT resources, visitors and visits. In history it might mean helping pupils devise and evaluate questionnaires that may be completed in a local home for the elderly.

8 *Pupil use of a range of language technology.* This is the opportunity for pupils to use technology to explore and express their ideas. In studying the second world war, the issue may be raised about the right of bombing another group of people. They would access images off the web from the war, watch recordings of current news programmes to consider how war works today and perhaps use music technology to express their feeling about the effects bombing might have on people in the past and today.

9 *Community involvement and use of the environment.* This is crucial to effective planning for citizenship. Pupils need to experience learning that is seen as relevant both to their lives and to the lives of other people. In their history enquiry they will work with older people in the community, the local library, perhaps a local group of immigrants who have settled in Britain due to a current dispute in another country and study websites offering various interpretations of

war, for example those from the holocaust. Griffiths (2000) argues that learning outside the classroom is essential if pupils are to leave school with both an understanding of and sensitivity towards the wider world. In the history topic it might involve visiting older people, a local air force base or an appropriate museum.

10 *A sense of audience*. Pupils are encouraged to present their enquiry findings in ways appropriate to different audiences. This does two things: it help them to become aware of the need for active citizens to communicate effectively. The other is to share ideas and return something to a wider community. In the history example they may return to the residential home to tell their stories in the form of songs and poems. They may prepare a small display that goes to the museum in which they did some research. A powerpoint presentation could be set up in the school foyer for parents and visitors to see what and how they have been investigating in history. In the Geography example, in researching sea defences, children can produce a poster of findings to communicate their ideas to a wider audience.

11 *Presentation in various forms*. Griffith (2000) suggests that a range of presentation methods should be used to demonstrate learning. Posters, plays, stories, hot-seating, video are just a few of the many ways that you will have knowledge of from your own professional development in assessment strategies.

12 *Reflexivity*. Griffith (2000) argues that this approach helps pupils to take the initiative over their education both in school and as life-long learners. The process helps them to think about their own learning through self-critical reflection. In the history topic it may work in two ways. The first would be how pupils reflect on their process of learning history, where the emphasis is on the activity of learning rather than just historical facts. The second is the extent that the history has been a vehicle for the development of their own understanding of the second world war and connections with life in the 21st century. This applies the work of Gee (1987) on the nature of discourse in which the social nature of language and thinking helps pupils to 'involve the uses of language and ways of thinking, of believing, valuing and behaving which may offer human beings new and different ways of seeing the world.' (Arthur *et al.* 2000:31).

In all these factors the role of the teacher is fundamentally that of a learning mentor who encourages pupils to develop enquiries relevant to their lives and to reflect on their learning and the ways in which it developed.

Picture 4.2   Preparing a poster to communicate findings to a wider audience

Practical and reflective tasks

Hopefully, you now have some understanding of Griffith's (2000) factors.

Level 1
Choose one curriculum area you have taught in school and set out your planning. Look back at Griffith's (2000) factors. Highlight where you used these in your planning and teaching. Consider how you could improve the planning to incorporate citizenship more effectively.

Level 2
Chose one learning experience that you currently offer to pupils, for example, a history study unit. Set out your current planning materials for this. Look back at Griffith's (2000) factors. Highlight where you already use these. Note any possible positive impact they may have on your pupils' perception of active citizenship. For example, visitors from the local community may work with them on aspects of their

cont.

historical enquiries in order to help pupils see life from the perspective of other people. The next stage is to read through your planning to see if there are other opportunities to integrate any more of Griffith's (2000) factors in order to embed active citizenship further into the curriculum.

Level 3

Look at your school's scheme of work in one subject area, such as geography or history and consider how you meet Griffith's (2000) factors through the scheme. Work with your staff to see if there are other opportunities to integrate any more of Griffith's factors in order to embed active citizenship further into the curriculum.

You will no doubt have identified a tension in all this. So long as we have a legally binding national curriculum, teachers can only go so far along the lines of genuine pupil-centred learning and experience of the learning to control and manage enquiry within an environment that identifies and promotes active citizenship.

The following sections examine various practical issues involved in planning for active citizenship. They also identify authors and resources that may be used to support citizenship education.

Freedom to think

At the start of this chapter we noted the non-statutory nature of Citizenship in primary schools and the affirmation that teachers have the responsibility to develop citizenship in ways that are meaningful to the pupils in their school.

It is really important to grasp the opportunity that this freedom gives us as teachers to be creative, and to work with issues that our pupils generate themselves, that emerge from what is happening in the outside world at any particular time.

(Claire 2004: 19)

We can draw on the many approaches to thinking that have emerged over the past few years. Fisher (2003) has written extensively on how thinking activities may be developed within the curriculum. In particular Fisher (2001) explores the relationship between thinking and citizenship. He argues that the development of values is central to citizenship education. They may be personal values relating to pupil's ability to understand themselves. They may be moral values linked to our relationships with others. They may be social values that could work at a range of scales. For example sharing space in the playground or sharing resources such as water around Britain within the context of climate change.

Reflective Task

Below are listed Fisher's (2001) views on personal, moral and social values.

Level 1
Consider how useful they might be in planning citizenship into your next work with children.

Level 2
Consider how useful they might be in planning citizenship into the everyday life of your classroom. Start with what you may already be doing.

Level 3
Consider how useful they might be in planning citizenship into the everyday life of your school. Start with what you may already be doing.

Personal values
- understanding of oneself, our own character, strengths and weaknesses
- developing self control, self respect and self discipline
- showing perseverance in making the most of our talents and abilities
- growing self confidence to stand up for what is right
- taking responsibility for the way we lead our lives.

Moral values
- respect for others, irrespective of race, gender, social group or ability
- care for others and the exercise of courtesy towards them
- loyalty, trust and friendship
- co-operation with others and the ability to share
- patience, tolerance and the ability to resolve conflicts peacefully.

Social values
- truth, justice, freedom, equality and human rights
- respect for justice and the rule of law
- recognition of the importance of love and commitment
- responsibility as active citizens within a democracy
- concern for maintaining a sustainable environment for the future.

Fisher (2001) suggests that using stories can be a very effective way of helping to create a 'community of enquiry' in your classroom. The personal, social and moral issues raised in stories can be useful as they do not need to focus on individual pupils. Of course the power here is that pupils can then reflect on how issues raised in stories may relate to what is going on in their lives. Their mental enquiries and thinking are then very much focused on what is important to them, but they are allowed to apply them in a personal way. The book includes many stories and support resources. In particular, it contains many practical activities to help you allow pupils to develop their perception of citizenship through 'values for thinking' lessons.

Another very valuable resource is the 'Thinking on the Edge' material (Rowley and Lewis 2003) published by Living Earth. The main aim is to, 'consider our relationship to the environment through challenging the assumptions that we might make in defining ourselves as citizens, of both our local area and of the planet.' (Rowley & Lewis, 2003:4). It contains many practical activities and resources to encourage children to think about what it is to be a citizen who may critically think about their relationship with the environment. The materials would also be very useful in a school's staff development work on citizenship. It relies very much on a reflective, content free approach to planning activities. Many of the activities are based on the 'Philosophy for Children' (P4C) approach to thinking from the UK Society for the Advancement of Philosophical Enquiry and Reflection in Education (SAPERE) (www.sapere.net). This organization consists of teachers, parents and other interested in helping children to develop philosophical enquiries in order to help them understand the world. Their website will provide you with many starting points. Again, the strength of their approach is that it begins with pupils asking questions that interest, challenge or excite them. The teacher uses philosophical methods to enable pupils to consider issues that are especially appropriate in developing their ability to become thinking citizens.

Further practical approaches are suggested by Clough and Holden (2002). Again, their resources provide staff development activities, case studies, research findings and many ideas for children to experience. They outline five useful learning outcomes (2002:3) that you may wish to use as a checklist when planning citizenship activities. These are based on the *National Curriculum in England* document (DfEE/QCA 1999: 10).

- *Truth.* They suggest that teachers and learners will research together in order to collect a wide range of evidence that will support decision-making and the best possible understanding of an issue.
- *Honesty.* Teachers and learners will always be looking at how fairly ideas and information are presented in order to avoid bias or stereotypes.
- *Justice.* Teachers and learners will examine how fairly resources are distributed around the world. They will also show an ability to empathize with the customs and values of other people.
- *Trust.* This involves teachers and learners allowing pupils voices to be heard in order that they may experience citizenship in action. Also, the need to work within the law and Human Rights Conventions. It also includes the ability to trust each other as we work to solve mutual problems at a range of scales.
- *Sense of duty.* This may be achieved as teachers and learners work together in school environments that actively promote citizenship in decision making and change.

School can of course add their own values. One that you may wish to consider in your planning is the concept of 'emotional literacy'. Potter (2002:59) suggests that in our present society young people have fewer social and institutional means of helping them to understand themselves both as individuals and within broader social groups. You will be familiar with the many techniques used in drama education for developing emotional awareness but may not have seen the links with citizenship. Methods such as hot-seating, forum theatre, flash backs and flash forwards, paired improvisation and thought tracking may all help children begin to understand what is happening in their lives and how their lives are closely inter-connected with others. Theatre in Education (TiE) groups can also provide you with events and activities to help pupils explore the more emotional aspects of life within a secure environment. They can help provide relevant and creative activities that help pupils better understand the more emotional responses they have as citizens.

Controversial Issues.

The scheme of work for citizenship (DfES/QCA 2002) provides some guidance on managing sensitive and controversial issues. It also highlights the importance of ensuring that partisan political views are not promoted in schools and that a balance of views in provided on any issue: this is a statutory requirement. Therefore, when you are planning or expecting controversial issues to arise you do need to have carefully thought through how you might respond, the language you may use and the style in which you may approach the issue. Children are very good at 'reading' adults so it important to ensure that your language and body language are as neutral as possible. Another point is that issues may also arise at times when you are not expecting them. Indeed, if we are to move forward with citizenship then perhaps we should be hoping that pupils will raise issues as they become relevant to them. Therefore, it is perhaps worth having ready in your mind some phrases that may at least give you some thinking time.

Relationships

Many of the standard texts and guides on citizenship focus on the rationale behind it. Only a few ask us to reflect on the environment that we create in the classroom for helping pupils begin to understand their place in the world as a citizen. Jackson (2000: 7) reminds us that 'citizenship education helps pupils develop their strategies to form affective and fulfilling relationships, which are essential to life and learning.'

Relationships will be established in your classroom. We often take out teaching environments for granted. It may, therefore, be worthwhile taking a close look at the physical environment in which you and your pupils will be developing citizenship skills and values. What might the environment be saying to them? Do you allow pupils to choose who goes into groups? Do you sometimes intentionally place pupils in particular groups for a specific reason? What does grouping tell pupils about themselves? How visible is everyone in the classroom? You may well have been in a social situation where you felt that you were not physically at the 'centre' of things, or that it was difficult to make your point because you were not as visible as might have liked. Are there times when groups would be mixed or single gender? If you have a mixed age group class, are there times when ages are best mixed or separated? Increasingly as teachers we find ourselves with a class containing pupils from many racial and global origins. How well do you know your pupils to ensure they feel they are in an environment in which they feel safe and secure? As effective professionals, we would take these things into account, but they can become especially important at times when the focus is on citizenship because we are modelling an environment that w hope they will take with them into their wider lives. Are there times when everyone needs to appear equal?

Circle time

Over the past few years the various techniques of circle time (Curry and Bromfield, 1994) have been used by teachers as one approach to developing some aspects of citizenship. There are many occasions when the environment created by circle time techniques is appropriate. For example, it can provide a physical environment where participants feel they are equal. It can focus attention on the need to accept rules that we all follow in discussions. The danger is that it can become a part of classroom routine, especially if it appears on a class, year group or school timetable. There is a danger that if we adopt the 'it's there so we must do it' approach to circle time, it actually becomes meaningless to everyone involved. I have observed sessions where pupils are simply playing the game they have all learnt. Even worse are the circle times when the issues being discussed have very little relevance for the pupils themselves. This may be an issue you wish to discuss with colleagues. Rather than seeing it as a part of the timetable, perhaps we should view it more of a learning approach that we move into as and when it is appropriate. Be creative in your use of the technique and perhaps devise your own variations on the approach.

Inclusion

Ferguson and Lawson (2003) suggest that pupils with learning difficulties experience a curriculum that is adapted, interpreted and extended to fulfill their own needs. The concepts of enablement and empowerment, which are the cornerstones of the concept of citizenship, can play a particularly powerful role in their development as individuals within society. If you are working with children who have learning difficulties and wanting them to gain maximum involvement in citizenship activities, it may be worth reflecting on the words contained in the United Nations Convention on the Rights of the Child (1989) in which it states that children should

> enjoy a full and decent life, in conditions which ensure dignity, promote self-reliance and facilitate the child's active participation in the community . . . and that the child achieves the fullest possible social integration and individual development.
>
> (United Nations 1989: Article 23)

In many ways this echoes very closely the type of experience we would hope pupils may have if the concepts of teaching for citizenship are adopted as fully as possible. Ferguson and Lawson (2003) offer many activities that may be used to support pupils with learning difficulties to become active citizens.

Global citizenship

This is a very important concept in the wider debate on citizenship. It has been left until this point in the chapter because you may wish to draw on the preceding ideas as you reflect on the nature of global citizenship.

Young and Commins (2002) offer a very thorough introduction to the principles of global citizenship, along with many practical ideas for planning it into the curriculum.

Reflective Task

Read the statements below that Oxfam suggest helps to define a global citizen. They are given as a model to be aimed for and do have very high expectations. However, you are probably already doing much in your own school to lead pupils towards them.
  Oxfam (1997) suggest a global citizen
- is aware of the wider world and has a sense of their own role as a world citizen
- respects and values diversity
- has an understanding of how the world works economically, politically, socially, culturally, technologically and environmentally
- is outraged by social injustice
- participates in and contributes to the community at a range of levels from local to global
- is willing to act in order to make the world a more equitable and sustainable place
- takes responsibility for their actions.

Level 1
Beside each item, note down opportunities that you have experienced to work towards this ideal. When you have read this chapter, return to the list and note down new ways that might help to extend your pupil's opportunities to develop their view of themselves as a global citizen.

Level 2
Beside each one, note down opportunities that your pupils already have to work towards this ideal. When you have read this chapter, return to the list and note down new ways that might help to extend your pupil's opportunities to develop their view of themselves as a global citizen.

Level 3
Beside each one, note down opportunities that your school already has to work towards this ideal. When you have read this chapter, return to the list and note down new ways that might help to extend your pupil's opportunities to develop their view of themselves as a global citizen.

In the decade since this was written we have perhaps become even more aware of how interconnected the physical and human world is becoming. Maiteny and Wade (1999) sum this up by suggesting that

> All such systems are much more than the sum of their parts; they are holistic systems where all parts are mutually dependent. The ability to think holistically is a key skill for active and responsible citizens.
>
> (Maiteny and Wade 1999: 37–8)

As with all aspects of citizenship, the ways in which you will develop global citizenship in your teaching will be affected by the school context in which you work. Ideally, the school will have a coherent and creative policy that actively promotes pupils understanding of how they might be a global citizen and develop it across the curriculum.

We will use Oxfam's (1997) view of a global citizen to set you thinking about the types of experiences you can plan to help pupils both develop a sense of their place in the world while at the same time encouraging pupils to become self-directing learners.

Many valuable geographical enquiries can be developed by pupils to help them become aware of the wider world and their role in it. They could choose their favourite meal and research the source of each ingredient. This helps to develop a sense of how we rely on people across the world and also the effect we may have on their lives. It can lead to moral discussions about their actions and helping them make decisions about how they want to participate in a complex and interrelated world.

When pupils are studying religions, teachers rarely plan a global dimension into enquiries. Where have various religions developed? How do they reflect the geographical, social, moral and cultural foundations on which they are based? Help pupils to make full use of geographical resources such as Google Earth (www.earth.google.com) to help them develop a sense of where they and other people actually are on our planet. Many school communities now reflect this global distribution of beliefs and values. Perhaps at the present time we have an even more urgent need for our pupils to develop a sense of respect and value diversity.

Using ICT may be a very effective way to plan ways of helping pupils to understand how the world works. If you can help pupils establish links with pupils both in Britain and around the world, they will very quickly raise many questions about economic, political, social and environmental processes work. They will see many similarities and differences by actually interacting with people around the world using them as their resource for learning. See the Fiankoma project on the web (www.fiankoma.org) as an example of how powerful such a learning process can be. This constantly evolving website demonstrates how pupils in Brighton and Ghana are developing their understanding of each others way of life using ICT to communicate.

As you help pupils develop such enquiries, they will see examples of social injustice that can be discussed. The BBC News website (www.bbc.co.uk/news) contains much news that cannot be fitted into TV and radio broadcasts and is a excellent source of information. Of course this also helps to raise questions of how accurate and fair the information actually is. It can encourage pupils to consider other points of view.

Active participation in a community is central to the notion of citizenship education. At a local level pupils might identify ways in which older people in the community could become much more involved in the life of the school. Schools that promote this active citizenship report that everyone involved gains much from the experience socially, intellectually and emotionally. At a more global level, pupils can begin to consider how their actions can have effects in distant places, but also raise issues. For example the pupils may fund-raise to buy animals for other countries instead of sending Christmas presents. Some NGOs support this approach while others do not. This then provides a foundation for discussing the complexities of being a global citizen.

It also gives them practical opportunities to act to make the world more equitable.

Sustainability is perhaps becoming an issue of increasing global importance. There are now many questions that pupils can develop and research that are affecting all of our lives. For example, may pupils fly in aeroplanes. Why do they do it and where do they go? Does this really have an effect on the environment locally and globally? Does it matter? This last question is central to citizenship activities in that it provides opportunities for pupils to make informed decisions based both on information and a set of developing and personal value systems. This in turn can enable them to take responsibility for their actions.

Conclusion

Hopefully, these examples will set you thinking about how you can begin to plan relevant and creative learning opportunities in which your pupil's understanding of what it is to be a citizen can evolve. All through this chapter we have been aware of the tension between a statutory national curriculum, prescribed teaching systems such as the literacy hour, national testing, school league tables and inspection on the one hand clear guidelines from official sources for the need to develop much more child-focussed and creative ways for young people to learn as developing and active citizens. It is perhaps time for the teaching profession to re-evaluate what it really believes in and why we put in all the commitment that we do. Potter (2002) concludes that

> In this context citizenship education is not so much a subject – with all the fuss and palaver about assessment criteria and inspection – as one small, but vital, means to create and sustain a vibrant and genuinely democratic society for our children and grandchildren.
>
> (Potter 2002: 45)

References

Arthur, J., Davison, J. and Stow, W. (2000) *Social Literacy, Citizenship Education and the National Curriculum*, London: Routledge Falmer.

Claire, H. (2004) (ed.) *Teaching Citizenship in Primary Schools*, Exeter: Learning Matters.

Clough, N. and Holden, C. (2002) *Education for Citizenship: Ideas into Action. A Practical Guide for Teachers of Pupils aged 7–14*, London: Routledge Falmer.

Curry, M. and Bromfield, C. (1994) *Personal and social education for primary schools through circle time*, Tamworth: NASEN.

DfEE / QCA (1999) *National Curriculum in England*, London: DfEE / QCA.

DfES / QCA (2002) *Citizenship. A scheme of work for Key Stages 1 and 2*. London: DfES / QCA.

Ferguson, A. and Lawson, H. (2003) *Access to Citizenship. Curriculum planning and practical activities for pupils with learning difficulties*, London: David Fulton.

Fisher, R. (2001) *Values for Thinking*, Oxford: Nash Pollock.

Fisher, R. (2003) *Teaching Thinking*, London: Continuum.

Gee, J.P. (1987) *The Social Mind: Language, Ideology and Social Praxis*, New York: Bergin & Garvey.

Giddens, A. (1991) *Modernity and Self Identity: Self and Society in the Late Modern Age*, Oxford: Oxford University Press.

Griffith, R. (2000) *National Curriculum: National Disaster? Education and Citizenship*. London: RoutledgeFalmer.

Jackson, E. (2000) 'What is citizenship education?' in K. Grimwade *et al.* (2000) *Geography and the New Agenda. Citizenship, PSHE and Sustainable Development in the Primary Curriculum*, Sheffield: Geographical Association.

Jones, (1990) 'Reader, writer, text: knowledge about language and the curriculum', in R. Carter (ed.) *The LINC Reader*, London: Hodder & Stoughton.

Maiteny, P. and Wade, R. (1999) 'Citizenship Education' in S. Bigger and E. Brown (eds) *Spiritual, Moral, Social and Cultural Education. Exploring Values in the Curriculum*. London: David Fulton.

Oxfam (1997) *A Curriculum for Global Citizenship*. Oxford: Oxfam.

Potter, J. (2002) *Active Citizenship in Schools*, London: Kogan Page.

QCA (1998) *Education for Citizenship and the Teaching of Democracy in Schools*, Final Report of the Advisory Group on Citizenship, London: QCA.

Rowley, C. and Lewis, L. (2003) *Thinking on the Edge. Thinking activities to develop citizenship and environmental awareness around Morecambe Bay*. London: Living Earth.

United Nations (1989) *UN Convention on the Rights of the Child*.

Young, M. and Commins, E. (2002) *Global Citizenship. The Handbook for Primary Teaching*, Cambridge: Chris Kington Publishing. / Oxfam.

Useful websites

BBC News www.bbc.co.uk/news

Fiankoma Project www.fiankoma.org

Google Earth www.earth.google.com

UK Society for the Advancement of Philosophical Enquiry and Reflection in Education: www.sapere.net

5

Behaviour Management

Mark Chater

Introduction

This chapter will address the skills and attitudes involved in managing behaviour in the primary classroom. The overall argument will be that, while there can be some consistent approaches and underlying values that benefit the promotion of 'good' behaviour, there is a considerable lack of consensus on what 'good' behaviour could be, and on how to achieve it. Expectations change as societies evolve; so do practical approaches to reward, motivation and punishment.

At the present time, most successful trainee teachers, newly qualified teachers, more experienced teachers and other colleagues working in schools agree that it is necessary to understand the *reasons* for behaviour as a prelude to calling it 'good' or 'bad'. Several well-established theoretical frameworks for explaining behaviour are discussed and evaluated. These include 'metanarrative' theories, such as emotional or economic factors, as well as 'micronarrative' causes, such as poor planning on the part of the teacher. Having a critical grasp on these factors is presented as a necessary preparation for dealing positively and constructively with difficult behaviour, and for reinforcing positive behaviour.

The more immediate environment in which good behaviour can be supported begins with the school as a whole, its communication, leadership, management and collective values. These are discussed for the impact they can have on the work of the classroom teacher. Even more immediately, the classroom environment, the expectations of the teacher, the daily routines and, crucially, the process leading up to the formulation of rules, can all have a powerful effect on behaviour.

Interactive tasks relevant to different professional levels are designed to stimulate thinking and to allow professional ownership of ideas, reinforcing the central point that there is no eternal definition of good (or bad) behaviour, and no permanently effective classroom method for getting it. Instead, there is a provisional definition: good behaviour is that which is conducive to the best possible learning in security and enjoyment, supported by consistent behaviour systems which provide the nurturing and the calling-to-account that the young need.

Where do our ideas about acceptable behaviour come from?

There is nothing either good or bad, but thinking makes it so.

(*Hamlet*, II. ii. 259)

Good behaviour in children is not a fixed or definite thing, any more than the good life is an agreed notion among adults. What we require of children will differ from one society or age to the next; therefore our present expectations must be seen as temporary constructs rather than certain solutions.

How a society defines the acceptable and normal in people's behaviour, and delineates these from the deviant or abnormal, has undergone many changes. In the nineteenth century, industrialization and mechanization led to a hardening of these definitions, so those identified as criminal or insane (and these two conditions were often conflated) would be sent to asylums or workhouses. There, they would be physically, socially and symbolically separate from the rest of society.

To identify as insane anyone whose behaviour deviates from the agreed norm may now seem an immoderate judgement, but less than a century ago it was common enough:

> The feeble-minded are a parasitic, predatory class, never capable of self-support or of managing their own affairs ... they cause unutterable sorrow at home and are a menace and danger to the community ... every feeble-minded person, especially the high-grade imbecile, is a potential criminal.
>
> (Fernald 1912, cited in Armstrong 1998: 33)

The schooling system that grew from that period was universal and compulsory, and has been, to some extent, the willing inheritor of those very clear delineations of the 'well' from the 'mad', and of the acceptable from the unacceptable. The harsh language and punitive measures have largely disappeared, at least from official thinking, but the widespread need for clarity about borderlines remains a reality. It can be observed, for instance, that teachers and parents frequently speak of the benefits of 'boundaries', 'clear rules' and the 'security' of knowing right from wrong; when confronted with 'difficult' behaviour, they voice the need for 'isolation', 'time out' or 'sanctions'. These language uses are constructs too; milder no doubt, and certainly moderated by a new professional awareness of the obligation to understand children's needs and respond to them – but even this new commitment to identifying and meeting needs is, itself, a constructed understanding of behaviour. The mental constructs within which we live, breathe and work are usually harder to identify as constructs, because we take them for granted as real and true. Yet it has probably happened to all of us, once or twice, that we privately wondered whether a particular school rule, lesson convention or teacher's judgement was, in the grand scheme of things, right – even though it did reflect the prevailing definitions.

To accept that there is a temporary and constructed nature to the way we manage and judge children's behaviour in school is not to admit defeat. Indeed, we are more likely to be able to see and understand the causes of unacceptable behaviour if we critically understand our own expectations and assumptions.

The present construction owes a great deal to the national curriculum framework. This is prefaced by a statement of aims and purposes (QCA 1999: 10–11) in which it is asserted that education aims at well-being, equality and values (p. 10) and that the purpose of the taught curriculum is, among other things, 'to promote pupils' spiritual, moral, social and cultural development, and prepare all pupils for the opportunities, responsibilities and experiences of life' (p. 11). A longer statement of values offers an ethical backdrop in the form of position statements on four cluster areas: valuing the self (self-esteem, health), valuing others (property, toleration, respect), valuing society (participation) and valuing the environment (sustainability, bio-diversity and repair of damage) (QCA 1999: 195–7). While it is not expected that every teacher, pupil or parent will be able to sign up to every statement – and that is not its purpose – the overall effect is to create a set of conditions in which it is felt that education is moral, not technical, and that schools care about behaviour because of its consequences for the whole person, more than caring about conformity and quiet so that the curriculum can be taught on time.

In our consideration of the causes of behaviour and the best responses to it, we will follow this construction and take the whole child as our focal point.

What affects behaviour?

Anyone can become angry – that is easy, but to be angry with the right person at the right time, and for the right purpose and in the right way – that is not within everyone's power and that is not easy.

(Aristotle 384–322 BC)

We begin this section with a consideration of two factors that are held to be major contributors to negative behaviour. These factors are identified as metanarratives to convey the idea that many teachers, researchers and others hold an overarching belief about the causes of misbehaviour. However, we must recall the discussion above, namely that all definitions and theories about behaviour are temporary constructs.

Metanarrative 1: Children's behaviour is conditioned by their emotional state and their early emotional experiences

Children's most basic beliefs about themselves and the world around them (including their self-esteem, capacity to hope and to grow in confidence, and ability to collaborate and seek help) may sometimes be in deficit for emotional reasons often connected with early childhood (Brearley 2001: 30). The ability to recognize, and transform, our negative feelings about ourselves and our life is often called emotional intelligence (EI). Users of EI will often refer to the three levels of the brain, controlling, respectively, our instinctive, social and intellectual functions. They argue that in moments of extreme emotion, the brain is literally flooded with one overpowering feeling (fear and anger are the most common negative examples) that comes from the instinctive (limbic) brain and bypasses the intellectual functions, drowning out any possibility of rational thought or action – an 'emotional hijacking' (Goleman 1996: 13). According to this theory, the pupil who engages in attention-seeking behaviour does so because his / her brain is flooded with feelings emerging from a basic belief that 'they won't notice me' or 'they don't want me'. The pupil who resorts to diversionary tactics instead of working (toilet, low-level disruption, helplessness) does so because his / her being is dominated by a basic belief that he / she 'cannot do it' and 'will always fail'. The pupil who has frequent fits of rage does so because of an overpowering wave of frustration stemming from a basic belief that 'they will never give me what I want' ('they' being any adult, or life in general). These basic beliefs are not articulated in words; if they were, they could be addressed rationally and more easily with skilled help. Instead, the basic beliefs are acted out through behaviour. Unfortunately, the negative behaviour tends to reinforce the negative self-belief because of its impact on others.

> If as a child we believe we are not liked, then we can spend all our time proving it. If we feel we are not lovable, then we may make sure no one will ever love us. This is now our truth, this is how we see our place in the tribe.
>
> (Corrie 2003: 35)

Thus, emotional intelligence theory understands the causes of behaviour to be in the person's self-image, and the cure to be in changing the feelings about self and about life – change from within. Therefore, the school's function should be understood not as enforcing conformity to rules but as empowering emotional maturity and self-acceptance. Many schools now aspire to be emotionally literate schools, using the research in EI to define the roles of their pastoral staff and senior leadership, and using the agenda of *Every Child Matters* and the Healthy Schools initiative to develop their work (Weare 2004: 169). Advocates of this approach will sometimes claim that the national effort to drive up standards of attainment, attendance and behaviour in schools will fail unless and until the emotional and intellectual relationships are improved, and that emotional well-being has become a casualty of the highly prescriptive drive towards excellence (Blum 2001: 137–8).

The weakness of this metanarrative is that it blurs the distinctions between teaching and therapy. Teachers have many calls on their time and skills apart from attending to emotional need, whether their own or their pupils'. The pace of reform, the nature of competitiveness and the hierarchical culture of the profession make EI approaches to behaviour inappropriate at times. A more fundamental objection is sometimes raised that schools, like societies, cannot always be attending to underlying causes, and must sometimes delineate the unacceptable, even if at the cost of excluding some individuals.

Metanarrative 2: Children's behaviour is conditioned by social, economic and political factors

There is a widespread and long-standing belief among teachers that difficult behaviours around attendance, social skills, interaction with other pupils and homework have roots in socio-economic factors (Watkins and Wagner 1987: 20). In analysing difficult behaviour, Blum (1998: 6–7) identifies a range of recurring factors: lack of English language; high unemployment; disunited parent, governor or staff bodies; and serious local clashes of clan, religion or race. Users of this collection of explanations may be interested in models of behaviour management that emphasize the entitlement of all to learning in peaceful, productive surroundings as an egalitarian measure to be valued for democratic and inclusive reasons (Hodgson and Spours 1999). However, others may take a more radical view, inherited from Illich (1971), that schooling itself is the root cause of behaviour problems, because school alienates and institutionalizes the young, teaching them to expect, and not to resist, further alienation and institutionalization throughout life. Countering this, the school democracy movement offers case studies in the transformation of primary schools in multiply deprived areas. The transformation is made effective by a major shift in teachers', heads' and local authorities' values (Apple and Beane 1999: 68ff). The focus is on collaboration between teachers and learners, on free and open discussion of contextual social issues in class, on directly addressing bilingualism and race, and on borrowing elements of the emotional literacy movement in order to ensure that human relations are a higher priority than the curriculum:

> So often, when we're in the middle of an incident, we want to fix it, make everything OK, and go on with the lesson. But here . . . we try to make sure that when you're in the middle of an incident, it gets processed. . . . Those are truly teachable moments in terms of human relations, and if you believe that's an important lifetime skill, you stop the lesson and deal with it.
>
> (Ahlgren 1993: 30)

Teachers who broadly accept this analysis of behaviour may also be interested in the approach to discipline as restorative justice, avoiding punishment and emphasizing the restoration of right relations in school after a misdemeanour (Hopkins 2004).

On the other hand, this metanarrative, like its emotional counterpart, may be too seductively simple. Perhaps it is too easy to explain behaviour as driven by social class:

> Such an approach can all too easily fall into the trap of romanticising the school pupils in question as working-class heroes, whose disruption is their expression of resistance to schooling.
>
> (Watkins and Wagner 1987: 20)

The other main objection is that what starts as a teacher's *explanation* of difficult behaviour may easily and subtly change into a school's *excuse* for low expectations in

behaviour. Schools would then end up tolerating that which impedes the progress of the poorest pupils. When teachers are heard to say things like, 'what do you expect of these kids, it's a tough neighbourhood', the shift from explanation to excuse has already begun. The Labour government's climate of high expectations was designed in part to counter this trend and to ensure that the highest standards were demanded from all pupils – for egalitarian reasons. The rhetoric of 'opportunity for all' and 'excellence for all' in part reflects this priority, but is not without its internal contradictions (Watson and Bowden 2001).

Both metanarratives, while attractive to some teachers, carry an additional danger: they have the potential to distract teachers from attending to the smaller, practical factors which can make a negative or positive difference to behaviour in class. At all levels of the profession, from the chalkface to policy making, the tide may have turned against metanarratives of behaviour: in a government circular of 1999, the identifying of underlying causes came eighth out of nine key principles of sound behaviour management, trailing behind much more practical measures such as setting good habits early, rewarding achievement and involving pupils (DfEE 1999). While some teachers can be aware that some behaviour problems are related to deeper emotional and / or wider political issues, many teachers agree that the classroom, as a safe, positive environment, is a good place to begin with expecting, teaching and reinforcing positive norms of behaviour in support of learning (DES 1987, DfES 2002). It is to these micronarratives of behaviour that we now turn.

The smaller causes of poor behaviour could include any combination of the following:

- schools not achieving the best possible match between the curriculum and the needs of pupils, for instance by not going far enough in differentiating schemes of work and lesson activities (DES 1989: 13);
- weak planning, in which objectives are unclear or inappropriate, or the lesson structure is monotonous, or the chosen teaching strategies are not matched to the needs and interests of the children (Ofsted 2003b: 36), for example by regularly favouring visual learners over aural or kinaesthetic;
- planning in which outcomes, activities or pace are pitched wrongly for some pupils, resulting in a failure to engage them effectively (Ofsted 2003b: 36) and in their feeling excluded, either by boredom (higher ability) or by confusion, frustration or alienation (lower ability);
- limited communication, or breakdowns in communication, between teachers and learners (Collins *et al.* 2002: 53);
- failure of teachers, teaching assistants and other support professionals to work together consistently and regularly on standards of behaviour (Ofsted 2003b: 36; Bentham 2006: 3);
- lack of consistency in establishing, reinforcing and applying rules early, positively and consistently (Constable 1998: 2–3);
- children's difficulties in specific social issues, such as making friends (Webster-Stratton 1999: 256) or regulating their own emotions skilfully (ibid: 285);

- children's social difficulties arising from a particular condition: for example, dyspraxia resulting in clumsiness; or attention deficit disorder resulting in restlessness, absent-mindedness or poor concentration; or autism resulting in difficulties in understanding and using social norms (Bentham 2006: 34);
- children's difficulties arising from a specific learning difficulty, for example, dyslexia, leading to feelings of frustration, incompetence, fear and anger (Dyslexia Institute 2006); the same applies to dyscalculia (difficulty with numbers, particularly mental arithmetic) and to dyspraxia (difficulty with physical coordination);
- specific behaviours brought on by diet, including food colouring or food / drink additives that may interfere with concentration or produce hyperactivity (Food Standards Agency 2005);
- individual, group and class factors, for example if pupils are unsettled by a change of teacher or of routine (Constable 1998: 2–3).

Picture 5.1 Motivating and involving children

Practical and reflective task

Is behaviour in primary schools a gendered issue?

Gender studies suggest that some forms of behaviour in school have at least as much to do with gender as they do with rules, teacher professionalism or pupil commitment. For instance, Blum (2001) believes that anger among pupils and teachers is predominantly a male problem, generally accompanied and supported by stereotyped gender roles and particularly exacerbated by the social expectation that males should suppress all but a very narrow range of emotions. It is known that bullying and violence take different forms between boys and girls in the UK (Smith 2003). Cultural expectations will sometimes create assumptions that girls are 'nice' and boys are 'tough'; and indeed parents can reinforce these views even when emotionally literate schools are trying to challenge them (Weare 2004). Could such assumptions be fuelling the problem identified by Blum? Nevertheless, it should not be forgotten that behavioural difficulties may have many causes, and can be divergently understood from medical, psychodynamic, behaviourist (i.e. here and now), cognitive and school-system perspectives (Cole 1998) as well as gender.

Try a small-scale research project to test these ideas with a primary class in a school.

Level 1

While observing a class being taught by an experienced teacher, keep a discreet tally of behaviour issues in the class for half a day. Organize the information so that it includes the gender of each pupil whose behaviour presents a problem.
- Does the number of issues differ between genders?
- Do the kinds of issues differ (e.g. physical / verbal)?

Level 2

If possible, discuss your class, and their behavioural issues, with the previous teacher. Over a one-week period, work with a teaching assistant to keep a discreet tally of behaviour issues in the class. Organize the information so that it includes the gender of each pupil whose behaviour presents a problem.
- Does the number of issues differ between genders?
- Do the kinds of issues differ (e.g. physical/verbal)?

Level 3

Follow up the Level 2 task by having a discussion with the teaching assistant. Together, consider any gender differences that may have arisen in the tally you kept. Consider why these differences exist, and evaluate the influence of home background, parental expectations, teacher / school expectations and cultural / media factors.

Every professional, from the training stage and throughout their career, will come face to face with situations that illustrate how behaviour difficulties are caused by a number of factors coming together, combining emotional, social and smaller specific factors. The most effective professionals are those who learn to find the solutions by understanding the causes, and who work with other professionals, rather than in isolation. For trainee teachers, the need to understand the factors that contribute to children's behaviour is clearly recognized in Standard 2.4, and is every bit as important as learning the 'skills' or 'tricks' of behaviour management from watching more experienced colleagues. For established teachers, the need for effective communication with parents and other professionals is reinforced in the inspection standards that ask about how well the school works in partnership with parents, other schools and the community (Ofsted 2003a). The following task is designed to give an opportunity to reflect on the importance of understanding causes and working together on solutions.

Reflective task

Considering an individual behaviour problem in a classroom

Think of one child in a class – a child who is seen as showing behavioural problems.
- Identify basic information on the child: gender, age, year group, size of class.
- Make a list of the specific behaviours that are seen as problematical, for example getting up and walking around without permission; kicking; talking.
- Write a sentence evaluating those behaviours. Consider why the child's behaviours are considered 'naughty'.

Level 1

If you are a trainee teacher: consult your mentor or class teacher about the child. Try to discover, and agree on, some reasons for these behaviours: for instance, is the child very young / old in his / her year group? Is the child socially isolated in the class? Is the gender mix balanced in the class?

Levels 2 and 3

Research the child's record in school, including communication with the home, attendance record, report from last school or performance data, as appropriate. Discuss the child with a colleague, such as a teaching assistant or health worker. Try to discover, and agree on, some underlying causes for these behaviours.

The school as an environment for positive behaviour

The issues of management and leadership in the school as a whole, and how they affect the ethos and values of the school, do not fall within the scope of this book, but clearly their relevance to the behaviour of individuals should be recognized. The atmosphere or ethos of a school can be shaped by the leadership group and governors. The quality of their working relationships with each other, of their communication and their expectations, will form part of the air that pupils breathe in the school. Management decisions will also concretely affect the range of 'micronarrative' factors which, in turn, affect behaviour: this is specially true of the appropriateness of the curriculum, the nature of communication, the quality of care, vigilance and guidance, as well as the consistency with which behaviour expectations are reinforced.

There is therefore a need for every school leadership team to think about its curriculum flexibility, its budget for forms of special support, and its inter-agency approach, so that there is a permanent focus on finding ways to achieve personalized learning, to be able to pay for appropriate support, and to gain trust and communication between the front-line agencies working with an individual child or a family (Clough 1998). School behaviour management policies should be working documents, regularly referred to and reviewed, informing the behaviour and practice of all staff (Blum 2001: 76).

In inspecting schools, Ofsted pays close attention to the school's communication and partnership. What has sometimes been called 'joined-up thinking' really implies a management culture that regularly and effectively communicates within and across professional divisions (teacher, nurse, teaching assistant, educational psychologist, chaplain, parent / carer), to ensure that knowledge of the child's needs is pooled, that consistent messages of challenge and support are reaching the child, and that a carefully built structure for social learning is in place. How well the school works with parents, other schools, other professionals and the community is a key inspection criterion (Ofsted 2003a). School handling of information and planning with teaching assistants, to ensure frequent reinforcement of school values, remains a crucial and sometimes neglected area.

It is worth remembering that all communication and management systems are there simply to create conditions for best possible professional knowledge of the child's needs. The systems can only work when they are used to create that knowledge, which is then used to help the pupil. For example, individual behaviour plans (IBPs) work best to back up and strengthen the conversation that pupil, teacher and parent have had. IBPs are not a substitute for relationships.

Practical and reflective task
Analysing a behaviour issue in the school

Think of one behaviour issue that has effects beyond the classroom, for example the behaviour of one difficult year group, or supervision / safety issues in one part of the school, or name-calling / exclusion in break time.

- Make a list of the specific behaviours that are seen as problematic, for example talking in Assembly, running in the corridor, play-fights that turn into real fights.
- Write a sentence evaluating those behaviours. Consider the impact of the behaviours on other children, the staff and the school environment.

cont.

Level 1

If you are a trainee teacher; consult your mentor or class teacher about the child. Try to discover what action has been / is being taken to deal positively with the issue(s).

Levels 2 and 3

Work with others to research the issue, by asking questions such as: Has this happened with previous year groups? Is there a causal factor in time of day, time in week, weather, diet? What communication strategies is the school using (parents, other agencies) to remind children about rules / values and to intervene?

The classroom as an environment for positive behaviour

A successful classroom in behaviour terms may be considered as a good ecological balance: an environment in which every organism is useful to the whole, and in which the factors leading to change are carefully balanced with the factors keeping things the same. In such an environment, pupils and teachers are constantly 'teaching' each other in the sense that they are letting each other know what is going on inside and between them about their behaviour (Rogers 2002: 5) and in regard to their feelings. Yet also, the teacher and other professionals in the classroom have the greater power to modulate the environment on the basis of what they notice and interpret about pupils' needs.

Most of the environmental modulating will consist of keeping a balance. Specifically, the teacher and the other adults in the room need to find the middle-way strategy of relaxed vigilance; between the extremes of overly vigilant behaviour (which may, at its worst, be aggressive, sharp-voiced, sarcastic, excessively picky, demanding, vengeful, punitive, humiliating or controlling) and non- or under-vigilance (which may, at its worst, be vague, evasive, indecisive, weak, whining, inconsistent or pleading (Rogers 2002: 7–9). Both extremes are equally undesirable. The adults in the classroom need to know their own and each other's tones of voice, body language and preferred strategies well enough to avoid the extremes and steer a productive middle course.

The adults in the classroom can work together to develop strategies that they will use for reinforcing rules and conventions in the classroom environment. When used consistently and regularly, the following short selection of strategies are just some of those that can maintain the desired ecological balance of behaviour expectations and emotional responses:

- Developing routines of explicit reminding on classroom rules, so that pupils all feel positively challenged and secure in their knowledge of what is and is not acceptable. With some classes, this reminding can include brief, frequent discussions of why a particular rule exists. With most classes, the reminding routines will be developmental, focusing on particular rules as necessary, and moving on to others when a point has been securely established.

- Tactical pausing, when teaching or issuing instructions, to signal that you are waiting for a particular rule or convention to be followed.
- Eye contact, which signals a positive regard for an individual pupil, perhaps mixed with a non-verbal message that the pupil should sit down and listen.
- Having a general preference for manoeuvring away from confrontation when possible, so that a positive experience of learning, rather than a negative experience of rebuke and clash, can be uppermost – but also accepting that this strategy will not be possible all the time.
- Making a general attempt to 'keep main thing the main thing', that is, to focus on the most important behaviour expectations for a class and an individual child, for instance the expectations as defined by an IBP. This will sometimes mean not challenging every single item of poor behaviour, especially if it is residual, accidental or if the challenge is likely to distract from larger and more important goals.
- A strong, positive and regular collaborative relationship between teacher, teaching assistant and other support professionals, maintained by regular eye contact, sharing of strategies and joint evaluations. A genuine coalition of two adults in the classroom is surely much stronger than the sum of its parts.

Strategies to gain and keep the pupils' attention should not be seen as 'tricks of the trade' that can simply be adopted by imitating more experienced teachers. As has been argued above, successful behaviour outcomes begin in the preparation and atmosphere of the whole school, and in the attitude of the teachers and other staff; these background items are of more importance than the foreground of teacher techniques, in the sense that values and attitudes are irreplaceable, whereas techniques and strategies vary.

As an example, let us consider an individual infant teacher who develops strategies for getting her class on task and refocusing them. She uses a number of non-verbal cues – hands in the air, clapping, eye contact, music and lights on / off. Over time, she finds that music works well and, as the class get to know her, they respond easily to a short snippet of music as a signal to end their play or their work activity and to pay attention to her. She also employs a graduated series of verbal cues, making her voice progressively softer as she looks personally at pupils in all parts of the room. The exact cues will vary, but this is one example: 'looking this way everyone . . . looking at me . . . this way Sophie . . . thank you everyone . . . looking at me, Krishan . . . everyone looking this way and listening . . . listening now . . . good, now we are ready . . .' (all the while her voice is becoming quieter, so that the class needs to quieten in order to hear her). Both she and the class come to be comfortable with this routine and this set of methods designed to uphold key expectations about paying attention. The behaviour of the class improves, and so does the teacher's enjoyment of her work with them. The teacher also pays careful attention to physical aspects of the classroom environment, particularly to space, display, heating, lighting, storage of liquids and sharp objects, organization of 'themed' areas to give coherence and routine to the experience of being in the room, and to furniture, seating and grouping (Moyles 1992: 34ff).

In due course the teacher is assigned as mentor to a trainee. The trainee starts by observing the teacher, and tries to imitate her manner of speech and her method of softening her voice, using music and other tactics. This takes place without any discussion, between the teacher and the trainee, about the teacher's philosophy. There is, therefore, no sharing of the psychological reasons behind her use of voice, nor is there any joint thinking about how the physical classroom promotes security, comfort, enjoyment and equality as prerequisites of learning. The trainee simply appears and tries to replicate the small part of the teacher's practice that she has seen. The class pays no attention to the trainee, even though, outwardly, the methods are the same. Their noise level does not go down; capturing the attention of the class becomes a struggle; the trainee resorts to raising her voice and rebuking individuals picked out more or less at random. The atmosphere in the class begins to be less positive.

In another example, a newly qualified teacher develops a highly successful behaviour management approach with his rather restless Year 5 class. He uses his 'big' personality, powerful voice, love of sport and sense of humour to jolly the class into paying attention and to cajole them into staying on task. Typical verbal cues are of the kind: 'Come on, we can do better than this! . . . That's right Alex, round it off nicely. . . . Oi, you lot, you'll never finish in a month of Sundays if you don't pipe down!'. The pupils like him. Some teachers have reservations about his 'joshing' and informal tone, but because the class never steps seriously out of line, and because the school has more pressing issues, the teacher is left to continue with these methods.

Then a teaching assistant is assigned to his class. She tries to engage him in discussions of strategies to support the needs of weaker and more easily distracted pupils, but he clearly has no wish to share his ideas, and his choice of approaches when in the classroom remains idiosyncratic and unpredictable for the teaching assistant. She is left struggling to adapt her methods to his from minute to minute. She suggests that they both use a noise meter (or 'shoutometer') to control talking levels in the class. (It can be used with, say, four settings with a dial, or three 'traffic light' settings.) He agrees to her making and installing it, but never uses it himself. She feels she cannot establish any authority or develop any coherent modus operandi of her own. She also notices that when he is out of school, the supply teacher is faced with a much harder task because of the lack of predictable, clear and reinforcable norms. Eventually, after several attempts to resolve the situation, the teaching assistant asks to be moved to another teacher.

In both episodes we can detect two strands: the apparent success of an individual teacher in establishing behaviour strategies, and the less than successful strategy of the teacher, or the system in school, in building outwards from their practice. Quiet or conforming classrooms are not the only indicators of a successful behaviour approach, and in some cases their appearance may be deceptive; the emphasis should be on the hidden power of routine in maximizing security and therefore minimizing off-task behaviour, attention seeking or aggression. Working in isolation, even with a strategy that appears to produce results, has serious drawbacks. There is a need to share good practice by asking why it works and whether it could work better, and by forming strategic alliances of adults and children. All teachers, even the most experienced, need the support, feedback and collaboration and advice of their colleagues, and should feel free to ask for it (Rogers 2002: 157). When teachers work in isolation, they are more likely to adopt notions of control, winning, standing on an abstracted concept of their own authority. Working with other adults will help them to start using adult, self-controlled behaviour that focuses on the pupils, and lays out expectations clearly without requiring humiliation or defeat.

An emotionally literate approach to behaviour problems includes making space for people to talk and establishing rules so that others do not feel blamed or victimized. Regular, stepped questions might be used with pupils aged 6 and upwards, whether in circle time or in special one-to-one conversations after an incident has occurred. Here is one example of the routine:

What is the problem?
How do you feel?
What do you need to do to change this?
Does anyone / anything else need to change?
What can you do differently?
Let's make a plan! If it doesn't work, we'll try again.

(Rae and Simmons 2002: 118)

Rules, once established, must be non-negotiable; questioning and discussion can be used to deepen the pupils' understanding of the reasons for the rules, and how they will be applied (Constable 1998).

Teachers should check their own body language for the unconscious messages it conveys. Body language can suggest calmness, being in control, friendliness and inner strength, or it can suggest any one of a range of less positive emotions, most commonly fear, aggression, tension, boredom or exhaustion. All teachers can check their body language, particularly in the way they greet pupils at the start of a lesson, the way they walk around the classroom and the way they respond to incidents. An increase in the teacher's tension or aggression, unconsciously revealed through the shoulders, face muscles or tone of voice, can be unconsciously read by pupils, whose behaviour will deteriorate as a result (Constable 1998: 5).

For evaluating your own approach to dealing with behaviour, use a regular set of questions, on your own or with a colleague. Here is one example:

Why did he / she behave in such a way?
What strategies did I use?
What worked? What didn't work?
How can I improve my practice?

(Bentham 2006: 57)

To this we should add a question designed to help the whole school system work better: How can I share with other colleagues my knowledge of the reasons for the behaviour, and my awareness of what works well with this pupil?

Teachers and other adults in the classroom need to monitor and evaluate their approaches regularly, but they should use common sense to judge the timing. Some aspects of behaviour-relevant classroom environment and planning that cannot be easily changed, such as schemes of work or classroom furniture, are best evaluated periodically; others, such as work with colleagues, or specific activities, are best discussed in daily or weekly sessions, while they are still fresh in the mind. Above all, there is a need to make sure that behaviour issues are addressed *in the context of* discussions of learning, and *in the presence of* appropriate professional colleagues, so that teacher isolation is prevented, knowledge of 'what works' is disseminated and best all-round support is available (Moyles 1992: 153ff).

An approach used with 9-year-olds upwards is to develop principles for discussion that emphasize the importance of every member's contribution. This is part of an effort, particularly in PSHE, to move away from hierarchies of teacher / teaching assistant / pupils, and also hierarchies of peer pressure generated as subcultures among the pupils. In this approach, each rule is stated as a 'core value', for example that 'everyone has the right to be heard', and is then made more concrete in the form of a 'pledge', for example 'we agree to give each other time to speak' (Hammond 2006: 5). This approach means that pupils benefit from the security of having clear, concrete rules, but also grow from the opportunity of discussing the reasons behind the rules.

Ofsted's indicators for assessing the effectiveness of classroom behaviour management are practical, but they do also give visibility to the values behind the practicalities. The Ofsted list includes: punctuality; pupils knowing right from wrong; pupils showing interest; freedom from bullying and harassment; pupils forming constructive relationships; and pupils having confidence and self-esteem (Ofsted 2003b: 34). One interesting exercise is to turn these indicators into core values (in Hammond's sense) and then into pledges.

Reflective task
Classroom rules

Think about classroom rules and the way they are agreed. Agree or disagree with the following statements. Where you agree, think of a concrete example where it has worked. Where you disagree, explore your reasons and test the strength of your evidence (for example, is it stronger than 'I tried that once last term, and it didn't work'?).

Level 1
- Classroom rules should always be negotiated and agreed with the class.
- Classroom rules should always be reinforced consistently by the teacher and other adults in the room.
- Rules should be specific and concrete, for example 'walk in the classroom' rather than 'behave safely'. *cont.*

Level 2
- The teacher should know, display and use the full range of strategies and sanctions that the school has agreed.
- Rules should be stated positively rather than negatively, for example 'we raise our hands to speak' rather than 'no shouting out'.
- If a teacher thinks that a school rule is unimportant or unfair, he / she should not criticize other teachers but can quietly not enforce it.

Level 3
- Rules should be few in number (4–6, maybe) and general, i.e. about values such as respect, safety, communication.
- Negotiated classroom rules should stay in place for a whole year or key stage.
- There should be a difference between rules about school conventions, such as uniform, and rules about moral issues, such as name calling.

The adult staff as personal models of positive behaviour

All adult staff working in classroom are human. This means that we have limits to our energy, patience, imagination and creativity in dealing with needy small people. Yet, however human and vulnerable we may feel, we need to remember that our behaviour is also on show, and is, indeed, a key factor in determining theirs. In dealing with pupils who are off task or defiant, there are a number of widely accepted small, crucial strategies that will help professionals to be the best possible role model:

- Comment on the behaviour or the rule, not the person.
- Avoid futile questions ('what are you doing?', 'why aren't you paying attention?') and put-downs (*'once again*, you are disrupting the class').
- Give the off-task pupil a choice that enables them to conform and also maintain their dignity.
- Do not get involved in time-wasting arguments that distract from learning and which unsettle other pupils.

In considering her work with children aged 4 to 8, Carolyn Webster-Stratton (1999) believes that teachers' negative reactions to what is perceived as poor behaviour will usually escalate the problem, and will also undermine our ability as adults to think strategically, learn from our mistakes and be proactive and steady. In order to uphold the best in children's behaviour, and also to protect teachers from the negative consequences of their own unconsidered reactions, she advocates:

- consistent limit setting;
- schedules for response;

- routines for the day;
- explicitly taught norms.

(Webster-Stratton 1999: 50)

Conclusion

Only the hypocrite is really rotten to the core.

Hannah Arendt, *On Revolution,* 1936)

The winning strategy in behaviour management is often elusive, because it is culturally determined to some extent, and also because it relies in part on personal
qualities and attitudes. Usually, a middle path between vigilance and negligence,
between assertiveness and aggression, and between concrete detail and broad-brush
values, makes for the most effective preconditions for behaviour.

Less experienced teachers can learn to go beyond merely imitating what they
think they see (techniques and rules) and can learn that techniques work only when
backed by inner authority, and rules are worthwhile only when supported by
understanding. More experienced teachers can understand that 'what works' in any
given situation needs to be professionally discussed and shared, so that 'why does it
work?', 'could it work better?', and 'could it be shared?' become regular subjects of
mutual professional conversation.

References

Ahlgren, P. (1993) La Escuala Fratney: reflections on a bilingual, anti-bias,
multicultural, elementary school, *Teaching Tolerance,* 2(2): 26–31.

Apple, M. and Beane, J. (eds) (1999) *Democratic Schools: Lessons from the Chalkface.*
Buckingham: Open University Press.

Armstrong, D. (1998) Changing faces, changing places: policy routes to inclusion,
Clough, P. (1998) ed., *Managing Inclusive Education: From policy to experience.*
London: Paul Chapman, pp. 31–47.

Bentham, S. (2006) *A Teaching Assistant's Guide to Managing Behaviour in the
Classroom.* Abingdon: Routledge.

Blum, P. (1998) *Surviving and Succeeding in Difficult Classrooms.* London:
Routledge.

Blum, P. (2001) *A Teacher's Guide to Anger Management.* London: RoutledgeFalmer.

Brearley, M. (2001) *Emotional Intelligence in the Classroom.* Carmarthen: Crown
House Publishing.

Clough, P. (ed.) (1998) *Managing Inclusive Education: From Policy to Experience.*
London: Paul Chapman.

Cole, T. (1998) Understanding challenging behaviour: prerequisites to inclusion, in
C. Tilstone, L. Florian and R. Rose (eds) *Promoting Inclusive Practice.* London:
RoutledgeFalmer, pp. 113–27.

Collins, J., Harkin, J. and Nind, M. (2002) *Manifesto for Learning.* London:
Continuum.

Constable, D. (1998) *Cracking the Code with Behaviour.* Brigg: Desktop Publications.

Corrie, C. (2003) *Becoming Emotionally Intelligent.* Stafford: Network Educational Press.

DES (Department of Education and Science) (1989) *Discipline in Schools* (Elton Report). London: HMSO.

DfEE (1999) *Social Inclusion: Pupil Support,* Circular 10 / 99. London: HMSO.

DfES (2002) *Classroom and Behaviour Management.* London: HMSO.

Dyslexia Institute (2006) www.dyslexiaaction.org.uk (accessed March 2006).

Fernald, W. (1912) The burden of feeble-minded, *Journal of Psycho-Asthenics,* 17: 87–111, cited in Armstrong, D. (1998) Changing faces, changing places: policy routes to inclusion, in Clough, P. (ed.) *Managing Inclusive Education: From Policy to Experience.* London: Paul Chapman, pp. 31–47.

Food Standards Agency (2005) www.food.gov.uk/science/research (accessed March 2006).

Goleman, D. (1996) *Emotional Intelligence.* London: Bloomsbury.

Hammond, A. (2006) *Tolerance and Empathy in Today's Classroom.* London: Paul Chapman.

Hodgson, A. and Spours, K. (1999) *New Labour's Educational Agenda.* London: RoutledgeFalmer.

Hopkins, B. (2004) *Just Schools: A Whole School Approach to Restorative Justice.* London: Jessica Kingsley.

Illich, I. (1971) *Deschooling Society.* New York: Harper & Row.

Moyles, J. (1992) *Organizing for Learning in the Primary Classroom.* Buckingham: Open University Press.

Ofsted (1999) *Principles into Practice: Effective Education for Pupils with Emotional and Behavioural Difficulties.* London: Ofsted.

Ofsted (2003a) *Handbook for Inspecting Primary and Nursery Schools.* London: Ofsted.

Ofsted (2003b) *Framework for Inspecting Schools.* London: Ofsted.

QCA (1999) *National Curriculum Handbook for Primary Teachers.* London: QCA.

Rae, T. and Simmons, K. (2002) *The Anger Alphabet.* Bristol: Lucky Duck.

Rogers, B. (2002) *Classroom Behaviour.* London: Paul Chapman.

Smith, P. (ed.) (2003) *Violence in Schools: The Response in Europe.* London: RoutledgeFalmer.

Watkins, C. and Wagner, P. (1987) *School Discipline: A Whole-School Approach.* Oxford: Blackwell.

Watson, D. and Bowden, R. (2001) *Can we be Equal and Excellent too?* Brighton: University of Brighton Educational Research Centre.

Weare, K. (2004) *Developing the Emotionally Literate School.* London: Paul Chapman.

Webster-Stratton, C. (1999) *How to Promote Children's Social and Emotional Competence.* London: Paul Chapman.

Part 2

Doing

6
Questioning
Jane Johnston

Introduction

This chapter focuses on questioning as a skill both for children and for teachers. It looks at what questioning is, how it develops and how teachers can develop both their own and children's skill.

Questioning as a skill

Questioning is an important skill throughout life. It is a primary component in problem solving (de Bono 1992), creative thinking (Beetlestone 1998) and moral decision making and citizenship, as a questioning mind is necessary in the consideration of different perspectives, making links between ideas (Duffy 1998) and development and change. As children, we use questions to learn about the world around us: the social, the physical, the natural, the moral world. As adults, we need to be able to question in order to be effective citizens: to question political, social, moral and economic norms and assumptions. As well as being a generic skill, necessary throughout life, questioning is a specific skill necessary in some areas for continued and effective development. In exploring and investigating the physical and natural world, as in geography and science, we need to ask questions in order to be effective in investigations, enquiry and the development of understanding. In history, literature and religious study, we need to ask analytical questions in order to understand historical events, the meaning of texts and the underlying beliefs in religions. In developing understandings, we need to move beyond the descriptive questions (what?, where?, when?, who?) and begin to ask analytical questions (why?, how?, so what?), which move us beyond the superficial to a deeper insight of issues and relationships. This is the case in any subject, curricular or otherwise.

Questioning as a skill is dependent on curiosity, an attitude that is essential for learning. Learners need to be curious about the world around them, asking questions and wanting to find out the answers to their own questions and those posed by others. Teachers working with children of all ages need to develop the children's skill of questioning by harnessing their natural curiosity and encouraging enquiry, explorations and problem solving.

Curiosity is arguably the most important factor in effective questioning in both young children and enquiry-based subjects, such as science (Johnston 2005a). Curious children are inquisitive about everything they interact with, and this leads them to raise questions and to investigate.

Children will display different abilities in their skills as questioner and in curiosity, and both need to be encouraged throughout their development by carers, practitioners and teachers working with them. Lack of curiosity has been identified as being due to temperament, experience, environment and social constraints (Harlen 1977), and these same factors can affect the skill of questioning. Children who are placid, reserved or lacking in confidence are less likely to ask questions, although this cannot be assumed, as can be seen in the observation described below. If the environment that children are interacting in is one that is not stimulating and does not encourage questioning, then the children are less likely to question. Socially, children may be discouraged from questioning, as a child who is persistently asking 'why' can be very wearing and I am sure we have all been irritated by overzealous and persistent questioning and been tempted to respond (if not actually responded, as I certainly have) with 'just because'. Sometimes the children's interest in the questions they ask is short-lived and they do not seem very concerned with the answers. However, even very young children can spend long periods of time exploring in answer to their internal questions and because they are curious enough to want to do this. For others, the number of differing and novel experiences may mean that they flit from one experience to another and their interest in their questions is transitory. As children develop, so will their ability to sustain interest and persevere in answering their questions.

Picture 6.1   Asking internal questions

Case study

Read the case study below and answer the following analytical questions:

1 How was the child demonstrating curiosity and questioning skills?
2 What does this case study tell us about the skill of questioning?
3 In this example, how was the skill of questioning affected by the factors identified by Harlen (1977), that is, temperament, experience, environment and social constraints?

A small group of pre-school children aged 4 years, part of a reception class, attending school two afternoons a week prior to entry to school, were playing in a garden centre role play area (de Bóo 2004). One child was observing seeds by picking up individual seeds and observing them closely using a computer microscope attached to a multimedia, thus projecting the image onto a large screen.

She was very solitary in her observations, having no communications with either her peers or adult practitioners. However, she showed evidence of observation of small details, working her way through the pile of seeds, from the smallest upwards. She also showed evidence of recognizing similarities and differences of size between the seeds. She persevered with this task for over 30 minutes, but did not respond to any questions posed by the teacher and did not talk about what she was doing and why, with either adults or children.

The impact of questioning on learning

Questioning skills are important in education for both learners and teachers (Kerry 2002). Questioning children are able to make connections between aspects of learning across the curriculum (DfES 2003); they develop thinking skills (Kerry 2002; Johnston 2005a) and develop understandings. In the Early Years Foundation Stage and Key Stage 1, children will often ask 'What is that?', 'Is it a ...?', 'Does this ...?', 'What can ...?', 'Will it ...?', 'What can I do with it?' and such like. Young children will pat you and wave their hands eagerly, wanting to ask questions, although there are always some children, like the child in the case study above, who do not appear curious or do not ask questions and who will patiently take on board what others say, sitting quietly while others ask questions. This, however, does not mean that these children are not questioning. Rather, it means that they are asking internal questions. As we have seen above, the skill of questioning is closely connected to attitudes such as curiosity and helps to develop understandings. As children get older they need to develop their ability to raise and answer questions to support analytical skills, as well as understandings and this will help to develop their thinking skills.

Raising questions in science

In primary science, children need to be able to raise questions, that is, questions that lead to further explorations, investigations and problem solving. This can begin with an initial exploration of scientific phenomena, such as gravity, dissolving and melting, plant growth, or a collection of items relating to the phenomena, a collection of paper aeroplanes and helicopters, salt, sugar, margarine and chocolate, a collection of plants or seeds. I have started with a box containing some objects which focus on a particular scientific concept, such as forces using a marble, polystyrene ball, ball bearing, plastic ball, all of similar sizes. The children are encouraged to observe the external appearance of the box, the size, shape, weight and sounds when gently shaken, before they open it and see what is inside. They can then explore the contents and begin to raise questions about them: 'What will happen when I drop / roll them?', 'Will they all fall to the ground at the same rate?', 'Will the heaviest fall / roll fastest?', 'What will happen if we put them in water?', 'Will the heaviest ones sink or float?'

Once the children have raised some questions, they need to examine which ones can lead to further explorations, investigations and problem solving, like the ones above, and which will not: 'Why are the balls different?', 'Can I play a game of marbles?' The children can then choose one question that they would like to investigate further. This has the advantage of giving them ownership of the direction of their learning.

I have taken this further and asked them a question to promote problem solving: 'Can you make a machine to sort the different balls?' (see Johnston 2005b). This will lead them into a problem-solving exercise. Using a cardboard box, junk materials and the balls, the machine can sort the balls by:

- weight: for example, heavy ones could drop down and lighter ones may stay up higher in the machine;
- buoyancy: when dropped into a container of water, those balls which are denser than water will sink and those less dense will float;
- whether they are magnetic: magnets on the ramp may separate the ball bearings from the others.

However, the criteria for sorting and the design of the machine are left up to the children.

Teacher questioning also has an important impact on learning. Firstly, teachers' ability to reflect and develop professional practice is dependent on their questioning skills. They need to question pedagogical practices and reflect on the effectiveness of different teaching and learning approaches in order to modify teaching for more effective learning. They need to analyse and evaluate their own teaching, and these skills are reliant on the ability to ask themselves questions such as 'How effective was this lesson?', 'Why did some children find this difficult?', 'What can I do in the next lesson to move the learning on and support the achievements of the learning objectives?' Secondly, teachers need to be able to ask questions of children to support their learning. Asking questions focuses the children's attention on the learning objectives and supports the development of understandings. Thirdly, teachers who ask questions are also modelling good behaviour and learning. Behaviour theorists (Bandura 1986) have shown the importance of modelling social behaviour, and teachers know that modelling learning behaviours will positively affect children's learning. If teachers question in learning situations, they model the questioning skills that we want children to develop. I was once told by a headteacher that you should never tell a child that you did not know something as it would undermine their faith in you as a teacher. My belief is that to lead children to believe that teachers are all-knowing is to undermine their future faith in adults as, and when, they discover that no one is all-knowing. If we ask questions alongside children we model good learning behaviour, illustrate our own curiosity and show our motivation for continual learning. I once observed a student teacher reading a story about Sir Walter Raleigh which contained the word 'discombobulate'. He did not question the children about the book or the word and no one seemed interested in the meaning of the word, except me. I questioned him about the word, asking him what it meant and discovered he had not looked it up. I went home that evening and checked the meaning in a dictionary and when I next saw the student teacher, I asked him if he had done the same. He had not. What surprised me most was that he did not seem to be interested in finding out himself and neither did he realize what a poor role model this was to the children he taught.

Reflective task

Do you know what the word 'discombobulate' means?

When you read the paragraph above, were you motivated to find out what the word means? Do you feel that your questioning behaviour is a motivating force for children's learning?

Level 1

Think of a recent time when you were motivated to find something out for yourself? Was the motivation intrinsic (internal to yourself) or extrinsic (due to outside influences)? What factors influenced your ability and motivation to find something out?

Level 2

Think of a recent experience when you asked a question of children that required them to find something out. What motivated the children to answer your question? Do you think that modelling questioning behaviour could have improved their motivation to answer your question?

Level 3

Think of something you are going to teach in the future and consider what questions you can ask that will motivate children to make enquiries themselves and will also model good questioning skills. Try out your questions and evaluate the response.

The child as a natural questioner

Children are natural questioners, but, as seen above, they may have different levels of natural curiosity. Asking questions in very young children takes the form of tactile exploration, in the course of finding out about the world around them, and occurs as soon as they are born. They soon begin to communicate their questions, through cries, babbling and gestures, and as they develop linguistically, they are able to articulate these questions. As they develop cognitively and linguistically, they will be able to articulate their questions more clearly, and if supported and encouraged by sensitively aware adults, they will continue to ask questions and develop both cognitively and linguistically (see Vygotsky 1978).

As children develop, if they are encouraged in their questioning and their natural ability is nurtured, then they will begin to develop their questioning skills. This is not a natural and easy process, and certainly not automatic. The barrage of questions facing teachers in the early years can often be replaced by silence when you want the children to be questioning. This is not because the children's skills are less developed or that they are less curious, but because of natural temperament and also the pressures of society and the classroom. For older children there are many influences on them which deter them from asking questions. In a sterile environment, children may not be encouraged to, or may even be discouraged from, asking questions. Peers may ridicule children who ask questions, because asking questions implies interest or lack of knowledge. Sometimes, asking questions can lead to extra work and children have found that life is easier to keep quiet even if they do not know something. Children may also have learnt from experience that their questions are not answered, so they do not waste their energy.

Reflective task

Level 1

Identify instances where you have seen children as natural questioners. This can be from school, your own life or in observation of children in everyday life. Did the age of the children make a difference to their natural ability? What do you think are the differences between the questioning skills of older and younger children?

Level 2

Consider different age groups that you have taught. Did the children show abilities as natural questioners to those in the exemplar? How did your teaching develop the children's natural ability?

Level 3

Consider one child in your current context? What natural questioning abilities do they demonstrate? How can you develop their abilities further in your future teaching?

Different types of questions

Questions have been categorized in different ways. Earlier in the chapter we identified productive questions that can lead to enquiry or problem solving, and
unproductive ones which it would be difficult to answer without outside help.
Kissock and Iyortsuun (1982) identified two types of questions: cognitive questions,
which involve higher-order thinking skills, and affective questions, dealing with
emotional responses (interests, feelings, beliefs and values). The authors consider
the relationship between the two types to be a close one, with the affective (curiosity
and interest) having an impact on the cognitive (analysis and understanding).
Sanders (1966), in a taxonomy of questions (see Figure 6.1), breaks down the
cognitive questions and identifies a hierarchy. Lower-order cognitive questions
requiring memory and recall are the most frequently used by teachers (Kissock and
Iyortsuun 1982), although rhetorical and organizational questions have been found
to form up to one-third of all teacher questions (Kerry 2002).

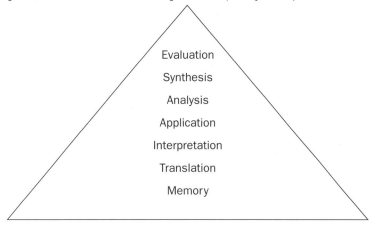

Figure 6.1 Taxonomy of questions (adapted from Sanders 1966)

The next levels of cognitive questions are those that require translation and
interpretation, involving a considered response, making sense of information
collected, observations, actions or events. For example, when reading a text, a
question such as 'What do you think will happen next?' requires a predictive
response, so information about what has happened previously needs to be assimi-
lated and considered.

Questions requiring an application response are at the next level of cognition.
Questions in this category include, 'How can you?' and 'Where can you?' These are
questions that can lead to a solution.

Questions requiring analysis and synthesis are at the next levels of cognition.
Analytical questions include, 'Why?', 'How?' and 'So what?' questions, and these
require the respondent to dig deeper into meanings and identify factors influencing
events and actions. Historically, we may ask children why Roman forts were built on

hills, which would involve knowledge of the Roman era and identification of the social and political tension of the time. Synthesis requires the respondent to reassemble ideas after analysis, so a child, having looked for evidence of weathering in the local environment, could be asked to draw conclusions about the main cause of weathering of gravestones in a churchyard. In order to do this the children must observe the weathering on the gravestones and analyse the influencing factors (for example, material, position, age, plant growth) and the possible causal factors for the weathering (sun, wind, anmals, plants, and so on). The highest level of cognitive questions comprises those that require an evaluative response. In technology, a question such as 'Which is the best paper towel?', would require children to test out criteria such as absorbency, strength and softness. In mathematics, a question such as 'What mental strategies did you find the most effective in solving this problem?' requires the children to evaluate the strategies used and involve an element of metacognition – understanding their own cognitive abilities and thinking processes.

Effective teacher questions are often those that are open-ended and personalized, as these are questions that help us to explore the cognitive abilities of children and link with the affective. Closed questions are ones that require a predetermined or limited-choice answer. Questions such as 'What is this?' and 'What will happen next?' are closed questions that can produce one-word answers or no answer at all. Changing the questions to 'What can you tell me about this?' and 'What do you think will happen next?' are more open and appear to value the respondent's opinion and will lead to answers of greater depth and insight into cognitive understandings. Personalized and open-ended questions can still focus on specific areas and support specific cognitive development and even inform us of children's skill development. For example, if we ask children to identify the differences between events, objects or ideas, we can begin to ascertain their skill in observing and classifying. If we ask them to consider why a historical figure took a particular course of action, then we can ascertain and develop their ability to hypothesize (provide a sensible explanation based on evidence). If we ask what they think the character in a book will do next, then we are asking them to interpret the evidence in previous chapters and make a prediction based on that evidence. If we ask them how they can explain something to others, then they will show their skill at communicating.

Questioning to develop thinking skills in geography
by John Halocha, Bishop Grosseteste University College Lincoln

Many teachers have based their planning on Storm's (1989) five questions for primary geography: these are discussed in depth in Chapter 10 in relation to the enquiry process. In this box we will look in more detail at the types of questions that pupils and teachers can ask. Use the ideas to:
* help you plan which types of questions match the learning styles you wish to promote;   *cont.*

- consider how a balanced experience of these questions and styles may help your pupils gain independence and confidence in asking questions.

Roberts (1996) offers the framework shown in Figure 6.2 for geographical teaching styles and enquiry. Closed, framed and negotiated questions can, of course, be used within one unit or topic of geographical study. By carefully selecting the appropriate type, you will also be modelling for pupils the way in which different questions can serve different purposes and types of information and ideas. Also, the

Stages of teaching and learning	Closed	Framed	Negotiated
Questions	Questions not explicit or questions remain the teacher's questions	Questions explicit, activities planned to make pupils ask questions	Pupils decide what they want to investigate under the guidance of the teacher
Data	Data selected by teacher, presented as authoritative, not to be challenged	Variety of data selected by teacher, presented as evidence to be interpreted	Puils are helped to find their own data from sources in and out of school
Interpretation	Teachers decide what is to be done with data, pupils follow instructions	Methods of interpretation are open to discussion and choice	Pupils choose methods of analysis and interpretation in consultation with teacher
Conclusion	Key ideas presented, generalizations are predicted, not open to debate	Pupils reach conclusions from data, different interpretations are expected	Pupils reach own conclusions and evaluate them
Summary	The teacher controls the knowledge by making all decisions about data, activities, conclusions. Pupils are not expected to challenge what is presented	The teacher inducts pupils into ways in which geographical knowledge is constructed, so that they are enabled to use these ways to construct knowledge themselves. Pupils are made aware of choices and are encouraged to be critical	Pupils are enabled by the teacher to investigate questions of concern and interest to themselves

Figure 6.2 Framework for geographical teaching styles and enquiry (Roberts 1996)

cont.

order in which questions are used may vary: enquiries do not always have to start with the more closed and factual style. If you find this grid helpful, you may wish to discuss with colleagues when pupils are introduced to these types of questions.

It is sometimes argued that young children should have their learning guided and focused by working from the teacher's questions and data. It may be that this approach instils in the youngest children a reliance on the teacher rather than on their own ability to ask questions, which we already know they do ask. We need to consider the extent to which the education system gives children the clear message to believe in themselves and their ability to ask big questions about the world. That will be an important foundation to support the notion that lifelong learning really is a valid and worthwhile concept. Geographical enquiries are an excellent way to start this as they can so easily be rooted in the children's experience of their own world.

We can also categorize questions as follows:

1 *Rhetorical questions which are comments, commands and require no answer.* These questions are used extensively by teachers (Kerry 2002) and must be very confusing to children until they learn the social rules of such questions. I once asked a Year 4 child if he would like to come and read to me, and he responded with 'No thank you'. Young children and those with special needs, such as Asberger's syndrome and autistic tendencies, will find these questions very difficult. Teachers should endeavour to think carefully about their use of such questions, to limit their use and to respect the answers to the questions if they are not what was expected. After all, I did ask the child 'Would you *like* to come and read to me?'.

2 *Questions requiring simple factual answers or lower-order cognitive questions* (Sanders 1966). These are questions often asked in school and require factual recall of knowledge and a degree of short- and medium-term memory. They are the sort of questions often used in national assessments at Key Stage 2 and form the focus of much teacher questioning in the primary school.

3 *Questions requiring more complex and analytical answers.* These are higher-order cognitive questions and ones we should be using increasingly as children develop, in order to support their thinking skills. Unfortunately, they appear to be ones we use least. I believe that this is because we are overconcerned with organizational and coverage issues in school and we also have not developed our questioning skills effectively in order to support thinking.

4 *Questions which can lead to an enquiry or investigation.* These are questions that encourage children to question themselves and support the development of their enquiry skills. They are particularly useful in mathematics, science, technology and geography.

Case study

Questioning to support understanding of dreams
by Kate Adams, Bishop Grosseteste University College Lincoln

Dreams are an integral part of the human condition. All humans dream, and in childhood, longer time is spent in the dream state than it is in adulthood (Foulkes 1982). For many children, some dreams can be particularly significant and be remembered for the rest of their lives. Teachers can draw on children's dreams in different parts of the curriculum to offer lessons which are relevant to children's lives and give voice to the children's experiences. However, such attention to dreams should not be superficial and the importance of hearing the children's views is paramount. One such example comes from Sarah, an 11-year-old girl, who reported a dream as part of a research project (Adams 2003). Sarah's dream occurred at a time when she was anxious about participating in a cross-country run at school. The night before the race, she dreamt that she was running the course without difficulty, completed it, and was not last over the finishing line.

The dream was not an unusual one and it is, at first glance, easy for teachers to explain the dream as a simple response to Sarah's concerns about the race. However, further questioning by myself in the context of the study revealed more interesting data regarding Sarah's understanding of her dream. Sarah was a Christian girl who believed that most dreams are created in the mind. However, she felt that this one was different. By asking her for more information about the context of the dream, she revealed that she believed that God had sent this dream to indicate to her that she had the ability to run the race successfully. Further, the dream made a positive impact on her waking life by easing her nerves on the day of the race. This enabled her to relax and to finish the race without being last.

The example of Sarah illustrates how children can often pay attention to their own dreams and make meaning from them. What is evident here is that Sarah had dwelt on her dream – on both its origin and meaning – and had taken those reflections into her waking life in the context of coping with a stressful situation. Without questioning her, this information would have gone unreported and unnoticed, despite its being a meaningful experience for her.

Questioning environments

A questioning environment is possibly the most important factor affecting the skill of questioning. A questioning environment is one which provides an atmosphere where children feel able to raise and answer questions, without fear of ridicule or comment. It provides an atmosphere in which children can be encouraged to examine their understandings and the questions they ask. They can be encouraged to ask more analytical and cognitive questions and develop their interest and enjoyment of learning. They can be encouraged to answer questions (their own and others') through research, enquiry, exploration or investigation, and this will lead to the development of understandings. A questioning environment can be achieved in the following ways:

- by the provision of motivating, new and different experiences or different ways of looking or thinking about something. All learners benefit from motivation and challenge and a motivating environment can provide the link between the affective and cognitive (Kissock and Iyortsuun 1982), as described above, and maximize learning. Learning that follows a strict and maybe imposed format, such as advocated by Literacy and Numeracy strategies (DfEE 1998, 1999) is less likely to continue to motivate (Johnston 2002). This possibly explains the success in practice of new cognitive acceleration practices, such as Brain Gym (Dennison and Dennison 1994);
- by the provision of motivating interactive displays and question tables. These may include historical or technological artefacts, collections from nature such as leaves, rocks and soil samples, or problem-solving puzzles such as word or numerical puzzles, or scientific problems. For younger children the displays and artefacts themselves support oral questioning. For older children, questions can be written on cards set on tables or on wall displays. Children can be encouraged to interact with the artefacts and questions and to try to find some answers which they can share with others. These can be written on Post-it™ notes and added to the display. Children may also raise new questions, leading to deeper thinking and these too can be written on Post-its and added to the display. Motivating displays will thus support development in the cognitive and affective domains, including helping children to respect the ideas of others;
- by the use of questioning strategies, designed to promote the development of questioning skills. These strategies include the use of a flipchart to enable children to jot down questions raised during discussions and explorations. Children can write these themselves with large felt-tip pens, or teachers can jot some down as they are raised by the children. These questions can be discussed later with larger groups or the whole class, and decisions as to which questions will be productive and can be answered and what to research, or investigate further can be made. Questions raised by children can also be pegged to washing lines or strung across the classroom (burglar alarms permitting). This helps to provide a more questioning atmosphere and focus attention on questions raised by children and encourage interaction with the questions of others. In science, I have used group explorations to raise questions about a scientific phenomenon (Johnston 2005a) and have used these questions to focus the explorations and investigations of other groups of children. Findings from the explorations and investigations are then discussed with the whole class and new questions raised which take the concept onto deeper levels and support cognition.

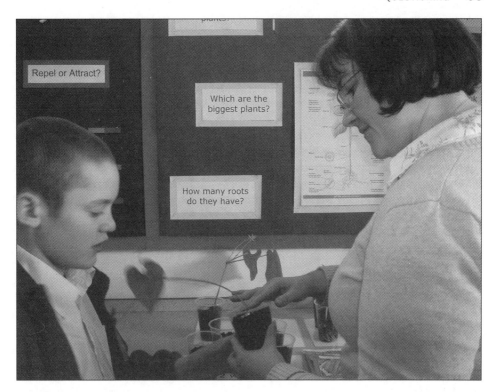

Picture 6.2   A questioning environment

How to develop questioning skills

In order to develop children's abilities to question, it is necessary to develop their curiosity and interest and provide a questioning environment. In addition, teachers need to develop their own pedagogical skills and to understand how to develop both their own and children's skills further. Analysing children's questions according to the level of complexity and skill can give us a valuable insight into their thinking, as well as their skill, and can help us to move their development on. If they ask higher-order, cognitive questions, we know that they need additional challenges and can gauge our next interactions with them accordingly. If they ask lower-order, factual questions, we can encourage them to be more analytical by asking analytical questions and modelling behaviours we wish to see in them. Sometimes it is best not to answer questions in a straightforward way, especially if the answer is complicated, as this may demotivate children if they do not understand the answers. Sometimes, questions do not require an answer or cannot be answered, and sometimes it is best to leave the children to find out the answers on their own, maybe with a little direction or support. Teachers need to have knowledge of the different types of questions, what those questions tell us about the children's knowledge, understandings and skills and how to support the children in the next stage of their development. Pedagogical decisions often need to be made quickly, but it may be better to consider questions rather than respond quickly, especially if this consideration will advance the children's learning. This is particularly the case with big questions (questions on abstract or philosophical issues, which usually do not have correct answers), which need careful consideration before answering. Questions during part of sex education come into this category and need to be carefully considered before answering. I use a question box, where children can post questions and I can consider these before deciding how to respond. It may be that the question is one that should not be answered in school, perhps because of legislation or school policy. It may be that the question should be given to the child's parents to answer, if it is a question best answered by the family. It may be that the question needs to be answered individually or it may be that all children would benefit from the answer.

Student teachers' ideas about teaching science

Research exploring 98 student primary teachers' ideas about teaching science (Ahtee and Johnston 2006) identified teaching approaches which did not generally encourage questioning skills and teacher questioning felt to support the development of conceptual understanding rather than the development of skills.

The students were in the autumn term of their third year of initial teacher education and, as such, had undertaken considerable work developing their scientific knowledge and pedagogical content knowledge, including 12 weeks on school placement; one specifically focused on scientific conceptual development. They were a mixed group of students who were specializing in many different subjects (mathematics with design and technology, English, drama, art, music, history, geography), with only 15 being science specialists.

As part of the research, the students observed a teaching episode and identified via a questionnaire their pedagogical knowledge (knowledge of teaching) and pedagogical content knowledge (PCK). PCK involves the combination of content knowledge and pedagogical knowledge to support pupil learning (Shulman 1987). The teaching episode involved balancing two unfilled balloons on a stick and then inflating one balloon and predicting what effect this will have on the balance. This was followed by the POE (prediction–observation–explanation) method introduced by White and Gunstone (1992).

The POE method was appreciated by the students and they identified that the rationale for the choice of teaching method was to encourage practical involvement of the child.

Despite this, 85 per cent of the student teachers emphasized content matters rather than thinking and process skills as the main objective of the teaching episode, and whereas 90 per cent mentioned practical work, few considered the importance of developing questioning skills and then only in conjunction with thinking skills: 'because they make their own theories and learn to question', '[they] develop their own reasons for things'.

cont.

The student teachers' were concerned about their lack of scientific knowledge, believing that it influenced their effectiveness in answering pupils' questions and giving good explanations. This lack of knowledge will also prevent them from concentrating on the development of questioning skills and lead to problems in the construction of questioning learning environments that enable pupils to 'take active control of their learning, express and support their ideas, make predictions and hypotheses and test them through explorations and investigation' (Ahtee and Johnston 2006). Effective content knowledge in science is considered necessary (Ginn and Watters 1995) in order to implement effective problem-solving and constructivist learning strategies (Yager 1991); in other words to promote and use questions, ideas and thinking to support learning, The challenge from the research is, how to support initial and beginner teachers developing both their own and children's questioning and problem-solving skills.

The pedagogical knowledge and skills that teachers need include not just what different types of questions can develop and how to question children to support their cognitive development, but also how not to question children. Closed and impersonal questions which make children feel uncomfortable are unlikely to be fully effective. Providing time for the children to respond to questions is also important. Kissock and Iyortsuun (1982) have identified that teachers do not wait long enough between a question and an expectation of a response; the average time being one minute. This is a very short length of time and will not allow children to give considered answers or engage in more analytical answers, whereas a greater time lapse will result in more thoughtful answers.

Kissock and Iyortsuun (1982) also identify that few teachers encourage children to ask questions themselves and this may be because they are concerned about being asked questions that they cannot answer. It is impossible and foolish for primary teachers to pretend that they know everything, and by doing so they do not provide good role models for children. However, when faced with a question that you cannot answer, there are some strategies we teachers can use: honesty, challenge and modelling. Being honest about your lack of knowledge in some situations is essential to enable children to gain a balanced view of the world and the people on it. More importantly, there are many questions we cannot answer: big questions about the birth of the universe, analytical questions about motivations in history, for example, why Henry VIII chose to divorce some wives and behead others, and questions about things of which we have little or no knowledge. Challenge involves the teacher in providing a challenge for the child to help them to answer the question for themselves; a strategy which involves quality individual time. For some children this may seem like too large a task and it may be appropriate to model the questioning behaviours and to explore the issue together. Some questions may not have a definite answer and this will help children to understand that not all questions can be fully answered. Questioning the children can model the questioning behaviours you wish to encourage in them, as good adult questioning can support 'thinking skills, language, problem-solving and cooperation' (de Bóo 2004: 12).

Reflective task

Level 1

Think about a recent situation where you have been a learner, such as a lecture, seminar, in-service course. During the session, did you pose any questions, or did you think of questions later? Were you asked any questions? If so, how long did you get to answer them and how did you feel? Are you encouraged to raise questions in learning situations?

Level 2

Think about a recent teaching situation and your questioning of learners. What types of question did you ask of the children? How long did you give them to answer the questions? How could you have improved your questioning of the children in this incident? How could you have encouraged children to raise their own questions?

Level 3

Think about some teaching you are planning. Identify higher-order cognitive questions which you can ask the children. Try out your questions but don't forget to give the children time to respond. Evaluate the effect of your questions on the children's learning, including their ability to raise questions themselves.

Giving children time to answer questions and providing quality time to raise questions for themselves is difficult because of the pressures of time and content. We need, however, to focus on the quality of learning rather than the quantity. Children who are given time to think and develop affective interests and curiosity, cognitive understandings and questioning skills will be more able to apply these in other contexts, advancing learning by making those connections that Duffy (1998) identifies as important.

Summary

- Questioning is an important skill necessary in learning and throughout life, for problem solving, creative thinking and decision making.
- Children are natural questioners, but their ability to answer questions is affected by their temperament, social interaction, age and cognitive ability. The skill does not necessarily develop with age and without support and encouragement.
- There are different types of questions, some being lower-order questions which do not lead to deeper understanding or skill development. Others are more cognitive and when linked to affective questions can lead to affective, cognitive and skill development.

- Teachers need to develop their own questioning skills and understanding of questioning in order to more effectively support children's development. The teacher is very important as a role model for questioning behaviours.
- The classroom ethos is important in providing a motivating, questioning atmosphere in which children feel able to ask questions and are given the time to answer both their own and the teacher's questions.

References

Adams, K. (2003) Children's dreams: an exploration of Jung's concept of big dreams. *International Journal of Children's Spirituality*, 8(2): 105–14.

Ahtee, M. and Johnston, J. (2006) primary student teachers' ideas about teaching a physics topic, *Scandinavian Journal of Science Education*, 50(2).

Bandura, A. (1986) *Social Foundations of Thought and Action: A Social Cognitive Theory*. Englewood Cliff, NJ: Prentice Hall.

Beetlestone, F. (1998) *Creative Children, Imaginative Teaching*. Buckingham: Open University Press.

de Bono, E. (1992) *Serious Creativity*. London: HarperCollins.

de Bóo, M. (ed.) (2004) *Early Years Handbook. Support for Practitioners in the Foundation Stage*. Sheffield: Curriculum Partnership / Geography Association.

Dennison, P. and Dennison, G. (1994) *Brain Gym*. Ventura, CA: Educational Kinesiology Foundation.

DfEE (1998) *The National Literacy Strategy*. London: DfEE.

DfEE (1999) *The National Numeracy Strategy*. London: DfEE.

DfES (2003) *Excellence and Enjoyment: A Strategy for Primary Schools*. London: DfES.

Duffy, B. (1998) *Supporting Creativity and Imagination in the Early Years*. Buckingham: Open University Press.

Foulkes, D. (1982) *Children's Dreams – Longitudinal Studies*. New York: John Wiley.

Ginn, I. S. and Waters, J. (1995) An analysis of scientific understanding of preservice elementary teacher education students, *Journal of Research in Science Teaching*, 32(2), 205–22.

Harlen, W. (ed.) (1977) *Match and Mismatch: Finding Answers*. Edinburgh: Oliver & Boyd.

Johnston, J. (2002) The changing face of teaching and learning, in J. Johnston, M. Chater and D. Bell (eds) *Teaching the Primary Curriculum*. Buckingham: Open University Press.

Johnston, J. (2005a) *Early Explorations in Science*, 2nd edn. Buckingham: Open University Press.

Johnston, J. (2005b) What is creativity in science education, in A. Wilson (ed.) *Creativity in Primary Education*. Exeter: Learning Matters.

Kerry, T. (2002) *Explaining and Questioning*, Mastering Teaching Skills Series. Cheltenham: Nelson Thornes.

Kissock, C. and Iyortsuun, P. (1982) *A Guide to Questioning: Classroom Procedures for Teachers*. London: Macmillan.

Roberts, M. (1996) Teaching styles and strategies, in A. Kent, D. Lambert, M. Naish and F. Slater (eds) *Geography in Education: Viewpoints on Teaching and Learning*. Cambridge: Cambridge University Press.

Sanders, N. M. (1966) *Classroom Questions: What Kinds?* New York: Harper & Row.

Shulman, L. S. (1987) Knowledge and teaching: foundations of the new reform, *Harvard Educational Review*, 57: 1–22.

Storm, M. (1989) The five basic questions for primary geography, *Primary Geographer*, 2 (Autumn): 4.

Vygotsky, L. (1978) *Mind in Society: The Development of Higher Psychological Processes*, eds M. Cole *et al*. Cambridge, MA: Harvard University Press.

White, R. and Gunstone, R. (1992) *Probing Understanding*. London: Falmer Press.

Yager, R. E. (1991) The constructivist learning model, *The Science Teacher*, 58: 52–7.

7

Differentiation

Jane Johnston

Introduction

Differentiation, that is matching teaching and learning to suit individual or groups of learners, is not a new concept in education and most books on differentiation appear to identify a lack of consensus about what it is. Teachers and other educational professionals also often share this confusion. There may be two main reasons for this confusion and lack of consensus. Firstly, it may be that the idea of differentiation conjures up an image of one specific way of differentiating (usually by providing different tasks for learners) rather than the generic idea of adapting plans and practice in different ways for different learners in different contexts. Secondly, the reality of differentiation is often more difficult than the theory and will be different in different phases of education.

In this chapter, we take the view that differentiation concerns changing aspects of teaching and learning, such as approaches, tasks, expectations and support, to enable the child to achieve the learning objectives or learning outcomes. In this way there needs to be coherence between what is being differentiated and the learning outcome for the child.

What is differentiation?

The idea of differentiation is well-established in theory (McNamara and Moreton 1997) and encompassed in Vygotsky's (1978) idea of the zone of proximal development, Bruner's scaffolding (Bruner 1983; see also Wood *et al.* 1976) and Gardner's (1983, 1993) multiple intelligences. Vygotsky's zone of proximal development identifies that learning occurs through the interaction of skilled adults (Vygotsky 1978) and through social interaction with peers. Bruner's scaffolding concerns the support (resources, tasks, guidance or models) an adult provides for the learner to support development and learning and gradually withdraws to encourage independent learning (Bruner 1983; also Wood *et al.* 1976). Gardner's theory of multiple intelligences identifies that different learners have different learning profiles and therefore different needs. While these theories help to provide us with a picture of differentiation and have led to very useful models of differentiation (McNamara and Moreton 1997), they do not really help to provide a clearer definition of it in practice.

Reflective task
Differentiation – the challenge for practice

Imagine a class of 30 Year 1 children. They may be in the early stages of their learning journey, but already there will be significant differences between them. Difference in gender, ages and maturity at this stage can make a significant difference as some children will be physically and cognitively more mature. Children whose birthday is in the earlier part of the academic year for example in September are one-fifth older than the youngest children, born in the latter part of the academic year (August). The class may also contain children who were born prematurely and so are physically less mature than those who were full-term births. Boys can often mature at a slower rate than girls and reach maturity up to 10 years after some children; some girls will reach physical maturity at 9 years of age, whereas some boys will be 19 years of age before they reach physical maturity. The children will also have different experiences during the first few years of their lives. Some children may have experienced the full range of challenging and stimulating pre-school experiences (home, playgroup, nursery); others may have limited and poor quality pre-school experiences. Some children may have started school in the Reception class and had a full year of experience before Year 1, whereas others may have only just started school in the Year 1 class. Some children may be part of large or extended families with many siblings and close relatives; others will be an only child in a nuclear family or a single-parent family. They will be used to different amounts of adult support and interaction and be at different stages of their language, social and cognitive development. Added to this, each and every child is an individual, with different skills and attitudes. Some children will be more independent than others, some will be more curious, some will be tolerant of a noisy social environment, and some will find cooperation easier than others.

There may also be some children with specific individual needs, such as physical disability, language delay or learning difficulties. The children may come from different cultural or social backgrounds or speak different languages. The result of these differences is a wide mix of abilities and experiences within even our first classroom, making the role of the teacher more challenging as every child has a right to have their difference taken into consideration. This may mean adapting, modifying or changing learning experiences for these individuals to accommodate their individual differences; in other words may have to differentiate learning.

Level 1
Consider a recent learning situation you have been in (school, university, and so on) and the people you were learning with. Try to group the individuals in different ways

cont.

(age, experience, qualifications, home backgrounds, and so on). How many different groups can you make? Remember that an individual can be in more than one group. How did the individual differences affect the learning within the group? How did the teacher accommodate the differences? How could these differences be better taken into consideration?

Level 2

Consider your own class of children and try to identify all the individual differences. Choose one child and analyse them as an individual learner. How does their individuality affect their development and learning? How do you currently accommodate the individual differences? How can you improve your differentiation for this individual?

Level 3

Consider your school or setting. What are the main areas of difference in the children (for example, age, race, culture, language, social background, physical ability). How does your school / setting accommodate learning for individuals with these differences? Choose the area of biggest challenge for your school / setting and identify how you could improve differentiation within the school / setting for individuals.

Why should you differentiate?

Differentiation is an integral part of legislation, from the Education Acts of 1981 and 2005 to the Human Rights Act 1998 and the Children Act 2004. The Primary Strategy (DfES 2003a: 39) recognizes that 'learning must be focused on individual pupils' needs and abilities' and *Every Child Matters* (DfES 2003b) is based on the principle that every child has the right to the same five outcomes, whatever their individual differences:

- health: enjoying a physical and mental well-being and living healthily;
- safety: being safe and protected from any form of harm or neglect;
- enjoyment and achievement: having access and benefiting from opportunities and developing important life skills;
- contribution: being involved in community and social life, so that they are able to make a positive contribution to society and take some responsibility for their own actions in society;
- economic well-being: being able to achieve their full potential and not be economically disadvantaged later in life because they have not had opportunities to fulfil their potential.

Parents also want their children's individual differences to be accommodated. Research into transition from the Foundation Stage to Key Stage 1 has identified that parents want early years teachers and professionals not only to know their children and to accommodate individual differences (PNS 2006) but also to consider the provision for the younger, the less mature, the less able or those with English as an additional language (EAL) (Sanders *et al.* 2005). Kerry (2002: 82) identifies that differentiation is an important skill for teachers, one that has a 'profound effect on the quality of learning'. Effective differentiation provides satisfaction for teachers, as they know that they are supporting effective learning. Children on the receiving end of effective differentiation are more likely to be motivated as the level of challenge and support will be empowering for them as learners. This will make a more effective learning environment, that is, one in which children are motivated to learn and in which the experiences are ones that are conducive to learning. Such an environment will enable children to progress through the learning experiences and develop their learning at a rate that is suitable for them. Such an environment is one that children, teachers, other professionals and parents will be happy to be part of and make the learning experience more pleasant for all involved.

Personalized learning

We noted above the many differences that can be observed or are inherent in different learners. These have been noted in different theories of personalized learning such as Gardner's (1983) theory of multiple intelligence and Johnston's (1996) interactive learning theory.

Gardner's (1983) idea is that there are a number of different intelligences, which may be unrelated. Each one is of equal importance, although some may be culturally or educationally favoured. For example, our education system favours linguistic and logical / mathematical abilities, whereas in some eastern cultures bodily / kinaesthetic and spatial abilities are more favoured. The different intelligences are:

- bodily / kinaesthetic or using the body to solve problems and express ideas and feelings;
- interpersonal, or the ability to gauge moods, feelings and needs;
- intrapersonal, or the ability to use knowledge about themselves and have a well-developed self-image;
- linguistic, or the ability to use words, oral or written;
- logical / mathematical, or the ability to understand and use numbers and reason well;
- musical;
- naturalist intelligence, or the ability to organize and classify both the animal and plant kingdoms as well as showing understanding of natural phenomena;
- spatial, or the ability to perceive the visuo-spatial world accurately.

Johnston's (1996) theory is that there are four interactive learning schemas, which combine together in different ways in individual learners:

- sequential processing, or the ability to be ordered, organized and having the desire for clear instructions and time to complete work;
- precise processing, or the ability to be precise and detailed and desiring information and enjoying acquiring knowledge;
- technical processing, or the ability to be practical, technical or scientific and liking hands-on projects and first-hand experience;
- confluent processing, or the ability to be creative or artistic and having confidence in oneself and liking to use imagination and take risks.

Johnston's theory identifies that most primary teachers are sequential and precise and therefore tend to teach in an organized and precise way. Indeed, our education system favours organization and the acquisition of knowledge, and children who are sequential and precise learners are more likely to navigate successfully through our educational system. Technical and confluent learners can be alienated by learning environments and teachers who favour sequential and precise learning and learners. They can find it difficult to progress through our educational system unless they can also be sequential and precise. On the other hand, learners who are not technical or confluent are unlikely to be disadvantaged and can progress through our educational system without the need to develop technical or confluent processing skills as these are not skills that form the core of our system nor are they assessed in statutory tests.

Reflective task

Identify how the following would fit into sequential, precise, technical or confluent processing.
- Finds sitting still difficult.
- A neat and tidy writer.
- Prefers to make a model rather than write about something.
- Knowledgeable and enjoys answering factual questions.
- Reads factual books.
- Would rather draw a picture or annotate a drawing.
- Is a leader rather than a follower.
- Likes to be given instructions to follow.
- Enjoys the unknown and unexpected.
- Likes a routine.
- Enjoys science and technology lessons.

Level 1

Think of an individual you have known who found school and learning difficult. Analyse the individual's behaviour and see if they are a sequential, precise, technical or confluent processor. How could the teacher have accommodated the individual learner more in their lessons?

cont.

> **Level 2**
>
> Think of a child you have taught whom you found it difficult to relate to. Analyse the child's behaviour and see if they are a sequential, precise, technical or confluent processor. How does this differ from you? How could you have improved your teaching to accommodate the individual?
>
> **Level 3**
>
> Identify all the children who find it difficult to settle into your school or setting. Are they sequential, precise, technical or confluent processors? How could you make changes which would better accommodate them and improve their learning?

Another very popular learning theory is VAK (visual, auditory and kinaesthetic) theory, which identifies that learners are of three types: those who favour visual methods, those favouring auditory methods and those favouring kinaesthetic methods (Dryden and Vos 1999). VAK theories identify that educational settings tend increasingly to favour the visual and auditory learners, although many practitioners say they advocate practical, kinaesthetic learning. There also seems to be little common understanding of what kinaesthetic learning means, with some activities being labelled as kinaesthetic when they are more visual or auditory and others believing that physical exercise before cognitive work equals kinaesthetic learning. There is a great deal of anecdotal evidence from teachers' practice to indicate the importance of VAK and other learning theories, although they do not appear to have a theoretical basis in research (Revell 2005) and there is concern that teachers are spending a great deal of time attempting to accommodate different learners without firm research evidence of the positive effects (Coffield *et al.* 2004).

In recent years we have become increasingly concerned about individual rights, as opposed to collective rights in all areas of life, from business and politics to education. This increase in personalization has led to a DfES initiative to improve personalized learning (DfES 2006), for, as David Miliband, former Minister of State for School Standards, has said:

> We need to engage parents and pupils in a partnership with professional teachers and support staff to deliver tailor-made services – to embrace individual choice within as well as between school and to make it meaningful through public sector reform that gives citizens voice and professionals flexibility.
>
> (David Miliband MP, quoted in DfES 2006)

Personalized learning is not a new idea. Rousseau, often called the 'Father of Education', believed that education should accommodate children rather than expect them to accommodate to the educational system, advocating a child-centred system, which emphasized expression rather than repression (Rousseau 1911). Personalized learning is about adapting what we offer children to cater for their individual need, interest and aptitude so that everyone can achieve regardless of personal circumstances, culture or ability, etc. It is at the heart of new DfES (2006) initiatives and has five components:

1 *Assessment for Learning* (AfL), that is, using evidence and dialogue to identify where pupils are in their learning, where they need to go and how best to get there. Decisions about individual or personalized learning need to be based on evidence, so that there is a clear link between children's learning and teachers' planning (see Chapter 11, Assessment for Learning).

2 *Effective teaching and learning* for personalized learning involves developing the competence and confidence of learners by actively engaging and stretching them and enabling them to understand themselves as learners and the way they learn (metacognition). In order to achieve effective teaching and learning, teachers need to develop whole-class, group and individual teaching, learning using ICT and other strategies to support the development of skills and attitudes, as well as of knowledge and understanding. They also need to accommodate different learners by enabling the pace of learning to be different for different learners (see also DfES 2003a).

3 A *flexible curriculum* enables breadth of study and personal relevance within the core curriculum provided by the introduction of the national curriculum (DfEE 1999b; DfES 2007), regardless of gender, social background, race, religion or disability. It also ensures that each setting or school provides high-quality opportunities to extend the learning experiences available in the curriculum. In primary schools this enrichment will hopefully be achieved through Excellence and Enjoyment (DfES 2003a) and the five-year strategies (PNS 2006).

4 *Organizing the school for personalized learning,* that is, thinking creatively about organization in the class and the school, as this supports quality teaching and learning and the development not just of educational aims but social aims too. This organization has a number of strands: workforce remodelling which builds effective teams of staff, with planning, preparation and assessment time (PPA); the effective use of ICT; the creation of clear and consistent behaviour policies; being informed by children and their parents about individual needs; the creation of a positive learning environment (both physical and metaphysical); guaranteeing a minimum level of standards; and perhaps most importantly, being child-focused, so that child needs are at the heart of the school and inclusion is seen as a guiding principle.

5 *Beyond the classroom* it is important that effective partnerships with children, families, communities and outside agencies are developed to enable the school to know, support and celebrate the achievements of individuals, provide effective pastoral care and provide for additional needs where necessary. Lunchtime and after-school clubs, extended services, including extended learning support, are part of the care beyond the classroom.

There are a number of principles at the heart of the government's personalized learning initiative (DfES 2006). For children, at the heart of the initiative, it means that they should have their individual and personal needs met in the school / setting and the home and community, so that they are supported in achieving their full potential in a safe and secure environment. Most importantly, it provides them with a voice, so they can identify the approaches which work for them. Through the initiative, parents should have a clearer understanding of their child's progress and how they can support them. They should be involved more in planning their child's educational pathway and have the opportunity to play a more active and valued role in their educational life.

For teachers, personalized learning means that they should have high, but realistic, expectations of individual children, informed by data about the child, which support planning for personalized learning. They should also have some quality time (PPA) to use this information to support teaching, learning and assessment. Effective continuing professional development (CPD) support for teachers will also enable them to develop a wide repertoire of teaching strategies, including ICT. Personalized learning means that schools will provide a professional ethos that acknowledges individual differences and attempts to assess and develop their talents through diverse teaching strategies, while the DfES and local education authorities (LEAs) have the responsibility to create the conditions to enable personalized learning to occur, through 'intelligent accountability' (DfES 2006). The overarching principle is that the various parts of the educational system share common goals of high quality provision and high equity and raise standards by personalizing learning, making it relevant to the individual child and removing obstacles to their achievement.

Differentiation by target setting

Personalized learning leads to differentiation by target setting, where children have differentiated targets, sometimes decided in partnership (teachers, child, carers), according to their specific needs and abilities. Some targets could be cognitive, such as learning to spell specific words or understanding a particular mathematical procedure. Some targets may be behavioural, such as listening attentively for a period of time, or working cooperatively within a group. Some targets may relate to attitudes, borne out through behaviour, such as persevering at a task for a period of time, or respecting others' ideas.

The advantage of target setting is that the work is closely matched to the child's needs and abilities; consequently the child, who is aware of their target and has helped to set it, is more likely to achieve it. The challenge is both to ensure the target is not too difficult or too easy, as this may demotivate the child, and to monitor the achievement of the targets effectively. Some teachers use learning mentors (teaching assistants or other children) to help monitor achievement of targets. Others use a degree of self-monitoring, where the child monitors their own achievement and sets new targets, with some degree of help from the teacher or a learning mentor. The disadvantages are that unless the targets are seen to be of value the children will not work towards them, and the time taken to monitor them can detract from quality teaching unless they are managed well. There are additionally some teachers who feel that having differentiated targets for behaviour leads to double standards and children will feel unfairly treated if some children are allowed to behave in a way that they are not. This has not been a problem in my experience, as children seem to accept that individuals need to have different expectations of them, because they are individuals. Another problem can be that targets set can be examples of negative reinforcement, so that a child is set a target 'not to' do something, for example 'not to shout out in class' or 'not to disrupt other children'. For more about target setting, see Chapter 12.

Ability grouping, setting and streaming

One way in which schools have managed to provide for individual differences is through setting and streaming. Setting involves children being taught together for individual subjects because of their ability, recognizing that an individual could be a high achiever in one area and a lower achiever in another. Streaming involves placing a child in a particular class with children of similar ability and teaching them together in all subjects.

A primary classroom of the 1960s and 1970s sometimes had children grouped according to their ability. As a child in the 1960s, I moved to a primary school in my last term of Year 6 and, because I had passed my 11+ examination in another local authority area, was placed at the front left-hand desk of the classroom. At the back of the classroom, on the right-hand side, sat the child deemed to be the least able, and in between were all the rest of the class in rank order. How that rank order was determined I have no idea, but there was some attempt at differentiation, in that, in mathematics, I was given an adding machine (this was pre-calculators) to make some complex calculation, while at the other end of the class children had more simple mathematical work. During the 1970s and 1980s, the more common form of ability grouping was children seated together and doing similar or the same work because of their ability. In secondary schools, setting and streaming were more common, but with the introduction of the primary literacy and numeracy strategies in the 1990s (DfEE 1998, 1999a), setting became more common in primary schools, particularly for mathematics and English (or numeracy and literacy). The advantages were that the more able could be stretched and the less able could be better supported if the gap between the higher and lower children was not too great. The disadvantages were threefold. Firstly, in large schools, much time was wasted as children moved between classes and got themselves organized for the lessons, whereas in smaller schools, especially where the class was vertically grouped (that is, more than one year grouping in the same class), the class teacher sometimes attempted to set the children within the class and give each set a different input, creating an organizational dilemma. Secondly, the sets are norm-referenced, that is they are dependent on the other children in the cohort, so that if the cohort is of generally high ability, you may be in a lower set, but if the cohort are of a lower ability, you may be in a higher set. While this does not appear to be much of a disadvantage for the school or teacher, it may be for the child as the work set may not provide the level of challenge or support they need. Thirdly, expectations and self-esteem can be affected by the set a child is placed in. A child who performs well in a lower set is likely to have a higher self-esteem than a child who is not achieving in a higher set. Conversely, expectations of a child in the lower set can be lower and this can lead to lower achievement, as the child performs according to expectations, whereas a child in a higher set may perform better due to higher expectations. Some teachers and educationalists will speak passionately for setting, while others will argue passionately against it, and each will be able to provide evidence to support their claims.

More common in many primary classrooms are ability groupings within the class, so that children are grouped around a table according to their ability. The advantage of this type of ability grouping is that children of roughly the same ability are placed together and the work can better match their needs and abilities. In reality though, the groups are often decided because of language ability (or even more commonly because of written language ability) and this can disadvantage individuals whose strengths lie in other areas, for example our technical and confluent processors (see Johnston 1996, and the discussion above), those with poor linguistic intelligences (see Gardner 1983, and the discussion above), or those with English as an additional language (EAL). I learnt this in my first teaching position, when a Year 3 child who was regarded as one of the less able, outshone the rest of the class in scientific thinking and problem solving, but was unable to communicate his ideas in writing.

Mixed-ability grouping

Common in the 1980s and 1990s and still common outside mathematics and English teaching, is mixed-ability groupings. These may be friendship groups or groups chosen by the teacher because the children work well together, either cooperatively or collaboratively. The advantages of mixed-ability groupings are that children can achieve at their own level, provided the work is well structured. Work is structured, usually through differentiation either by task or by outcome (see below), and if this is effective then the more able can be stretched and the less able can be supported. There can even be an element of the less able being supported by the more able. Remember, too, that a child may be more able in one area and less able in another. Indeed, in some subjects, such as science, a child may be more able in one area (perhaps growth of plants, or light) because they have an outside interest in it (e.g. gardening or photography). The disadvantages are that the work does need careful structuring and monitoring to ensure it is well suited to individuals, as too big a challenge can lead to demotivation and too little challenge to boredom, and both can lead to behavioural problems.

Problems can occur with mixed-ability groupings if the groupings remain for long periods of time, as they may not be to the advantage of all the children. I once sat Debbie, a very serious, motivated and high-achieving Year 4 child, next to John, a lower achiever, with concentration problems and a poor diet. My rationale for this was that Debbie was able to concentrate despite John's interruptions and her distain for him meant that he was more likely to get on with his work. However, a colleague pointed out to me that Debbie kept a tally on the back of her hand of the number of times she was distracted by John 'passing wind' and I subsequently reorganized my groupings!

Differentiation by task

Differentiation by task is where children are given different tasks depending on their ability. This is common in both mathematics and English, where children's abilities can be well assessed and these assessments can be used to inform planning of tasks for different learners.

Practical and reflective task

Level 1

Use a collection of buttons, postcards, sweets or money and plan three differentiated tasks (higher ability, middle ability and lower ability) for children of a chosen age, with the learning objectives being in problem solving, reasoning and numeracy / mathematics – sorting and classifying. Use the curriculum guidance document (QCA 2007) or national curriculum (DfES 1999b) to help you match the learning objectives with the age of the children.

Level 2

Use a collection of buttons, postcards, sweets or money and plan three differentiated tasks (higher ability, middle ability and lower ability) for the children in your class, in mathematics and English (objectives: problem solving, reasoning and numeracy / mathematics – sorting and classifying; communication, language and literacy / English – description / using adjectives).

Level 3

Consider how you can use a collection of buttons, postcards, sweets or money to plan three differentiated tasks (higher ability, middle ability and lower ability) for different year groups in your school in mathematics and English (objectives: problem solving, reasoning and numeracy / mathematics – sorting and classifying; communication, language and literacy / English – description / using adjectives).

The advantage of differentiation by task is that the tasks can be well matched to individual needs and abilities. There are disadvantages, however: we often do not know details of individual abilities in every area; some children may continually underachieve because the tasks are not correctly designed for their abilities; the differentiation may not be closely linked to the learning objectives and may not support individuals to achieve them.

Differentiation by task is much more difficult in subject areas where you do not have enough information about the child to make decisions as to ability. For example, a child may have a particular interest in Roman history and so in work on the Romans would be at a higher level of ability than in work on modern history, a subject of which they have no knowledge. Similarly, in science a child may have particular interest in biology but no expertise in physics, or, as mentioned above, they may understand about plant growth but not about other aspects of biology. It is very easy to group children according to their literacy ability and then to give tasks in other subjects which are differentiated in the way they are recorded, instead of focusing on the learning objectives / outcomes. In planning differentiated tasks, it is essential that there is coherence between the planned learning objectives / outcomes and the differentiated tasks.

Reflective task

In one school, four Year 4 classes planned together and delivered the same lessons. During a history topic on the Romans, they had planned a lesson with objectives to understand the life of the Romans. The lesson was differentiated into three tasks three levels of ability. The higher achievers were asked to write a piece of prose about the Roman army and their fighting techniques. The middle achievers were asked to complete some cloze procedure (fill in the missing words in a piece of prose) on the same theme. The lower-ability children were asked to match a piece of prose to pictures of the Roman army, cutting them out of a sheet and sticking them into their books.

Level 1
What are the main problems with differentiation such as this? How could the differentiation be improved to provide better coherence between the tasks and learning objectives?

Level 2
Look at your own planning in history and see how you provide for different learners. Identify if you differentiate by task or outcome. How could you modify the differentiation to achieve coherence between the task and the learning objectives?

Level 3
Consider how you and your colleagues differentiate in history, geography and science. How could you improve your differentiation to better support achievements of the learning objectives?

The main problems with the differentiation described in the reflective task above are that:

- there is no coherence between the historical learning objectives and the literacy tasks, so that children who have good understanding of historical concepts may not be able to achieve well in the task;
- it is unlikely that the teacher has detailed knowledge of the children's abilities in Roman history and so it is impossible for them to plan tasks that will support the less able and stretch the more able.

In such cases, differentiation by outcome is more appropriate as there are more opportunities to match the work effectively and achieve greater coherence between the activities and the learning objectives.

Differentiation by outcome

Differentiation by outcome is where all children undertake the same activity but there are different outcomes for different learners. The advantages of this type of differentiation is that every child has the opportunity to achieve at a level appropriate to them and children do not feel labelled as poor achievers or that they are doing something of less worth than others. The disadvantages are that the activity can be successful only if it is well constructed with open-ended outcomes and there are opportunities to achieve at different levels, with clear expectations (success criteria) identified for individual learners and support for individuals.

Practical and reflective task
Key Stages 1 and 2

Level 1
Use a collection of buttons, postcards, sweets or money and plan three levels of expected outcome (success criteria) for three different groups of children of a chosen age (higher-ability, average-ability, lower-ability) in history, geography or science. You will need to use the national curriculum (DfES 1999b) to help you plan learning objectives *before* you start. What support would you need to give the lower-ability children to help them achieve?

Level 2
Use a collection of buttons, postcards, sweets or money and plan three levels of expected outcome (success criteria) for three different groups of children in your class (higher-ability, average-ability, lower-ability) in history, geography and science. Consider what additional support you need to help the lower-ability children to reach their success criteria and how your interaction can stretch the higher-ability children.

Level 3
Consider how you can use a collection of buttons, postcards, sweets or money to plan three levels of outcome (success criteria) for higher-ability, middle-ability and lower-ability) in different year groups in your school in history, geography and science. Consider how you could support children who are performing well below expected or stretch those who are gifted or talented.

The argument for differentiation by outcome is that it is most effective when:

- used in subjects where you do not know the details of children's abilities (all areas except mathematics and English);
- the activities are skilfully planned to enable children to achieve at different levels;
- professionals are very clear about what the success criteria are.

A well-planned, open-ended activity has an element of self-differentiation, as children will enter the activity and choose what to do based on their own experience, knowledge and skills. They will choose to consolidate, develop or modify ideas or skills, taking ownership of their own learning, setting their own targets and progressing at a rate appropriate to them. The key to success in such an activity is threefold. Firstly, the planning and preparation need to be of the highest quality to ensure there are opportunities to achieve at a number of different levels. Secondly, there needs to be clear success criteria or expectations of different levels of achievement, so that achievement can be recognized. Thirdly, interaction needs to be of the highest quality to support the less able and stretch the more able. Interaction can be through role modelling of learning behaviours and through questioning which supports, encourages and stretches children (see Chapter 6, Questioning).

Practical and reflective task
Foundation Stage

Look at the lesson plan for Garden Centre Play in Figure 7.1.

Level 1
Identify the expected outcomes (success criteria) for either Foundation Stage 1 or Foundation Stage 2 / Reception children in either knowledge and understanding of the world or personal, social and emotional development. Use the objectives in the plan as a guide or look at the early years curriculum documentation (QCA 2007) and *Foundation Stage Profile* (QCA 2003). What support would you need to give the lower-ability children to help them achieve the objectives?

Level 2
Identify the expected outcomes (success criteria) for the children in your class in both knowledge and understanding of the world and personal, social and emotional development. Consider what additional support you need to help the lower-ability children to reach their success criteria and how your interaction can stretch the higher-ability children.

Level 3
Identify the expected outcomes (success criteria) for both the Foundation 1 / nursery and Reception children in your setting in both knowledge and understanding of the world and personal, social and emotional development. Identify the practitioner's role in these play activities; that is, how should the professional interact with the children / what questions would focus on the objectives / success criteria?

Title of session Garden Centre Play (see de Bóo 2004)	Year group Foundation stage
Date of session	Practitioner
Length of session Ongoing play activities	Method Play in role play area

Outline
Set up a garden centre in the role play area. Children can sort seeds, plant seeds and potatoes in the garden, write labels, make purchases from the garden centre etc.

Area	Learning objectives	Resources
1 Garden centre	**Communication, language and literacy:** Eric Carle (1987) *The Tiny Seed* Writing labels for plants Vocabulary (plant, seed, soil, grow, root, shoot, leaf, flower) **Problem solving, reasoning and numeracy:** Counting, sorting and buying / selling seeds and plants **Knowledge and understanding of the world:** Parts of plants, variety of seeds and plants, growth of plants **Personal, social and emotional development:** Social interaction, taking turns Care for living things Awareness of the needs of others including plants	Book Eric Carle (1987) *The Tiny Seed* Collection of seeds, seed packets, plants and flowers, potatoes Plastic lolly stick labels (some blank and some with vocabulary on) Laminated white labels Dry-wipe pens Sorting hoops Shop front Till and money Trowel, wheelbarrow, rake etc. Compost and pots

Figure 7.1 Early Years Foundation Stage Lesson Plan

Picture 7.1 Playing in the garden centre

Differentiation by support

Whether we differentiate by outcome or task, we need to support children in their learning, and this involves differentiation by support. This means supporting different children in different ways. Some children may need very little support, although an occasional challenging question can engage them and help to support their development. Some children will need extensive physical or cognitive support because of special needs and this will involve teachers and other professionals supporting them, by giving them more time to complete an activity, assist them in undertaking some physical tasks that they are unable to do and putting different questions to them because of their individual needs. I always find that planning questions to ask of different learners helps me to focus on the differentiated success criteria and ensures that in a busy classroom I will ask those questions and support different learners. Other adults working in the classroom can also support children and it is common for teaching assistants to work with individuals who have particular needs or with groups of children.

In order for other adults to be effective in supporting different learners, they must be familiar with the planning for the lesson, sharing plans, success criteria and individual targets to support assessment for learning. Individual Education Plans (IEPs) are a form of individual target setting for children with particular needs and identify how individuals can be supported, although they are thought to be more appropriate for groups of children rather than individuals and it can be difficult to find the individual within the IEP (O'Brien and Guiney 2001).

For some children with particular needs, or who are gifted (are generally achieving well above the expectation for their age) or talented (are achieving particularly well in one or two areas), support may take the form of teaching them in special schools, classes or programmes. For gifted and talented children this may involve cognitive acceleration, which involves removing artificial obstacles in the way of the developing child. For many gifted children this means removing the brakes (Evans 2002) to allow them to develop in accordance with their ability rather than their age and the notion of cognitive stage. In this way, children with special educational needs or who are gifted and talented may be supported by:

- starting school early or later;
- skipping or extending time spent in one year group;
- telescoping (setting work over a shorter than normal period of time) or extending work (setting longer periods of time to undertake work, as for dyslexic learners);
- subject acceleration or special classes or programmes (Mulhearn 2006; National Academy for Gifted and Talented Youth 2006);
- in-class or content acceleration (allowing individual children to progress at their own rate in a subject or part of a subject);
- whole-class acceleration (classes of gifted children) or special needs classes (classes of children with particular needs);
- curriculum compacting (elimination of material from the curriculum that the child has already learnt) or narrowing the curriculum for children with particular needs;
- 'brain gym' activities (Dennison and Dennison 1994) which advocate drinking plenty of water and performing short exercises to support left / right brain hemisphere coordination and cognitive development.

There are arguments against separating children from their peers to support aspects of their development, since it is unlikely that all areas will need the same level of support, and separating children can lead to social and emotional problems in later life. Additionally, some types of support, such as cognitive acceleration, are not convincingly evidence based.

Reflective task

Gifted and talented

by Chris Johnston, St Mary Magdalene Primary School, Sutton-in-Ashfield, Nottinghamshire

In the days before all schools were expected to identify gifted and talented children we had a child in school, Rachel, who was most definitely talented and, in particular, gifted at mathematics.

Throughout Foundation Stage and Key Stage 1, Rachel's abilities were very apparent, being demonstrated time and again as she explored with apparatus, recorded and computed on paper. The general feeling in school was that if Rachel was shown a technique once, she would be able to use it thereafter; give her a problem to solve and she would apply known techniques and invent new strategies to find the solution. The important issue was that during these key stages it was perfectly possible to meet Rachel's needs by differentiated work within the classroom and by the teacher. It should also be noted that she was a very quiet, unassuming and particularly modest girl.

At the end of Key Stage 1, Rachel's test results were exceptional. The school tests Key Stage 2 children in February of each year using NFER maths and English tests and non-verbal reasoning tests in Years 3 and 5. Her scores in Maths at the end of Year 3 were exceptional, and it was at this point that we felt Rachel needed extending beyond the range of the class. In Year 4 for maths and English she was put up one year group, working and exceeding the achievement levels of the top group in the class. This worked very well in as much as Rachel continued to be challenged and she developed accordingly. We did consider moving her up another academic year for maths, but did not do so since she would have been in the same group as her brother. This was likely to put him under pressure having a sibling two years his junior in his class so we took the decision to give Rachel one-to-one tutoring for two sessions every week with a teacher who was a maths specialist. The specialist set Rachel additional follow-up work to be completed in class during maths sessions. The work presented was of a higher level but focused particularly upon problem solving and investigative maths. This kept Rachel in her classroom and in more contact with her classmates and helped to avoid some of the growing social problems, especially with her female peers, who were withdrawing from her and becoming antagonistic towards her.

This level of personal tutoring continued throughout Years 5 and 6. In her end of Key Stage 2 SATs in maths Rachel only dropped one mark – a silly arithmetical mistake. Achieving a level five in her maths completely misrepresented Rachel's ability. Unfortunately, by then, the option to take Level 6 tests had been withdrawn.

We wrote to the secondary school that Rachel was to transfer to, giving them a full account of her abilities and asking that they made immediate special and specific provision for her on transfer into Year 7. Sadly, they chose not to pursue this. When I spoke to Rachel's parents and to Rachel some time afterwards I was told that she

cont.

was totally bored repeating work she had done in this school some time before. Subsequently they made an appointment to see the head of maths and he was unaware of the contact we had made in advance of her transfer. It was not until the end of Year 7 tests that the school recognized her ability and made arrangements to provide appropriate challenges for her.

Level 1

Can you think of any gifted or talented children or adults you have known. How were they supported in their learning? Did the support have any effect on other areas of their development? How do you think the children could have been better supported? Explain why you think this support would have been advantageous for the individual.

Level 2

How could you have supported a child like Rachel within your class? How could you ensure that this support did not have an adverse effect on other areas of the child's development? What additional support do you think the child would need from the school?

Level 3

Can you think of any other ways the school could support a child like Rachel? How would you support the child, ensuring that no aspect of their development is adversely affected? What additional outside support could you access to support a gifted or talented child?

References

Bruner, J. S. (1983) *Child's Talk: Learning to Use Language.* Oxford: Oxford University Press.

Carle, E. (1987) *The Tiny Seed.* London: Hodder & Stoughton.

Coffield, F., Moseley, D., Hall, E. and Ecclestone, K. (2004) *Should we be Using Learning Styles? What Research has to Say to Practice.* London: Learning and Skills Development Agency.

Dennison, P. and Dennison, G. (1994) *Brain Gym.* Ventura, CA: Educational Kinesiology Foundation.

DfEE (1998) *The National Literacy Strategy.* London: DfEE.

DfEE (1999a) *The National Numeracy Strategy.* London: DfEE.

DfEE (1999b) *The National Curriculum: Handbook for Teachers in England.* London: DfEE / QCA.

DfES (2003a) *Excellence and Enjoyment: A Strategy for Primary Schools.* London: DfES.

DfES (2003b) *Every Child Matters.* London: DfES.

DfES (2006) *Personalised Learning.* Available at www.standards.dfes.gov.uk/ personalisedlearning/

DfES (2007) Statutory Framework for the Early Years Foundation Stage; Setting the Standards for Learning, Development and Care for chioldren from birth to five. *Every Child Matters, Change for Children*. London DfES.

Dryden, G. and Vos, J. (1999) *The Learning Revolution: To Change the Way the World Learns*. Auckland: The Learning Web.

Evans, S. (2002) *Acceleration: A Legitimate Means of Meeting the Needs of Gifted Children*. Available at www.nexus.edu.au.teachstud/gat/evanss.htm

Gardner, H. (1983) *Frames of Mind: The Theory of Multiple Intelligences*. London: Heinemann.

Gardner, H. (1993) *The Unschooled Mind: How Children Think and How Schools should Teach*. London: Fontana.

Johnston, C. (1996) *Unlocking the Will to Learn*. Thousand Oaks, CA: Corwin Press.

Kerry, T. (2002) *Learning Objectives, Task Setting and Differentiation*. Cheltenham: Nelson Thornes.

McNamara, S. and Moreton, G. (1997) *Understanding Differentiation: A Teacher's Guide*. London: David Fulton.

Mulhearn, D. (2006) The sky's the limit, *Primary Teachers*, 43 (March). Available at www.teachernet.gov.uk

National Academy for Gifted and Talented Youth (2006) www.nagty.ac.uk

O'Brien, T. and Guiney, D. (2001) *Differentiation in Teaching and Learning: Principles and Practice*. London: Continuum.

PNS (2006) *Primary National Strategy: Foundation Stage*. www.standards. dfes.gov.uk

QCA (2007)

Revell, P. (2005) Each to their own, *Education Guardian*, 31 May.

Rousseau, J-J. (1911) *Emile*. London: J. M. Dent & Sons (first published 1762).

Sanders, D., White, G., Burge, B., Sharp, C., Eames, A., McEune, R. and Grayson, H. (2005) *A Study of the Transition from the Foundation Stage to Key Stage 1*. London: DfES / Sure Start.

Vygotsky, L. (1978) *Mind in Society: The Development of Higher Psychological Processes*, eds M. Cole *et al*. Cambridge, MA: Harvard University Press.

Wood, D., Bruner, J. and Ross, G. (1976) The role of tutoring in problem solving, *Journal of Child Psychology and Psychiatry*, 17: 89–100.`

8
Using ICT in Teaching
John Halocha

Introduction

> *Learning with computers in school is a social activity in which the teacher plays a crucial role.*
>
> Wegerif and Dawes (2004: 1)

The purpose of this chapter is to help you think about how you use information and communication technology (ICT) in your professional life as a teacher. The chapter raises questions and encourages you to develop your own philosophy about how you will plan, use and evaluate the learning opportunities for your pupils that are supported by ICT in its many guises. The theories and initiatives that are discussed have been chosen to help you stand back from your fast-moving day-to-day life and reflect on precisely why ICT may or may not be a valuable tool in twenty-first century primary schools. As Muirhead (2005: 167) suggests:

> The challenge therefore is for our country to develop a policy which takes on board the aspirations of the digital generation and presents opportunities for [the children] to learn in a flexible, interactive and meaningful way.

ICT – the bigger picture

As a headteacher committed to using ICT to support pupil learning and social interaction, Muirhead argues that, as developments such as wireless technologies develop, teachers need to reconsider the ways in which they both construct the curriculum and support learning environments for their pupils. In order to set this in a broad context we begin by examining some underlying concepts in ICT.

When we talk about ICT the image of a PC often comes to mind. However, ICT includes a very wide range of equipment and technologies. These include digital cameras, light sensors, videotapes, digital keyboards, mobile phones, iPods and fax machines. The central focus of this chapter is how teachers may understand the unique ways in which such technologies can support pupils in their learning and understanding about the world. The artefacts do not necessarily have to have digital technology to be included: the humble television should be included in the list, even before it is transformed into the new digital beast that manufacturers are increasingly promoting.

Although ICT is included in National Curriculum documents, its visibility in schools varies enormously, as seen both by teachers and by pupils. As Kirkman (2000) states:

> Whilst the ICT National Curriculum has made a useful contribution to the development of ICT in schools, the original vision of delivering ICT across the curriculum has not been realised in the majority of schools.

Before reading on, it may be worthwhile considering the following activity in relation to your teaching experience.

Reflective task

Level 1

Think of a recent school experience and note down all the ICT equipment you were aware of. Identify which items you or the pupils used. Refer back to this list as you read through the chapter.

Level 2

Think back over a recent half term of teaching experience. Make a list of the variety of ICT equipment that you and your pupils used. You may well be amazed at how extensive this list is. Beside each item note down why that particular piece of equipment was chosen and what special qualities it had for supporting pupil learning. Keep these ideas and refer back to them as you read through the chapter.

Level 3

Make a list of the variety of ICT equipment that you have in your setting. You may well be amazed at how extensive this list is. Beside each item note down what special qualities it has for supporting pupil learning and how often it is used. Keep these ideas and refer back to them as you read through the chapter.

In order to understand how recent thinking on ICT has developed, it is necessary first to briefly look back at factors that have helped to create the current state of affairs in our primary schools.

Learning from the past

Books will soon be obsolete in the schools. Scholars will soon be instructed through the eye. It is possible to teach every branch of human knowledge with the motion picture. Our school system will be completely changed in ten years.

New York Dramatic Mirror, 1913, quoted in Saettler (1968: 98)

Almost a century after the *New York Dramatic Mirror*'s claim was published, we can see the pattern repeating itself in our schools where ICT has perhaps not brought about the radical and transformational changes that were predicted when primary schools first introduced computers in the 1980s. To a large extent, many of the government-led initiatives provided money for equipment but not for the effective support for teachers to use new technology. Leadership in many primary schools lacks a vision of how ICT can support the curriculum. ICT cannot be seen in isolation if we are genuinely to move into a world in which pupils, teachers and technology are more seamlessly integrated in the goal towards meaningful and independent learning. Finally, there are many instances where ICT is still regarded as a subject rather than as a range of tools and techniques to aid learning and social interaction. However, much innovative work is taking place in our understanding of the pedagogy of ICT in primary education. The following section analyses a broad range of perspectives and initiatives that are moving forward our thinking in this significant area of education.

ICT as a pedagogical skill

Charles Clarke, Secretary of State for Education and Skills, offered a government perspective on ICT as a pedagogical skill when, in 2003, he stated:

My vision is one where schools are confidently, successfully and routinely exploiting ICT alongside other transformational measures. By doing so they will be delivering an education that equips learners for life in the Information Age of the 21st Century.

(DfES 2003a)

The National College for School Leadership (DfES 2003b) has published a framework for developing e-confident schools in which this pedagogy might develop. Its emphasis is on clear leadership that sees ICT as central in any twenty-first-century learning organization, especially as both the role and nature of schools as organizations are beginning to change. The 'Every Child Matters' strategy is one part of this much larger jigsaw of innovation. What, then, is happening in the fields of pedagogical theory and practice?

Technology has always been a part of schools, but if we are to suggest that ICT is special, and perhaps unique, within our range of professional tools, we need to be clear about some of the characteristics it holds. Loveless (2002) suggests that ICT may have five distinguishing features that can help us inform our pedagogical approaches: *Interactivity* (1) is seen as the process where a child becomes a dynamic user and thinker of technology. For example, if a child is using a photo package to manipulate their digital photos, they can see how one change gives the photo a new meaning. This example also helps to explain the idea that ICT helps children understand the *provisionality* (2) of knowledge and information. Cropping their photograph can turn the image into a totally new product. By being able to manipulate a digital image, a child can experience how the *capacity* (3) of ICT can be utilized: the example here shows how the vast processing power of modern computers can make changes to an image that might be almost impossible with more traditional photographic processes. If a child then emails their new image to a friend in another country, the process demonstrates the *range* (4) of power that the technology has to distribute information. Finally, this experience illustrates the *speed* (5) at which ICT can operate, where their friend almost instantaneously receives the image.

Reflective task

Level 1

Choose one example of how you have used ICT in your own learning.
- To what extent do you think that you have understood the five aspects suggested by Loveless (2002)?
- Do you agree that they are valid features of ICT?
- Is there another feature that you might wish to add if we are to create a rigorous pedagogical model?

Level 2

Choose one example of how you use ICT in your teaching.
- To what extent do you think the five aspects suggested by Loveless (2002) have been understood by your pupils?
- Do you agree that they are valid features of ICT?
- Is there another feature that you might wish to add if we are to create a rigorous pedagogical model?

Level 3

In a staff meeting, get your staff to analyse Loveless's (2002) five aspects.
- To what extent do you think the five aspects have been understood by your pupils in your recent teaching?
- Are they valid features of ICT?
- Are there other features that you might wish to add if we are to create a rigorous pedagogical model?
- How can you move forward in your ICT teaching in school?

In order to help us understand how teachers might exploit these features of ICT, Somekh (1997) suggests that teachers adopt one of three ways of using computers in the classroom. The first example is where a teacher sets up a computer so that a child (or a small group of children) sits at a computer and the computer will act as their teacher and require no intervention from the human teacher. An example of this might be where a teacher selects a piece of drill and practice software in which the child obtains all their instructions from the program and may even get some form of score. Another way in which teachers might use computers is where they view the computer as a neutral tool that replaces another set of equipment: word processing is one example of this, where the child is in essence completing the same activity but using ICT instead of traditional technology. The final example she cites is where teachers arrange for ICT to provide an active learning environment that would not be possible without the use of ICT facilities. An example here might be the ability to access webcams to observe, at first hand, wild animals in Africa. Clearly, her model is not fully convincing, especially with regard to the second category. The word processing example might apply only where the pupil uses the computer as electronic writing paper and pen. As soon as they start using the more advanced facilities of word processing they are moving along her scale to a more thinking and creative use of the technology. Rather than three separate models of pedagogical use of ICT, you may prefer to imagine Somekh's positions as sitting along a continuum of how pupils actually benefit from a particular piece of technology.

In essence, Somekh (1997) is encouraging us to stand back from the increasing range of technology that can now be used in primary schools in order to alter our pedagogical approaches to teaching and learning. We need to be clear about the specific qualities the technologies have and how those can be applied. Various pieces of hardware and software can help pupils and teachers think in new ways. Jonassen (2000: 4c) suggested that this ever increasing range of technologies could be viewed as a set of 'mindtools'. This can be a useful way of thinking about the ICT experiences we offer in school as it relates to recent developments in thinking skills and philosophy for children. He suggests five possible groups of mindtools that ICT offers.

1 *Knowledge construction tools* are those that help children and teachers build up their own version of knowledge and the interrelations between aspects of it. Children selecting and editing information for a PowerPoint presentation would be an example of how the power of ICT as a mindtool encourages children to consider their thinking in new, flexible and creative ways. Of course, it could have been done in the past by cutting up pieces of paper with writing and pictures on: the argument Jonassen (2000) offers is that by being able to adapt knowledge and make non-linear connections between pieces of understanding, pupils can gain greater insight into the nature of knowledge and their current understanding of it.
2 *Semantic organization tools* are software that enables pupils to ask questions about the world in flexible and creative ways. An example here might be a database where, once pupils have input a certain amount of data, they can then ask new questions and devise new models to test out ideas. A creative example here would be the ways in which music keyboards can record children's compositions for which they can then change key, add new instruments, alter pace and so forth.

3 *Interpretation tools* are seen by Jonassen (2000) as software that allows children to collect and analyse information from a wide variety of sources. The world wide web and CD-Roms are just two examples. He argues that children need to use such tools in order to understand that the information they find might be contradictory and biased, depending on the creator and context in which it was developed. For example, a community website debating the proposal of a new wind farm in the area might contain very different information from that placed on the website by the energy company wishing to build the facility.

4 *Dynamic modelling tools* are seen by Jonassen (2000) as opportunities for pupils to develop open-ended and creative thinking by being able to look at a whole range of possible solutions to an enquiry or problem. The classic software is Logo, or one of the many derivatives now available, including some very easy-to-program robots for early years children. These mindtools place pupils in learning environments where they can also discover that there is often no one fixed solution to a question or problem. If set up carefully in the classroom, they can also be effective environments for social learning as described by Vygotsky (1978) and illustrated through examples by Agar (2003), who suggests that 'Vygotsky, originally writing in Russian in the 1930s, has some very influential insights into the ways in which children learn that have vast implications for children and their use of ICT' (p. 18).

5 *Conversation tools* would be seen by Jonassen (2000) to include email and video-conferencing, which allow children immediate access to each other's thinking, information and ideas. He considers that the social activities involved in using these tools are at least as important as the technical ones. They help children to develop discussion skills, consider other people's points of view and change their perspectives on issues. One powerful example of this is the Fiankoma Project (www.fiankoma.org) in which English and African children have access to each other through live links and use a wide range of ICT to share information, ideas and views on many real-life events and issues.

To this list Loveless (2002: 19) adds *communication tools* which group together applications such as desktop publishing, graphics packages and multimedia presentation software. This might be a worthwhile discussion activity in which to engage with colleagues when you discuss the validity of Jonassen's (2000) grouping of tools as one framework through which to analyse your use of various pedagogical approaches to the use of ICT in your school, perhaps based around the notion of mindtools for thinking.

If these tools are to be used successfully, it may be necessary for us to think anew about the context in which they are used.

> ICT has fundamentally changed the way we do things in our everyday lives and business. However, although this is evident all around us, schools and education policy seem to be caught in a 'time warp' and continue to adopt the practice of mapping the new technologies on to old curricula with tired pedagogy.
>
> (Yelland 2002: 85)

The point that Yelland is making is that we often start with our existing curriculum and pedagogical beliefs and try to use some technology within them. Perhaps it is time for us to take a much closer look at the technology we have available and find new and innovative ways of building a curriculum around it. That is not to say that technology should dominate the design and philosophy of the whole curriculum; rather, we need to be aware of ways in which it may provide new, creative and enjoyable ways of learning. This can be illustrated by an example from geographical enquiry. Photographs and video are often used in geography teaching. They are often taken by people not connected with the school and may represent outdated or biased perspectives on a place. By getting children to locate appropriate live webcams or even children transmitting live pictures back to school from phones or cameras, we are instantly able to develop new kinds of geographical enquiry based on up-to-date information that is more meaningful to the pupils.

This whole process of designing a curriculum based on the potential of the technology opens up opportunities for children to become much more aware of the benefits and pitfalls of such technology. It can also build in elements of citizenship in that if the imaging technology is used to link pupils around the country, and indeed the world, it enables children to reconsider their knowledge, understanding and values as they become more aware of how people in other places understand their world views.

The example cited above illustrates how the use of ICT can change the nature of the learning environment. Yelland (2002: 93) suggests that this environment has five key elements. The first is *learners* who are actively engaged in using and developing their own ideas. The second is *teachers* who do not see themselves as providers of knowledge. Rather, they are supporters of children who are learning to construct their own view of the world. The third is that both children and teachers are working in a *context* that encourages children to enquire and investigate problems. The fourth is a sense in which the learning environment is an *integration* of questions, information and skills that are being explored in a holistic way. The children are at the centre of the learning process, using ICT as appropriate and supported by the teacher in their learning. Finally, the element of *communication* is very apparent in that ICT is being used to gather, store, analyse and communicate information and ideas.

Practical and reflective task
Consider how these five elements could be used to develop your own pedagogy.

Level 1
Select an activity that you have done during a placement.
- How could the activity be changed so that children become more active learners through using appropriate technology that places them more at the centre of the learning process?
- How does the ICT help you and the children to achieve the learning objectives in a more dynamic way?   *cont.*

Level 2

Select an activity that you do with your class. Draw a grid with Yelland's (2002) five elements as headings. Think about how the children might become more active learners through using appropriate technology that places them more at the centre of the learning process. When you have selected the ICT, note down what it enables you and the children to do in a more dynamic way than you have perhaps done in the past. It may take a while to think in this way when planning. The key is to take your learning objectives and consider how ICT can actively support them, rather than taking the objectives and seeing when ICT can simply be fitted in somewhere to ensure those boxes of the curriculum get ticked off.

Level 3

As a school, consider Yelland's (2002) five elements. Draw a grid with the five elements as headings.
- How do you currently use ICT in your school in each area?
- How can you develop ICT further to ensure that *learners* are actively engaged, *teachers* support children, the *context* encourages children to enquire and investigate problems in an *integrated* learning environment, and that ICT is being used to gather, store, analyse and *communicate* information and ideas.
- What factors hinder this development?
- How can you overcome these hindrances?

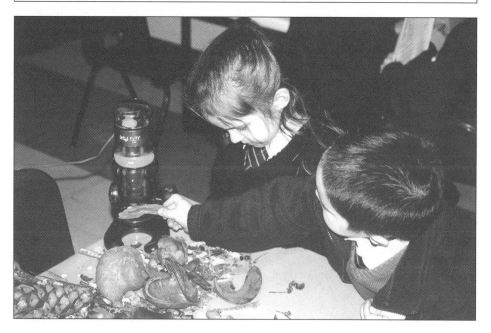

Picture 8.1 Key Stage 2 children using a digital microscope to develop observational skills

Another pedagogical consideration linked to developing ICT within the curriculum is how you plan for the children's various preferred learning styles. Riding *et al.* (1993: 269) suggest two main styles of learning:

- The holistic–analytic style: whether an individual tends to process information in whole or in part;
- The verbal–imagery style: whether an individual is inclined to represent information verbally or in mental images.

These ideas are now well rooted in pedagogical considerations. However, research reported by Meadows and Leask (2000: 8) suggests that various types of hardware and software, if carefully selected, can provide children with learning environments that are most suited to their learning styles. Clearly this could not be done across the whole curriculum at present, but you may wish to consider how this and visual, auditory, kinaesthetic and tactile forms of learning might be supported by appropriate ICT. For example, there are now many easy-to-use programmable robots that offer children a very visual and tactile way of developing both their understanding of space and direction and their mathematical interpretation of the world. This example also raises the issue of continuity in ICT experiences: it may well help pupils if they are able to regularly revisit and build upon their ICT skills and understanding, which is a point not fully emphasized in the ICT National Curriculum.

This section has emphasized the need for a deeper understanding of how pedagogy can be developed through integrating ICT in appropriate ways into the curriculum. The starting point is not the acquisition of ICT for their own sake, but rather how those skills will be developed and applied as pupils ask and resolve questions. The idea of information literacy is also important here. Almost all uses of ICT can place children in positions where they can, at a level appropriate to age and ability, begin to critically analyse what is being provided through their use of ICT and how it is affecting their learning (metacognition). For example, how is information on a webpage really suitable for their learning and how well are they able to use and interpret that information? Such skills also address current interest in assessment for learning and involve pupils in their progress.

Finally, we need to consider how ICT is beginning to change the roles of teachers and pupils. Abbott (2001: 63) takes a look at the broad educational picture and suggests that ICT enables everyone involved in the educational process to work much more collaboratively. The teacher is not seen as the giver of knowledge but as being there to support pupils in their learning and to make appropriate uses of ICT to that end. But this greater collaboration also involves pupils working together in more meaningful ways, whether they are sitting beside each other or on opposite sides of the world. It can also support teachers working together more effectively: an example of this is how the Geographical Association now has a place on its website to which teachers, indeed anyone, can contribute geographical images that can be shared. You may well be doing this already if you work in a school that provides you with laptops that enable you to communicate with colleagues in your planning and administration activities. All of this fits well into current developments in education at a national level. The 'Every Child Matters' (DfES 2003a) agenda will see professionals working more closely together in environments, currently called schools, that will soon encompass a much wider range of facilities and expertise. The radical rethinking of curriculum and pedagogy currently taking place at Key Stage 3 will probably move across the key stages as politicians begin to understand that centrally created and controlled curriculum and pedagogical philosophy currently do little to motivate an increasingly alienated and dissatisfied body of pupils. Within all these changes

> One of the effects of the emergence of ICT as a dominant player in primary education will surely be, if it has not already happened, a dramatic change in the role of the teacher and their working relationships with the child.
>
> (Torjussen and Coppard 2002: 163)

Good practice in incorporating ICT in teaching

The previous section provided an overview of some current thinking about the pedagogical issues surrounding ICT in the primary school. This section offers three case studies in different subjects where some of these concepts are put into practice. As you read them, consider how the use of ICT may affect the roles of both teachers and children and how ICT can be used to help create both the content and the structure of a curriculum.

Case study
Geography

For many years the study of localities has been central in primary geography. Localities include the school locality, another UK locality and one in a less economically developed country. This curriculum was created long before even the current power of ICT could have been imagined. Teachers needed resources for teaching about localities. As a result, many organizations began to offer locality packs. These normally consisted of a set of A4 colour photographs, teacher's notes, maps and perhaps some other appropriate paper-based materials. Many were well constructed and helped children to understand places around the world. However, they were not cheap and the information in them dated very quickly. The actual location was controlled by the producers of the materials. Non-specialist teachers also found it hard to decode much of the geography that had been built into the resources: for example, there could be a photograph of an Indian river bank with people going about their daily lives. The teacher often only had the information in the teacher's notes for support.

Today, we still have the requirement that primary children study this range of localities. However, today's information technology can provide totally new resources and learning approaches to the study of other places. Instead of a whole class having to study one locality based on a paper pack, groups and individuals can follow

cont.

geographical enquiries into places that are of interest to them personally, so that they are motivated to make investigations. The world wide web gives primary children the opportunity to investigate a place from a wide range of perspectives. There may well be web material produced by people in their place of study; but it need not stop there. Google Earth will help them locate that place within a wider global setting. Weather sites will let them study the climate there and how it changes. Travel information will help them see that place through one particular lens. Religious websites will help them understand the beliefs, customs and values held by the people living there. Environmental websites may help to explain current environmental issues affecting that place. Each one looks at the place but from a different perspective. Hopefully, the information will be at least as up to date as that in a traditional pack. Instead of the teacher being the provider of information and worksheets to colour in, they are now able to guide and support children in their geographical enquiries. This can be backed up with other ICT resources such as CD-Roms as well as traditional atlases, books and globes.

So, what might be happening in those geography lessons, and does it map back to the pedagogical issues developed earlier? The role of the teacher will have changed dramatically. Instead of having to find materials to teach, they are much more involved in ensuring that pupils gain a balanced insight into other places. If they base this on the five key questions approach to geography (Storm 1989) they are very likely to provide effective learning experiences for pupils. Children are placed at the centre of their learning: for example, if a child has a current fascination with China, there is every chance they can pursue this through a web-based study of a place there. Pupils will need to use a range of ICT to record, edit and present their findings. Perhaps most of all, pupils will begin to see how the many varied parts of their enquiries are connected: the Chinese village does not have enough water today because so much is being diverted to feed the rapidly growing cities of China. From a geographical perspective, children will be less likely to see their place as an isolated bubble in the world, which has so often been the case when study packs are used.

Case study

Music

by Vanessa Richards, Primary Music Consultant in Lincolnshire and Leicestershire

QCA Unit 18 (DfES 2007) suggests that children create a Space Soundshape. The description below has been provided by a primary music specialist and explains what the pupils did.

The children were part way through a topic to create a soundscape of space. They began by watching footage of the first moon landing and discussed the sounds they could hear. In the focus lesson children listened to a piece of music called 'Atmospheres' by Gyory Ligeti. Ligeti's composing technique relies heavily on musical clusters. A cluster is a collection of closely pitched notes all played at the same time. Using chime bars the teacher demonstrated the effect of clusters. A group of five children were each given a chime bar with closely pitched notes and were asked to play their notes individually. The children were then asked to play their notes one after the other but keep their note playing until all the notes were playing together. When all the notes were playing together the children were then asked to stop playing until only one note was left playing.

Children were then allocated groups. Using electronic keyboards children were able to experiment with creating their own clusters. They were able to explore the different sounds available to them on the keyboard and change the voices to create different moods. Children found that some voices on the keyboard did not last long and they were able to choose sounds which they felt had a longer note decay in order to get the desired effect. Children were also able to see the possible limitations of using keyboards in this way as some keyboards were able to play fewer notes simultaneously than others. When the children had created their own clusters and chosen their voice, the clusters were recorded using the keyboard's own record function. All groups then recorded their experiments directly onto CD which was able to be used as evidence for assessment.

This example shows how ICT was used in three ways. The first was to research the internet to find moving images of the moon landing. The second was the use of keyboards to experiment and compose in a variety of critical ways. The third was the use of two digital recording methods to store the compositions and provide assessment evidence.

Case study
Design and technology / science

For many years, primary children have studied materials and structures. The current QCA (2000b) schemes of work includes Unit 6a, Shelters. It encourages teachers to choose interesting structures on which their pupils may base their investigations. One of these is bridges. Enquiries often go through a number of stages: design, construction, testing and analysis. The design stage might begin with some web-based research into how bridges are designed around the world: the BBC Education site is a good starting point, but there are many others.

As pupils find various types of bridge design, the teacher's role becomes one of encouraging pupils to think about why certain designs have been used and the clues they can get from photographs and other information. Pictures can be printed or stored in a folder for future reference. This leads onto the design stage when simple draw and paint packages can be used to develop design ideas. The key point here is that because they can change, adapt and improve their ideas on screen, children are much more likely to be willing to think creatively and divergently because it will not involve rubbing out, 'spoiling' the first attempt or producing a messy finished product. They will, of course, also be learning the relevant ICT skills associated with drawing and paint packages within a real context. As they are building their bridge structures, they can take their own digital photographs to record how they adapted and improved particular parts of their bridge; for example, they could record how they tried creating various shapes in paper and card for the road part of the structure. Such activities normally involve testing their completed bridges to destruction. If a video camera is set up near their bridges they can record the whole testing process. The video can be played back frame by frame and in slow motion: both will reveal different information that the children can then attempt to explain. The video could be projected onto an interactive whiteboard for use within whole-class discussions. If a digital video camera is used, the video can be downloaded onto class computers: children can then annotate and manipulate the images as they analyse what happened during the experiment.

The real benefit is that they are using ICT to gain a much greater understanding of what actually happened to their structure and offer explanations as to why. This can be a valuable part of the assessment process as well as helping the children to take their learning on to new situations. By organizing the curriculum in this way and placing the use of ICT at the core, the teacher shifts from the role of instructor to that of learning facilitator and the pupils take on the active roles of designer and engineer.

New technologies in education

The focus of this section is on how new technologies may be used to support the changes in curriculum and pedagogy discussed earlier. Regardless of what is currently happening in your school, it will hopefully encourage you to think critically about your use of ICT.

The world wide web

Many teachers make effective use of the web to support their planning and to extract teaching resources such as photographs, diagrams and text. Much of this then gets printed off and used in ways where the teacher retains their traditional role of presenter of information and giver of instructions. Many of the examples in this chapter have placed pupils in the role of researcher and the teacher in that of learning guide. Although the content of the web is not perfect, there is an enormous amount that can be used by primary school pupils to support and structure their learning. Teachers who spend less time researching information that they will then use in traditional roles and more time on establishing what is on the web for pupils to study, may be in a stronger and more confident position to rethink the place of ICT. The web is included in this section because, although it is not new technology, there may be much that is new for you to discover within it.

Rethinking old technology

Many schools are now dismantling their computer suites and sharing the PCs out across the classes. This has occurred because some schools failed to manage curriculum and timetables in such a way that the suites were actually a useful tool for learning. Teachers now need to consider how they can best use a number of class-based computers. Another model that can be seen is where perhaps two classes or a year group have permanent access to a small number of computers. Where ICT has been carefully integrated into curriculum planning, my experience on school visits is that this can be a very effective way of using ICT facilities within the learning environment.

Wireless nomadic networks

The use of wireless laptop and notebooks is becoming the norm in many primary schools. The timetabling issue remains as most schools cannot afford one machine for every one or two pupils. However, those times when your class has access to such technology need to be used to the full. I recently observed a student who planned an afternoon of historical research for a Year 6 class knowing they would have access to 15 wireless laptops. All the activities were carefully planned: pupils knew exactly why they were using the web, CD-Roms and non-ICT resources. She deliberately chose historical evidence that required the children to compare what they found through ICT and more traditional resources. Pupils were totally absorbed in enquiries they had created, and historical learning was seamlessly integrated with developing and applying their skills in ICT. Muirhead's (2005) research into the use of wireless laptops in primary schools provides further ideas for consideration.

Interactive whiteboards

We have only just begun to understand the power of using interactive whiteboards in the classroom. The key to integrating them into your teaching is to learn about them a little at a time and use them when you see opportunities that will make the most of what they can offer.

Hooper and Reiber (1995) suggest that teachers go through five stages in embedding ICT into their professional work. In essence their message is that learning new technology is like learning to ride a bike: as soon as you want to travel somewhere, you gradually build up the skills needed to operate the whole machine. Before long, you have evolved into a cycle-riding person who almost finds it hard to explain what they are doing because it is a natural process to them.

Children's technology

Finally, spend time talking to your pupils about the technology they use in their everyday lives. They will enjoy being the experts and keen to explain how things work and what they do. You may even find ways of building their technology into the curriculum. Camera phones may be a way into exploring the wider world, while iPods can bring you closer to your pupils through their interest in music and then on into the broader music curriculum. As teachers, we cannot turn away from ICT, but we can work alongside the digital generation as we all rethink the roles we will have in schools of the future.

References

Abbott, C. (2001) *ICT: Changing Education*. London: RoutledgeFalmer.

Agar, R. (2003) *Information and Communication Technologies in Primary Schools: Children or Computers in Control?* London: David Fulton.

DfES (2003a) *Every Child Matters*. London: DfES.

DfES (2003b) *Towards a Unified e-Learning Strategy*, Consultation Document. Nottingham: DfES.

Hooper, S. and Reiber, L. P. (1995) Teaching with technology, in A. Ornstein (ed.) *Teaching: Theory into Practice*. Needham Heights, MA: Allyn & Bacon.

Jonassen, D. H. (2000) *Computers as Mindtools for Schools: Engaging Critical Thinking*. Upper Saddle River, NJ: Merrill / Prentice Hall.

Kirkman, C. (2000) A model for the effective management of information and communications technology development in schools derived from six contrasting case studies, *Journal of Information Technology for Teacher Education*, 9(1): 37–52.

Loveless, A. (2002) ICT in the primary curriculum, in A. Loveless and B. Dore (eds) *ICT in the Primary School*. Maidenhead: Open University Press.

Meadows, J. and Leask, M. (2000) Why use ICT?, in M. Leask and J. Meadows (eds) *Teaching and Learning with ICT in the Primary School*. London: RoutledgeFalmer.

Muirhead, G. (2005) Why wireless – why laptop? The case for wireless laptops in primary schools, in S. Wheeler (ed.) *Transforming Primary ICT*. Exeter: Learning Matters.

QCA (2000a) *A Scheme of Work for Key Stages 1 and 2 – Music*. London: QCA.

QCA (2000b) *A Scheme of Work for Key Stages 1 and 2 – Science*. London: QCA.

Riding, R. J., Glass, A. and Douglas, G. ((1993) Individual differences in thinking: cognitive and and neurophysiological perspectives, *Educational Psychology*, 13 (3 / 4): 267–79.

Saettler, P. (1968) *A History of Instructional Technology*. New York: McGraw-Hill.

Somekh, B. (1997) Classroom investigations: exploring and evaluating how IT can support learning, in B. Somekh and N. Davis (eds) *Using Information Technology Effectively in Teaching and Learning*. London: Routledge, pp. 114–26.

Storm, M. (1989) The five basic questions for primary geography, *Primary Geographer*, 2 (Autumn): 4.

Torjussen, M. and Coppard, E. (2002) Potential into practice, in A. Loveless and B. Dore (eds) *ICT in the Primary School*. Maidenhead: Open University Press.

Vygotsky, L. S. (1978) *Mind in Society: The Development of Higher Psychological Processes*, eds M. Cole *et al*. Cambridge, MA: Harvard University Press.

Wegerif, R. and Dawes, L. (2004) *Thinking and Learning with ICT: Raising Achievement in Primary Classrooms*. London: RoutledgeFalmer.

Yelland, N. (2002) Asdf;lkj: challenges to early childhood curriculum and pedagogy for the information age, in A. Loveless and B. Dore (eds) *ICT in the Primary School*. Maidenhead: Open University Press.

Useful websites

BBC Education: www.bbc.co.uk/education

BECTA: www.becta.org.uk

Fiankoma Project: www.fiankoma.org

Talking Teaching: www.talkingteaching.com/

Teacher Resource Exchange: www.tre.ngfl.gov.uk

9

Supporting Children in Recording Work

Jane Johnston

Introduction

Why do children need to record their work? Throughout my educational career, I have recorded my work. As a child in school I drew pictures, wrote in my workbooks and wrote essays. As a student teacher I wrote reports, essays, made presentations. And as a teacher I recorded my plans for learners and their assessments. Why was it necessary to record at all? This chapter considers the purposes of recording and looks at different types of recording (writing; oral discussions, debate and argumentation; cartoons and annotated diagrams; concept maps; pictures, photos and video; audio; plays, assemblies and presentations), before finally looking at how recording can support and extend learning.

The purposes of recording

We record for a number of reasons:

- to help us to remember;
- to demonstrate our strengths and weaknesses;
- to enable others to see what we have achieved;
- to enable our work to be assessed and compared over short and long periods of time;
- to extend our lessons;
- to extend our learning and consolidate understanding.

Early in our primary education, we rarely use the records of our work to help us remember, and it is only when children get to the stages of revising for tests and examinations that recorded work is used in this way. More commonly, records of work are used for assessment and reporting purposes and, I suspect, as a result of observations of practice over many years, that recording is also used as a time-filler rather than as a teaching and learning tool. In the primary school, recording that is of great educational value should form part of the learning process, extending understanding and developing skills. It should also support assessment for learning, enabling practitioners to modify, extend and develop future learning experiences, by providing information, but without taking precedence over teaching and learning. When planning for learning, there should be clear coherence between the learning outcome or objectives and the way of recording. If there is no coherence, we should question why we are recording at all. If it is for assessment purposes, but does not extend learning, then it should be a small part of the total learning time, so that it does not detract from the main purposes of the lesson. Effective practice involves questioning, reflecting on and challenging assumptions about the purpose of recording and the methods we use to record children's work.

Different types of recording

As a preliminary to looking in some detail at the different types of recording, carry out the reflective task below.

Reflective task

Writing, discussion, debate, cartoon, annotated diagram, concept map, picture, photo display, video, audio, plays, presentation.

Level 1
Look at the list above and identify the different ways you have been asked to record work during your time as a learner. Put a number beside each one to indicate how often you have recorded in that form.
- Why do you think some forms are used more than others?
- What form of recording do you think was most effective for you? Why?

Level 2
Using the list above, identify how many times in the past year you have recorded children's work in different ways.
- Are some forms of recording used more than others? If so, why?
- Do you use different forms of recording for different purposes? If so, why?
- Looking at your planning for next term, should you, and can you, use other forms of recording more?

Level 3
Consider a child moving through your setting. Using the list above, identify when they might use different forms of recording: In what year? What context? For what purposes? How often? Why do you think some forms of recording may be more effective for some learners and in some contexts?

Writing up

Written work is the most common type of recording used by children in school. For many children, every lesson throughout the day will have an aspect of written recording. Such recording usually takes place at the end of the lesson in a very repetitive format of teacher input to the whole class, followed by some individual or group activity including or followed by individual writing and a whole class plenary. This is fine if the purposes of the written work are to aid communication – an important skill to develop in young children (DfEE 1999b; DfES 2007). Communication has been described as 'an outward extension of thought' (Harlen 1985: 39), enabling children to sort out muddled thinking and understanding (Harlen 2000), and as such can extend learning and support achievement of learning outcomes or objectives. If, however, the writing does not support the learning outcomes and demotivates the children, who like active learning but do not like having to 'write about it', then the lesson can be deemed to be less effective.

After the introduction of the National Literacy Strategy (DfEE 1998), teachers were encouraged to raise standards of literacy by incorporating writing in other subjects, and this led to concerns that literacy was dominating primary education and detracting from the learning in other subjects (see, for example, ASE 1999). Cross-curricular work, which achieves learning objectives in a number of subject areas, is regarded as creative (DfES 2003) and can be extremely effective, but it is important that one subject does not dominate and that children are motivated to write and see the relevance to the task and purpose for their learning.

Case study

Story sticks

by Karen Harding, SENCO and class teacher, St David's Primary School, Moreton-in-Marsh, Gloucestershire

I was attempting to stimulate a class of extremely dynamic Year 1 children to write a recount piece of prose for their monthly writing assessment. It was the summer term so the obvious activity to my colleague and I was to take the children on a walk, rambling through sheep fields, over streams and a local farmer's yard. How could I keep the children motivated to walk with their observational eyes open and, even more challenging, get them to remember what they had seen on their travels the following day.

Searching the internet for inspiration I decided to try doing what I have called story sticks with the class. This required a substantial stick about the length of a ruler and lots of pieces of wool. The children were to have their sticks throughout the walk and wrap pieces of different coloured wool around the stick to represent the colours they saw and the objects they passed. All the children took part in the task with enthusiasm. The sticks started bare; then, as we walked along the pavement, we all stopped to wrap a piece of grey wool around the bottom of the stick. We moved on to a field and so we wrapped green wool around the stick. And so the activity continued

cont.

and the wool grew up the stick. As the children gained in confidence the task became less teacher-directed – 'What colour is the grass?', 'What colour wool shall we use?' and more child-led – 'I can see some yellow flowers, can I have some yellow wool?'. I even stood back and watched one child take this to the next level and incorporate into the wool wrapped around his stick a small piece of sheep's wool, a feather and a flower he had come across on his walk. The outcome was a class full of 'story sticks', sticks that told the story of their afternoon walk.

What struck me was the children's interest in what they were seeing and the sense of pride they all had. The conversation on the walk back to school was about what each child had put round their stick. They were asking each other questions and saying things like, 'Did you see the sheep?' and 'We saw a lot of grass today.' It was an activity that every child could reach, from the child who struggles to produce any piece of work to the articulate and self-motivated child collecting and weaving items into the wool on the stick.

It was therefore not surprising that the following day the children were able to sit down and recall their walk in detail, and went on to want to write about their walk and all the things they had seen.

Some children can use a learning journal to informally record their ideas, thoughts, plans and things they need to remember. These journals can be used in future work: using their ideas to make something, undertake a piece of formal writing, conduct an investigation, or revise for a test. I have used learning journals in design and technology and in science, where children make annotated diagrams and use them to help in the final design or investigation. I once asked a class of Year 4 children to work in small groups to make a rubber-band vehicle. These vehicles use a cylindrical object (such as a bobbin, drinks can, washing up liquid bottle or cylindrical container). The children had 30 minutes one afternoon to design their vehicle and decide what resources they needed to make it. Most children chose to draw an annotated diagram in their learning journal, whereas some wrote a list of items needed to make the vehicle. The lists of resources were helpful as the children could use them to collect resources from around school and to decide what they needed to bring from home to achieve their design. The next day the children used their designs to make their vehicles.

I have also used learning journals to enable children to identify their inner thoughts, ask questions they do not want to ask in front of their peers and to identify their thinking. These can be used in a formative way by identifying children's ideas and to help support future learning. They can also support emotional development by providing an informal outlet for children's concerns and motivations. In addition these journals can provide an element of metacognition, helping children to identify what and how they think, how they solve problems, what helps them learn, and so on.

Sometimes, ideas, thoughts and emotions can be expressed and recorded through creative writing. Conceptual understanding can also be recorded through creative

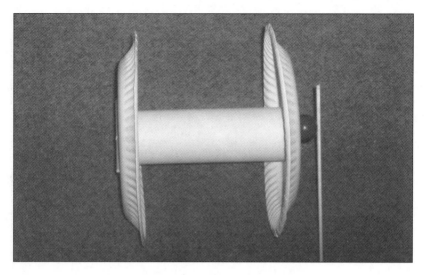

Picture 9.1 A rubber-band-powered vehicle

writing, so that children can use creative prose as a vehicle to apply understanding from another context. For example, with Year 6 children engaged in sex education, I have used the fictional task of writing a letter from a robot alien who is visiting Earth to investigate how human beings reproduce. The children are told that the robots on the alien planet are made in factories and are therefore very interested in human reproduction. The aliens also like technical terms, and so these must be used in the letter. The resulting letter helps the children to articulate their understanding of a very difficult area in a non-threatening way. This letter can take the form of a formal report to the alien planet.

Other opportunities for report writing occur in history, geography, religious education and science. In history, children can write a report in character, writing from a historical perspective, or compare the lives of children historically with their own. In geography, children can compare localities in a formal report or a database. Comparative religion can lead to formal report writing in religious education; and in science, exploration and investigation may be reported using formal headings such as:

- Question (what we were trying to find out)
- Resources (what we needed)
- Method (what we did)
- Results (what we found out)
- Conclusion (what we learnt).

Such formal reports require children to examine their use of words and be precise in what they say, to justify their statements using evidence to support them, and also to be tentative. For example, if a child decides that one type of material is the best insulator, they need to be precise as to what they mean by 'best' (keeping something warm or cold or both or something else?). They also need to justify this statement using the evidence from their investigations, but they also need to be aware that there may be other factors affecting the results of their investigation.

Even before the report stage, children can record their plans for an investigation in science using a planning board or ladder (see Figure 9.1). The planning ladder helps the children to plan a successful investigation, helps them to articulate their ideas and thus consolidate their learning, and helps achieve learning objectives / outcomes.

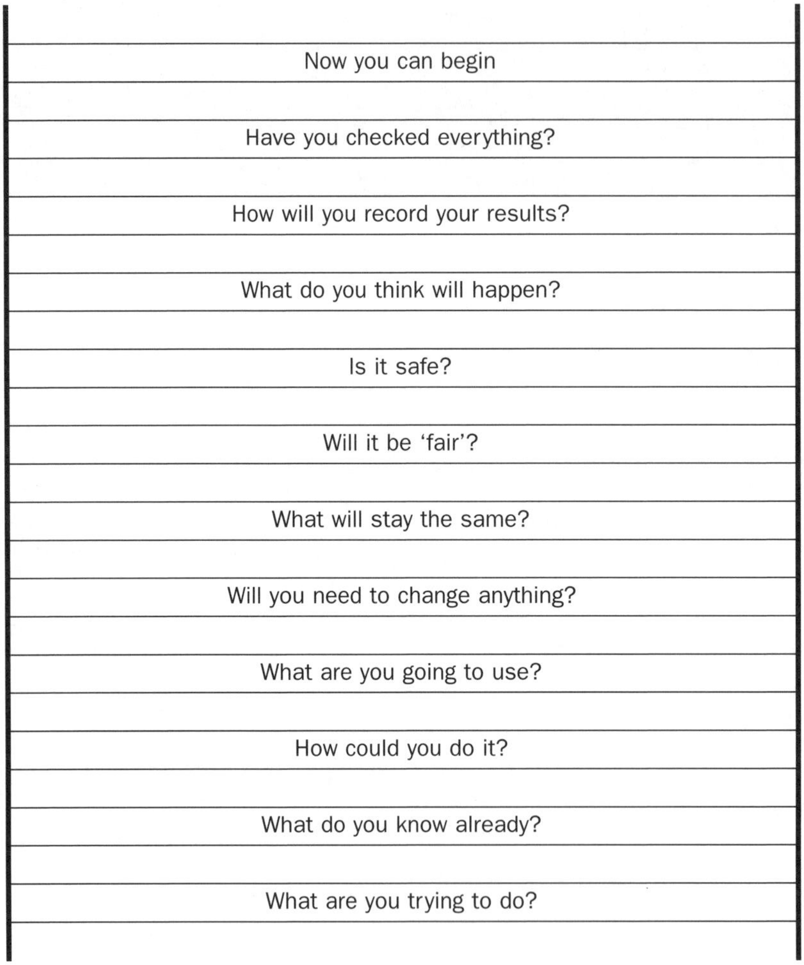

| Now you can begin |
| Have you checked everything? |
| How will you record your results? |
| What do you think will happen? |
| Is it safe? |
| Will it be 'fair'? |
| What will stay the same? |
| Will you need to change anything? |
| What are you going to use? |
| How could you do it? |
| What do you know already? |
| What are you trying to do? |

Figure 9.1   A planning ladder in science

As children's skill in writing progresses so we can expect greater detail, precision and understanding to be evident in their written recording. Written records can thus be used to help make assessments of children, but care is needed to ensure that difficulties in writing do not affect assessments of cognition (see Chapter 11, Assessment for Learning).

Discussions, debate and argumentation

Not all work undertaken by children needs to be recorded in a written format. Sometimes the best way of developing, consolidating and assessing understandings and skills can be oral. Oral communication is an important part of development (DfES 1999b; QCA 2007) and helps children to understand how they think (metacognition). Pressurized classrooms, where teachers are looking at the clock and worried about coverage, can mean that there are few opportunities for real discussion. The formats of Literacy and Numeracy strategies (DfEE 1998, 1999a) provide opportunity for children to respond to questions and can challenge their understandings. However, there are few opportunities for them to engage in deep discussion and sharing of ideas. Oral communication gives children access to the ideas of others and can help them to see alternative ways of thinking, as well as understand their own thinking. Discussion enables children to share ideas, evidence for these ideas and challenge both their own beliefs and the beliefs of others. In active classrooms, this communication involves general talking while children are working. Generally this is constructive talk, enabling children to express and clarify their ideas and, in the process, reach a deeper understanding. Children may sometimes be 'off task', but this is natural and occurs with groups of adults working together as well as among children. The disadvantages of this classroom discussion are greatly outweighed by the benefits in terms of learning.

More formal means of oral communication occur in plenary sessions, which can, if structured effectively, move children's learning forward through enabling children to share ideas, so that each child can communicate and the teacher does not dominate. Unfortunately, the whole-class plenary tends to be adult dominated, involve some of the children in answering questions and are far too long for meaningful learning. Moreover, they are increasingly a compulsory part of each and every lesson but serve little purpose. They can be used in a developmental rather than informative way, with children discussing ideas or findings from explorations and setting challenges for further work (Johnston 2005).

Whole-class, group debates or discussions which involve an element of argument are proven to be successful in developing skills and understandings (Osborne *et al.* 2001, 2004). Cognitive acceleration research in science, mathematics, technology and the arts involves debate, discussion and argument in order to develop cognitive skills (King's College London 2006). With primary children, science discussions have been initiated by a concept cartoon (Naylor and Keogh 2000; Naylor and Naylor 2000) which provides the focus and different ideas that children will discuss (see Figure 9.2).

In history and English, the discussion can take the form of 'hot seating' (see Ginnis 2001; DfES 2006), where the teacher, another adult or a child can be in role (often identified by a costume or a prop) as an historical figure or character from a book or play and can be questioned by the children as to feelings, motivations, and so on. In this way the children can better understand the character and the context.

I have used the story of *Jim and the Beanstalk* (Briggs 1970) with Foundation Stage and Key Stage 1 children (Johnston and Herridge 2004; see also Figure 2.4 and Picture 2.1 in Chapter 2) making use of a story sack and the props inside (the book, Giant and Jim puppets, a wig, some false teeth, a tape measure, a climbing Jim (see Johnston 2005), a collection of glasses, some gold coins, writing paper and envelopes).

Figure 9.2 A concept cartoon (Naylor and Keogh 2000)

After telling the story and using the props in the story sack, the children can question Jack, his mother and the giant about how they felt at different times during the story and why they decided to take certain actions. I have also seen Key Stage 2 children question an adult in role about the motivations and feelings of famous historical figures, such as Van Gogh, Mozart and Sir Walter Raleigh. Whatever the learning objective underpinning hot seating or any discussion, opportunities need to be provided where children can discuss their ideas. Small-group discussion has the advantage that quiet children are not intimidated by the more orally dominant, whereas large groups are advantaged by having a potentially greater level of challenge. The use of a 'talking buddy' or the use of puppets can be effective in allowing quieter children to express their ideas through a more orally confident peer or the puppet (Keogh *et al.* 2006). What needs to be avoided are discussions where all children take turns in expressing their ideas, as this can be a time-consuming and demotivating ritual for children. Discussions should be a maximum of 10 minutes for young children and 30 minutes for the eldest Key Stage 2 children and paced so that children are engaged and motivated to learn.

Oral recording can be the end process in a learning sequence and not a prerequisite to written recording. Children may describe how they worked out a mathematical problem, or explain how they would describe the process of dissolving to an alien or discuss a newspaper article, historical document or citizenship issues. It is more effective if questions asked are open-ended to initiate the discussion or debate (see Chapter 6), as this will allow greater depth of discussion and the expression of the children's real ideas, rather than the ideas they think they should be expressing. The learning atmosphere should also be one that is conducive to children's oral expression; their responses should be accepted, they should feel able to discuss and they should be given time to respond and think. This does not mean that the children should not be challenged or that the teacher should not play devil's advocate, to make the children think more deeply about what they are saying and what they mean.

Cartoons and annotated diagrams

Children can effectively record a process or sequence of events, such as in a geographical, mathematical or scientific investigation or a religious, historical or literary story, through a cartoon. For some children, cartoons can be more effective than a piece of written work as they are able to accurately record the sequence in the process and do not disadvantage the children who find written work difficult.

Practical and reflective task

Level 1

Choose a story (fictional, historical or religious) and identify up to ten cartoon frames that would tell the story. Draw these on paper or on PowerPoint slides.

- How could your cartoon be used to develop understanding of the story?
- How could you use the cartoon to illustrate how the children can record using cartoons?
- How could cartoons be used by children to record a story?

cont.

Level 2

Choose a story (fictional, historical or religious) from your future planning, that can be recorded in a cartoon format. Make sure that the recording is integral to the learning objectives.

- How could you best introduce the cartoon task to the children in your class?

Try out your idea and evaluate the use of a cartoon for recording.

- Did the cartoon help to achieve the learning objectives?
- What were the advantages and disadvantages of using a cartoon recording format?
- How could you adapt the use of the cartoon for better effect?

Level 3

Analyse the recording methods used in your year group / key stage / setting (see the reflective task on page 136) and identify methods of recording work that could be replaced by the use of cartoons.

- Identify how the cartoon can support the learning objectives;
- How do you think children will respond to the task?

Try out the ideas for using cartoons and evaluate their effect.

- Did the cartoon help to achieve the learning objectives for some children? If so which ones?
- What were the advantages and disadvantages of using a cartoon recording format?
- How could you use cartoons in future teaching?

When children are planning, designing or making models they can record their ideas and finished model in an annotated diagram (see page 139). Annotated diagrams can also be used to record and communicate children's ideas. They could draw a picture of a house from a historical period and label the period features (windows, doors, shapes, materials used in construction). They could draw a picture of a geographical feature (urban or rural location, street, valley) and annotate to show main geographical features. They could draw a diagram of a model they have made and annotate to show how it works. They could annotate a diagram of a scientific investigation, recording their results and conclusions. In Figure 9.3 a 10-year-old child has produced an annotated diagram to explain what they think will happen in a balloon balance investigation. Two balloons are stuck onto the ends of a stick and the children find the point of balance and mark it with a felt-tip pen. They were asked what they thought would happen when they blew up one of the balloons and put it back on the point of balance. They then produced an annotated diagram of their predictions. In Figure 9.3 the child predicts that the inflated balloon will rise, rather than fall (as air has mass) and so the annotated diagram can be used to aid assessment of the child's thinking. After the child has completed the activity, they can continue to annotate their diagram and this can help to ascertain the development of their understanding.

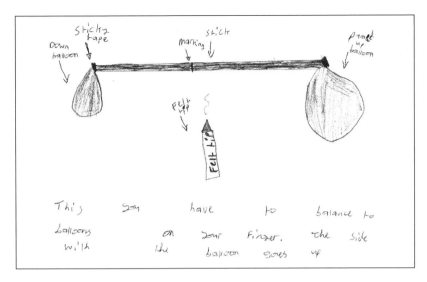

Figure 9.3 A Year 5 child's annotated diagram

Concept maps

Concept maps can be another way for children to record their conceptual ideas (Novak and Gowan 1984). In a concept map, a child identifies their thinking by writing down the perceived conceptual links between ideas in a 'brainstorm type' map, which can be used to set out ideas for planning.

For young children, concept maps can be undertaken as a group and / or pictorially. A group of Key Stage 1 children could be given a set of pictures or artefacts linked to a concept and asked to sort them onto a large piece of paper, explaining how they link together. An adult could annotate the paper, with words and phrases which explain the links between the pictures or artefacts. Older children could work in a group and be given a set of words on a theme or concept and asked to agree how they group together. Each child can add their ideas using a different coloured felt-tip pen, so individual ideas can be ascertained. The advantages of group concept maps is that they not only record ideas but also involve discussion and debate and support further conceptual development.

Older children can work individually, either using a given set of words or brainstorming their own words. The advantage of using a prepared set of words is that the words can stimulate ideas, and if the child cannot use a word, then the next learning step for them is clearly signalled. The advantage of brainstorming words for themselves, is that the words used can indicate conceptual understanding and areas for development. Some teachers in top Key Stage 2 classes have used concept maps to ascertain the children's individual learning needs (see Chapter 11, Assessment for Learning) or to help the children to ascertain their own learning needs. At the end of a sequence of work, these maps can be altered or a new map prepared and then the children and / or the teacher can assess the learning that has taken place.

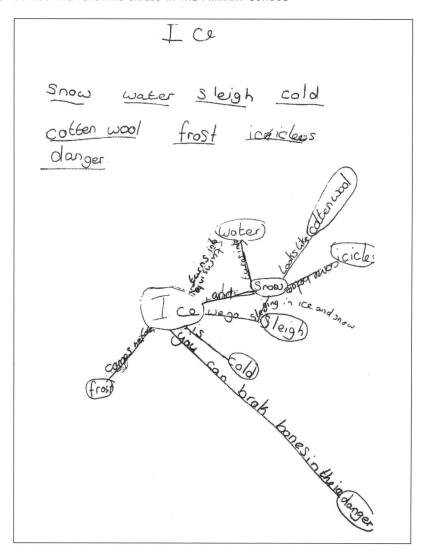

Figure 9.4 A concept map

Practical and reflective task

Level 1

Choose a concept and brainstorm words connected to it. Now try to link the words into a concept map, identifying along the linking lines, the reasons for the connections.

- Analyse your concept map and highlight areas that you found difficult to link or links you found difficult to explain;
- Do you think the concept map is an accurate record of your conceptual understanding?
- How could you introduce concept mapping to a class of children?

Level 2

Choose a concept you are developing in your next term's work. Plan how you could introduce concept mapping with your class. Try this out and analyse the children's maps.

- How do the maps record the children's thinking and conceptual understanding?
- How can you use the maps to develop the children's conceptual understanding?
- What do children feel about recording their ideas in this way?

Level 3

Discuss with colleagues how you can use concept maps within your school / setting to record children's conceptual understanding. Use concept mapping in different classes and different areas of learning / subjects.

- Are there certain areas of learning / subjects that lend themselves to concept mapping?
- Is concept mapping as effective with all ages and abilities?
- How could you improve your use of concept mapping as a recording tool?

Pictures, photos and video

Young children often record work by drawing a picture, although, like written work with older children, it may be uncertain how this extends the learning objectives and adds to the children's learning. Sometimes this distorts their image of the subject (Johnston 2005) and they make links between the activity and art; for example, science involves drawing because they always draw after a science activity. Pictures are not always good ways to record conceptual understandings, as successful pictures are dependent on physical and creative skills and do not always show understandings. However, they can help children to articulate ideas, promote discussions and be used to display and celebrate achievements. Children's pictures can be displayed formally together with written records and models. Children are justifiably proud when their work is displayed.

As well as recording understandings and action, pictures can also be a good way for children to record their emotions, and analysis of pictures can help adults to understand and support children through emotional trauma (Malchiodi 1998; Cooper 1999). However, care is needed to ensure that unqualified practitioners do not assign meanings to pictures and make judgements based on assumption rather than expertise. I knew of one 8-year-old child who, when asked to draw a picture of something he hated, drew his sister. When asked why, he explained that he knew that this picture would give him extra attention from the teacher. The teacher used the picture as evidence that his home life was unhappy, an incorrect analysis which took some time to unravel and caused difficulties in the partnership between the parents and the school.

Photographs provide a good opportunity to record an individual or group action, practical activity or visual outcome. They are a recognized assessment tool for young children (QCA 2003), providing a snapshot of an instance in action as evidence for assessment. Photographs can also be used on displays to record and communicate children's work to a wider audience and to stimulate further development as a discussion point within the whole class. This is especially the case when photographs are used as part of an interactive display, which encourages child interaction with objects, records of work, and questions.

Reflective task

A class of Key Stage 1 children were undertaking a mathematical and scientific classification task, sorting toys according to criteria chosen by the children. They decided that the toys could be put into five groups; spinning, magnetic, wind-up, jumping and ones with a spring. From this they were encouraged to develop a simple branch or hierarchical database, that is, one that distinguishes between objects in answer to certain questions (the answers to which are either yes or no). The first question the children decided to ask was 'Does it spin?', and this divided the toys into those that spun and those that did not. The next question for the group of toys that did spin was 'Is it magnetic?', which separated out one toy from all the spinners: a magnetic gyroscope. Questions for the group of toys that did not spin were:

1   Does it wind up?
2   Does it jump?
3   Does it have a spring?

The teacher wrote these questions down and the resulting database was photographed (see Picture 9.2).

Level 1
How else could you record a group database? Consider the advantages and disadvantages for each way you decide.

cont.

Picture 9.2 A Key Stage 1 group record of a classification task (annotations by teacher)

Level 2

How could you extend this activity so that the learning objectives / outcomes can be further developed? How could you record the results of any extension activities?

Level 3

How could you extend this activity to develop other learning objectives / outcomes in mathematics, science and other areas of learning? How could you record these other activities?

Some activities lend themselves to video recording, and these recordings can also be used to provide evidence for assessment as well as to record children's work for communication to a wider audience or to extend learning. For example, a piece of drama can be recorded and at a later date the children could analyse the performance or suggest modifications to the performance. Hot seating scenarios (see page 141 and Ginnis 2001; DfES 2006) can also be recorded and used later so the children can analyse the questions posed and the responses and consider new aspects of the context or person being studied and thus deepen their understandings.

Children can make their own videos of work to record what they have done and what they have learnt. I have asked children to make their own television news or current affairs programme, where they can report on findings from a geographical, technological or scientific investigation or summarize book or internet research. These can be motivating ways for children to record and communicate their learning and provide opportunities for the development of social skills and enable the less literate children to succeed.

Videos and photographs do need to comply with the school's ethical and child protection policy. Some schools will not allow any photographs to be taken of children; others wish the school or children to remain anonymous, and yet others require the faces of the children to be digitally disguised. In addition, there are some children who are not able (for child protection purposes) to be photographed, and this may make them feel singled out and excluded. It is therefore important to check what the school's policy is before planning any photography or video recording.

Audio

An alternative to videotaping is audio recording. Children can make a radio programme to record findings in a similar way to the current affairs television programmes described above. They can also record music they have composed, poems they have written and stories they have created. Copies of these are always gratefully received by parents and grandparents. My own son would sometimes produce audiotapes for his grandparents, who lived long distances away, with music and readings on, and these were treasured possessions which all parties, child and adults, enjoyed. Like the group video programmes, the audiotapes are collaborative exploits, which enable children to work together and to develop social skills such as cooperation and independence, and important social and behavioural attitudes such as tolerance for others' ideas and suggestions, collective responsibility and persever-ance (Johnston 2005).

Plays, assemblies and presentations

Schools have a long history of performances, from Nativity plays or pantomimes at Christmas to summer concerts, recitals and class assemblies for the parents. The frequency of these was reduced in some schools during the 1990s when the curriculum was so burdensome that the schools felt it was unachievable unless something else was omitted. However, the need to achieve performance as an outcome (DfES 1999b) in drama, dance and music has helped to reinstate it for some children although class performance and assemblies have often replaced whole-school performance and plays.

There are many types of work that lend themselves to performances of some kind. The obvious ones are drama, music, dance and story, but these can be combined in a meaningful way with other subjects, such as science, mathematics and history. Performances which tell the life of historical figures, such as Mozart, Van Gogh, Captain Cook or Galileo, will combine performance with history and link to music, art, geography and science. I have asked children to research difficult and abstract scientific concepts and present their findings in a performance of a poem, song or drama. For example, ideas researched about the movement of the planets can be presented as a drama; understandings of the three characteristics of sound (loudness, pitch and timbre) can be presented through a piece of performed music; and knowledge of fossils can be encompassed in a poem and read out. Stories (mythical, religious, historical or fictional) can be retold through finger, shadow or string puppets in a performance, and this will help children to articulate their ideas and understandings.

Other work can be recorded and communicated through presentations and displays. These can be visual, such as ideas presented on a poster in any chosen form; pictorial, written, graphical, diagrammatic, or a combination. Children can also produce adverts to:

- show understanding of health issues in personal, social and health education (PSHE);
- advertise a product or design in technology;
- produce a piece of persuasive writing in literacy;
- advertise a location in geography.

Oral presentations can enable children to articulate understandings in a variety of areas. They can tell small or large groups of their peers what they have discovered in a piece of factual research using secondary sources, such as books, journals and the internet. They can tell others the results of their investigations, presenting findings and posing new questions for their peers to answer or consider. Small-group presentations can take the form of jigsawing, where a class of 30 children is divided into 5 groups of 6 children and each group researches a different aspect of the same area, for example, Roman life (roads, houses, baths, food, army) or the geography of a street (houses, people, vehicles, industry, flora and fauna). Then one child from each group joins together (6 groups of 5 children) and presents their findings to the others, so that each child gains a holistic knowledge of the subject being studied.

ICT can be used to make PowerPoint presentations or present findings using an interactive whiteboard. These can incorporate tables, graphs, scanned or digital pictures and hyperlinks to webpages. In this way, the recording can support learning outcomes in ICT as well as the area being researched and presented.

Making recording support and extend learning

Whatever way is chosen to record and communicate learning, it is important that the learning objectives / outcomes are not overshadowed by the recording and that the time spent recording is not excessive, detracting from the planned learning. Effective recording is an integral part of the lesson and supports and extends the learning. Meaningless recording has little relevance to the learning outcomes and has no real learning purpose (see the beginning of this chapter). Effective recording does not always involve children in the same task and it engages the child in a meaningful way. It is therefore important that children do not always use the same method of recording, as this would be demotivating.

Reflective task

The importance of varying recording methods

Level 1

Look through a scheme of work in one subject. This could be a QCA scheme of work (QCA 2000), another published scheme of work or a downloaded scheme from the internet (for example, from the DfES website, www.dfes.gov.uk).

• In how many different ways is work recorded in the scheme?
• Does one method of recording dominate?
• Does the recording extend learning?
• How could you change the methods of recording to make them more effective?

Level 2

Look through your medium-term planning for the next term and analyse how effective your chosen methods of recording are.

• In how many different ways is work recorded in your planning?
• Does one method of recording dominate?
• Does the recording extend learning?
• How could you change the methods of recording to make them more effective?

Level 3

Look through the long-term planning for your year group / key stage / setting / school and analyse how effective your chosen methods of recording are.

• In how many different ways is work recorded in your planning?
• Does one method of recording dominate?
• Does the recording extend learning?
• How could you change the methods of recording to make them more effective?

References

ASE (Association for Science Education) (1999) *ASE Survey on the Effect of the National Literacy Strategy on the Teaching of Science*. Hatfield: ASE.

Briggs, R. (1970) *Jim and the Beanstalk*. London: Penguin (Picture Puffin).

Cooper, P. (ed.) (1999) *Understanding and Supporting Children with Emotional and Behavioural Difficulties*. London: Jessica Kingsley.

DfEE (1998) *The National Literacy Strategy*. London: DfEE.

DfEE (1999a) *The National Numeracy Strategy*. London: DfEE.

DfEE (1999b) *The National Curriculum: Handbook for Teachers in England*. London: DfEE / QCA.

DfES (2003) *Excellence and Enjoyment. A Strategy for Primary Schools*. London: DfES.

DfES (2006) *Key Stage 2 Framework for Literacy*. Available at www.standards.dfes .gov.uk/primary/publications/languages/framework/oracy/

DfES (2007) Statutory Framework for the Early Years Foundation Stage; Setting the Standards for Learning, Development and Care for children from birth to five. *Every Child Matters, Change for Children*. London: DfES.

Ginnis, P. (2001) *Hot Seating*. Available at www.english-teaching.co.uk

Harlen, W. (1985) *Teaching and Learning Primary Science*. London: Paul Chapman.

Harlen, W. (2000) *The Teaching of Science in Primary Schools*, 3rd edn. London: David Fulton.

Johnston, J. (2005) *Early Explorations in Science*, 2nd edn. Buckingham: Open University Press.

Johnston, J. and Herridge, D. (2004) *Heinemann Explore Science: Reception*. Oxford: Heinemann Educational.

Keogh, B., Naylor, S., Downing, B., Maloney, J. and Simon, S. (2006) Puppets bringing stories to life in science, *Primary Science Review*, 92: 26–8.

King's College London (2006) *Cognitive Acceleration Programmes*. Available at http://www.kcl.ac.uk/education/case.html

Malchiodi, C. (1998) *Understanding Children's Drawings*. London: Jessica Kingsley.

Naylor, S. and Keogh, B. (2000) *Concept Cartoons in Science Education*. Sandbach, Cheshire: Millgate House.

Naylor, B. and Naylor, S. (2000) *Snowman's Coat and Other Science Questions*. Sandbach, Cheshire: Millgate House.

Novak, J. and Gowan, D. B. (1984) *Learning How to Learn*. Cambridge: Cambridge University Press.

Osborne, J., Erduran, S., Simon, S. and Monk, M. (2001). Enhancing the quality of argument in school science, *School Science Review*, 82(301): 63–70.

Osborne, J., Erduran, S. and Simon, S. (2004) *Ideas, Evidence and Argument in Science*, in-service training pack, resource pack and video. London: Nuffield Foundation.

QCA (2007)

QCA (2003) *Foundation Stage Profile*. London: QCA.

10

Developing Investigative Work / Enquiry

John Halocha

Introduction

The purpose of this chapter is to help you to develop your understanding of the nature of enquiry in primary education in the twenty-first century and to reflect on how you believe it might be an active part of your own professional practice. The first section places enquiry within the current national picture for primary education. The second examines some current perspectives and theories on the nature of enquiry in teaching and learning. It considers why enquiry may be an important part of the educational process and what it helps pupils to develop. This is followed by an evaluation of the role of enquiry in out-of-classroom activities and how enquiry may be used within geography, science and primary mathematics. Finally, you will be able to consider how these perspectives may be integrated within your everyday working environment.

Enquiry today

Various notions of enquiry have been in and out of fashion in English primary education for almost a century. The Hadow Report of 1931 (Hadow 1931) encouraged teachers to allow pupils to explore various aspects of the world using their own curiosity. This was less favoured in the post-war years as political pressures for the education system to support economic growth came to dominate. The 1967 Plowden Report (DES 1967) took up the ideas mooted in the Hadow Report and strongly recommended that teachers adopt more innovative ways of working in primary schools. It suggested that topic work enabled pupils to develop more independent enquiry skills and encouraged teachers to plan the curriculum in a more cross-curricular way. Where this was carefully planned and teachers were confident in what pupils were meant to be learning in this more self-directed way, many exciting initiatives were developed and pupils could begin to understand the world in a more holistic way. However, much of the topic and project work carried out in the late 1960s and 1970s was vague and undirected. In some cases, pupils experienced an unbalanced curriculum and could spend many hours doing very little. This was picked up by HM Inspectorate in the late 1970s and early 1980s. There were attempts to offer primary teachers structured guidance on how subjects might be planned and taught: the Bullock Report (DES 1975) on the teaching of English was one example of this policy. However, by the mid-1980s, politicians began to take a much firmer control of education policy. They were unhappy about the experiences of pupils and the effect this was having on 'standards'. From 1987 to about 2000 the national curriculum (DfEE 1999b), the Literacy (DfEE 1998) and Numeracy (DfEE 1999a) strategies and various other initiatives prescribed both what and how primary school children should be taught. Enquiry was mentioned in documents, but in practice Ofsted and national testing ensured that many schools spent the majority of time in direct teaching, with little opportunity for pupils to plan and direct their own learning.

At the time of writing (2006), the picture is a little different. Strategies such as *Excellence and Enjoyment* (DfES 2003) and Ofsted's report *Expecting the Unexpected: Developing Creativity in Primary and Secondary Schools* (2003) and many others are suggesting that teachers should plan more imaginative learning experiences and interpret the curriculum in more innovative ways. There are a number of issues preventing this from taking place on a large scale. The first is that teachers and school leaders are unsure how the revised Ofsted inspection regime will operate: is there a genuine belief at Ofsted that a more child-centred curriculum is the way forward and that schools will be encouraged to take this route? Another is that many primary teachers in their 20s and 30s have never experienced a school environment that is not dominated by the national curriculum and the pedagogical methods it promoted.

However, the world is changing. Politicians are beginning to realize that much of the disillusionment with education felt by both pupils and society at large exists because of an increasingly irrelevant and outdated curriculum. The current initiatives at Key Stage 3 demonstrate both their concern and approach to change. This is further reinforced by teaching methods and learning environments that do not reflect society's expectations. Finally, the advances in ICT provide new ways in which people may learn and interact at an ever increasing global scale. Does the model of education as it currently stands really motivate pupils into a 'lifelong learning' culture? Do teachers need to reconsider their role? Should pupils be placed at the centre of the learning debate? How might this be developed in practice? The rest of this chapter considers how the concept of enquiry may be a part of new approaches to learning and teaching. Adey and Shayer (2002: 16) consider that, now,

> We are talking here about re-focussing the main aim of the whole enterprise of education from being primarily concerned with content – knowledge, understanding, skills and attitudes –towards a primary concern for intellectual development per se.

What is enquiry?

In her thought-provoking book *Children's Inquiry*, Judith Wells Lindfors (1999) argues that language is central to the learning process and that pupils and teachers need to adopt new social roles in this process.

> No enquiry was ever born in a vacuum. These acts arise in what we do know, including the fact that our knowledge is limited and something lies beyond it. Our inquiry act is the articulation of our sense of what may lie beyond what we presently know.
>
> (Lindfors 1999: 93)

Lindfors' view of learning is that we do not start with a prescribed view of curriculum content and process as we do now. Children come to school already knowing a great deal. This view is included in the vast majority of teacher education courses through the analysis of how a 'constructive' approach may be effective in helping pupils learn. The social theories of Vygotsky (1978) are also well rehearsed in suggesting that pupils learn best working together in the learning process. However, in practice, teachers find that they work in a school environment where they are expected to deliver certain content and often using prescribed methods such as the literacy hour strategy (DfEE 1998). The theory is fine but it gets left at the door of the classroom. The position that English teachers currently find themselves in is one of having to reconsider their philosophy of how pupils learn best and then how to turn this into practice within the working context. Lindfors' (1999) model of learning is one where pupils arrive in school having a clear idea of what they know and wanting to build upon that. She also suggests that they are perhaps aware of the transitional nature of knowledge and understanding. In her book she provides many transcripts of children talking with adults and attempts to analyse the language to uncover how dialogue can gradually help children develop their understanding of the world. The talk may be with adults or peers.

Lindfors (1999) also suggests that enquiry may not always be based on questions. The currently accepted wisdom in many primary school subjects often proposes that enquiries begin with a question or series of questions. Storm (1989), for example, set the agenda for much geographical investigation by offering a series of questions to help pupils develop an understanding of the world. We do need questions, but we may also need to consider the type of dialogue in which we engage with pupils to help develop their enquiries into the world.

Reflective task

It may be worth reflecting on the way in which you use language and questions to help pupils develop their understanding and enquiries. As teachers, we quickly get into habits and ways of teaching that we take for granted the language and questions we use.

Level 1

Choose a lesson you have already taught. Reflect on your planning and consider how you could have developed your teaching to establish more of a dialogue and discussion with the children. Could you also include the notion that you too are trying to find out something together.

Level 2

In the coming days, choose a lesson where you would expect to ask pupils a fair number of questions. In your planning, consider how you might establish more of a dialogue and discussion with them. Could you also include the notion that you too are trying to find out something and perhaps begin to puzzle it out together. This might be in a science or maths session, but it could work for any subject. For example, if you were to set an enquiry within a music lesson, put yourself in the same position as the pupils and demonstrate that you are also trying to move forward your musical understanding. Ask the children to help you. This role reversal can be an effective means of helping pupils to identify and clarify their own learning. If you have the courage, try recording these sessions so that you may reflect on what took place.

> Because we inquire of others in order to further our understanding, inquiry is as much a social act as it is an intellectual one.
>
> (Lindfors 1999: 2)

Level 3

Reflect on the medium- or long-term planning for your setting or a year group / key stage within your setting. How could your scheme of work be developed to include more dialogue and discussion with the children and some element of problem solving or enquiry?

Another way of thinking about the nature of enquiry is to reconsider how we perceive the children when they come to school. To what extent do you think your school really starts with the knowledge the children already have? Or, does it give the impression that children come with ignorance about something that needs replacing with knowledge? Also, with your questioning may children gain an impression that teacher's questions are there to demonstrate their lack of knowledge or a sense of 'wrongness'? Lindfors (1999: 53) takes this a stage further by suggesting that, as teachers, we use many strategies that pretend that children are engaging in an enquiry. She cites the example of showing a picture of Eskimos and asking pupils to devise questions they would like answers for. She suggests that, 'the board would fill up with what I now recognise to be an extraordinary list of non-inquiries' (p. 52). Her key point here is that, to be a genuine enquiry in the purest sense of meaning, the desire to move knowledge and understanding forward has to start with the child's own curiosity. This is certainly an extreme position and probably very hard to instigate within the current educational climate. But it does make us sit up as educators who play with the word 'enquiry' to ask just how far we are committed to the concept. What may be even more interesting is to consider the long-term effect on pupils' desire to learn and extend the boundaries of their understanding. If they are regularly placed in a so-called learning environment where it becomes obvious that they have to follow the teacher's definition of what needs to be learnt, do they eventually end up just playing the game, or, more seriously, give up on the learning process? To place this in context, Chapter 8 includes an example of how, instead of using a commercially produced locality pack for geography, a teacher has very clear ideas of the geographical concepts and learning approaches she wishes children to develop but allows them much more choice in their selection of the place for study.

The above example leads us on to the notion that 'the process of learning is not, therefore, about the accumulation of material of learning, but about the process of changing conceptions' (Moon 2004: 17). Moon argues that genuine personal enquiry can be a powerful way in which to achieve this. Especially important in this process is the idea that the enquiry experience has real meaning for the learner and that it may be difficult for an outsider to judge the quality of learning, especially if we accept the notion that understanding and knowledge are temporary as we are always refining our understanding of the world. Again, it may be difficult for teachers to adopt this approach in all aspects of their teaching at the current time. However, as professionals, do we perhaps need to consider how we might begin to make a difference to pupils' learning experiences? What opportunities might there be within your teaching to provide an environment in which pupils can experience being able to develop a genuine personal enquiry while at the same time you can justify their actions from the more pragmatic perspectives of timetable, curriculum, assessment and so forth?

If you are able to provide opportunities for pupils to develop their enquiries, you will also be putting them in an environment where they can begin to think about their own thinking and learning (metacognition). One aspect of this could be their ability to better understand how they are actually developing their understanding of the world. This may be at a very practical level, such as time management: if they have taken a lot of time on a web search, they may be able to consider how better to plan a web-based enquiry in the future. This is where the role of the teacher may be reconsidered, as it moves away from the notion of instructor to one of a learning guide or mentor. Using the enquiry process can be a powerful way of seeing your role in a new way. It may also enable you to discuss learning in new ways with your pupils.

Providing pupils with opportunities to both develop personal enquiries and reflect on their learning may also help them begin to understand that what we know and learn is in fact a part of ourselves and what it is to be human (Kelly 1955). If we never provide such learning opportunities, can pupils begin to hold up this type of mirror to their lives? Shayer and Adey (2002) report on the cognitive acceleration projects in which such approaches have been used with pupils aged between 5 and 15 to promote their own understanding of learning, motivation and achievement. However, if we are to achieve this, it is important that students preparing to become teachers have opportunities to analyse the nature of enquiry and how it will become a part of their professional philosophy and practice. Halocha (2004) studied student teachers' perceptions of geographical enquiry and found a variety of factors that affected their interpretation of the concept.

The cognitive acceleration project builds on the work of Lipman *et al.* (1980) with the Philosophy for Children (P4C) approaches to education. This also uses an empowering learning environment in which pupils are actively encouraged to take control of their learning through enquiry. Fisher (2003) provides many interesting examples from English schools where this approach has been developed. It leads us to a consideration of the role of thinking skills within the enquiry process. 'Thinking skills' has been a fashionable educational term over the past 15 years and indeed can be found in recent official curriculum and policy documents. Smith (2004) provides a thorough discussion as to whether there are identifiable thinking skills or whether particular subjects and disciplines actually have their own range of thinking skills that pupils need to encounter during their time at school. You may wish to discuss this with colleagues. Higgins and Baumfield (2001) provide many practical ideas for developing thinking skills across the primary curriculum and grounded their work in much classroom-based research. The strength of their ideas is that they integrate the main concepts of encouraging children to think actively and also to think about how they approach their enquiries within open-ended enquiries across a range of curriculum subjects.

Fisher and Williams (2004) build on the concepts of enquiry and thinking skills by relating them to recent interest in creativity in schools. Ofsted (2003) and other official documents are currently promoting creativity. Many teachers do see it as a way of re-engaging both pupils and teachers with the learning process. Some exciting projects can be found in primary schools. Hardy (2006) describes how all the classes in a large primary school mapped a part of their village. In the weeks following their fieldwork each class chose a modelling method for building their part of the village. When all the parts were brought together in the hall, there was much excitement and interest from pupils, teachers and the wider community about their creative approach to geographical enquiry in the locality. Fisher and Williams (2004: 12) sum up this approach to creative enquiry as being

What we need is teaching not trapped in defence or routine thinking, but teaching that is innovative. We need our children to experience paradox and uncertainty. They need lessons that produce effective surprise. They need also to reflect the processes of creativity – to plan, do and review their learning activities.

They suggest that the combination of enquiry approaches that are developed in an environment where both pupils and teachers are encouraged to be creative can help develop more creative people. They justify the need for this in two ways. The pragmatic approach is that our future citizens will need to be creative and confident enquirers in an ever increasingly complex, interrelated world where knowledge and problem solving will be the keys to survival. They also argue that such citizens will also have a greater capacity to feel and act as humans. They suggest that creative people have the following characteristics:

- they are flexible;
- they connect ideas;
- they are unorthodox;
- they show aesthetic taste;
- they see similarities and differences;
- they question accepted ways of doing things.
                    (Fisher and Williams 2004: 13)

You may wish to add to this list or disagree with their points. The key question is the extent to which we actually encourage or discourage pupils from developing these traits. What can help or hinder the process: curriculum content and structure, learning approaches, timetabling, assessment methods, pupil ownership of learning, the role of the teacher, external pressures such as Ofsted, teacher experience and confidence? Within the current educational climate, it may not be possible to transform learning overnight. However, it may be possible for you to take one of the traits and look at how you might create learning environments in which that trait could be encouraged. For example, in art when you are studying art styles from other countries and cultures you might help children to connect ideas by not just looking at the art but also relating it to the landscape and culture from which it came. Ask pupils for their ideas on why they interpret the art the way they do. Be brave enough to move onwards and upwards from just what the national curriculum (DfEE 1999b) and QCA schemes of work (QCA 2000) dictate. This chapter is all about empowering yourself and your pupils to learn in new and creative ways where you are much more in control of what is learnt and how it takes place.

Out-of-classroom activities

Many subjects and cross-curricular activities can take place outside the classroom. Before concluding this chapter, we will consider some generic ways in which enquiries based on pupils' desire to learn may be effectively planned into out-of-classroom activities.

The key question is the roles that you and the pupils actually take during the three stages of the fieldwork: before, during and after. Halocha (2005) reports on a longitudinal study of how teachers modified a field visit over a number of years. As pupils became more involved in these three stages and the overall planning, they began to develop a greater understanding of the geographical processes they were investigating.

Reflective task

Level 1

Identify an out-of-school activity that you have been on as a pupil, helper or teacher.
- What roles did the teacher play in the three stages of the visit?
- What roles did the learner play in the three stages of the visit?
- To what extent was enquiry a main focus of the visit?
- Did all pupils have the same experiences on the visit? If so, why?
- What did pupils actually do during the visit? For example, did they spend time listening to instructions or completing worksheet tasks?
- How could the experience be improved to make it more enquiry based?

Level 2

Identify an out-of-school activity that you run with your pupils. Note down your answers to the questions below. Consider how you may be able to adapt the experience by encouraging pupils to take greater ownership of the planning, what they do out of school and in the follow-up activities, while still covering the objectives (external factors) by which you justify the trip.
- What roles do you play in the three stages of the visit?
- What roles do pupils play in the three stages of the visit?
- To what extent is enquiry a main focus of the visit and to what extent is this based on pupils' questions and stages of development?
- Do all pupils have the same experiences on the visit? If so, why?
- What do pupils actually do during the visit? For example, do they spend time listening to instructions or completing worksheet tasks?
- How do you encourage pupils to develop emotional literacy (Tanner 2004) through a sense of awe and wonder while they are in the field?

  Be realistic and identify some ways in which you might modify the fieldwork experience by providing a learning environment in which pupils' enquiries are more centre stage. Indeed, you may decide that it can only be done with a full-scale revision of the process.

Level 3

Consider what out-of-school activities your school is involved in during any one year. Note down your answers to the following questions.
- What roles do teachers and other adults play in the three stages of the visit?
- What roles do pupils play in the three stages of the visit?
- To what extent is enquiry a main focus of the visit and to what extent is this based on pupils' questions and stages of development?
- Do all pupils have the same experiences on the visit? If so, why?
- What do pupils actually do during the visit? For example, do they spend time listening to instructions or completing worksheet tasks?
- How do you encourage pupils to develop emotional literacy (Tanner 2004) through a sense of awe and wonder while they are in the field?   *cont.*

Consider how you may be able to adapt the experiences by encouraging pupils to take greater ownership of the planning, what they do out of school and in the follow-up activities, while still covering the objectives (external factors) by which you justify the trip. Modify your plans to accommodate out-of-school enquiry.

It may appear daunting but the results can be dramatic. On a recent school visit, I was told of a Year 6 day visit to London which pupils had chosen for a contrasting locality. The teachers had moved some way along the path to placing pupil enquiry at the heart of the visit. Pupils were asked to form groups, allocated adult support, agreed a budget and timescales for the day. Each group was then allowed to plan their day in London within those practical parameters. They had to research where they were going, means of transport, what they would be investigating, how they would collect data, and how those data would be analysed and presented. The staff complied with all external demands of curriculum and safety but the pupils had ownership of their geographical enquiries. Teachers reported that it also made the day much more enjoyable in that they were not there as instructors but as learning mentors, and indeed learning alongside the pupils. In many ways the ideas discussed in the theoretical part of this chapter were addressed by using such an approach in which social learning, language, thinking skills and creativity were used by pupils and adults throughout the process. Tan *et al.* (2005) also report encouraging results by using group investigation methods in geographical fieldwork with 14-year-old pupils in Singapore where the children also took greater control of their enquiries.

Enquiry methods in subjects

This section includes a variety of ways in which the concept of enquiry is developed within different curriculum subjects. As you read it, consider the following questions:

- In what ways are the education objectives and processes of enquiry similar across the subjects?
- How might you help pupils, understanding of learning to develop in an integrated way, whether your school uses discrete subjects for teaching or prefers a more integrated approach?

Geography

We live in a world that is becoming interconnected in so many ways: we rely on people across the world for things we want; we can watch news events happening live on the world wide web; we are beginning to understand that what happens in one part of the world can have a considerable effect elsewhere; children use game stations to play together around the world; we are travelling more and more for work and pleasure. Almost every item of news has a geographical or spatial element to it. All this raises many questions and enquiries for us as individuals, members of communities, countries and organizations. Geography in school can help children ask questions about what is happening in the world, why it is happening and how the world is changing.

Picture 10.1 Children engaged in geographical investigation – sampling materials on a beach cross-section

To start them off on this process, Storm (1989: 4) offered five basic questions to use in primary geography:

- What is this place like?
- Why is this place as it is?
- How is this place connected to other places?
- How is this place changing?
- What would it feel like to live in this place?

Clearly, these are only a starting point and pupils should be encouraged to think of their own enquiry questions. Also, it would become very mechanical if every geographical enquiry simply worked through these questions. Each one will have a different strength and emphasis depending on where and what your pupils are investigating.

Dinkele (2004: 97) suggests a possible framework for you and your pupils to manage geographical enquiry:

Stage 1a Awareness raising
Stage 1b Generating enabling questions
Stage 2 Collecting and recording information
Stage 3 Processing the gathered information
Stage 4 Drawing conclusions from the processed data
Stage 5 Evaluation by all concerned

We now consider what these may look like in practice. In raising awareness, you will have to decide how much autonomy pupils will have in actually devising the key and follow-up questions. Don't forget that it may not just be a question: it might be a point of view. For example, in a class discussion, pupils might say that they think their playground is a very boring place and that is why there are arguments at break times. Now look at Storm's (1989) questions and you will probably see how they might be used to structure a genuine enquiry into their place, the playground. At other times, you may need to be more of a catalyst, but be so in a subtle way. Perhaps quite 'innocently' you begin discussing a news item that people share in your class. The 2004 Asian tsunami would be a useful example. Instead of asking a question, you might say that perhaps such disasters cannot be helped because local people need to live and work on coasts and tourists like to visit those places. From my experience being a geographer (as you've probably guessed by now!) your class would take up this challenge to see how far you were correct.

Immediately, this helps pupils to develop further enabling questions they can follow. Indeed, they do not all need to follow the same questions because you will know the key geographical skill and concepts you wish to develop. Also, in stage 5 there will be ample opportunity to share information, ideas and values. Thus, pupils will want to know where such disaster areas exist, how a tsunami is formed, what happens to people, why they live where they do?

These enabling questions then allow individuals, groups and sometimes the class to collect and record information. Your planning will ensure they are using a wide range of geographical sources, resources and recording methods. You do this by acting as a learning mentor, not as a geographical expert with all the answers. Indeed, simply voicing your own thoughts (Lindfors 1999: 9) rather than asking other questions may help children to reflect on their own changing understanding of the world.

Processing the gathered information probably goes on as it is being collected and you may therefore wish to challenge Dinkele's (2004) separation of stages 2 and 3. Indeed, Lindfors (1999) argues that the discussion taking place both in a social context and quietly within the child's own mind is perhaps a crucial stage of the enquiry. You might prefer to redraw Dinkele's model and perhaps place information processing across each of the stages. In the example offered, pupils will have gathered personal accounts of the tsunami from local people and tourists (the BBC News website at www.bbc.co.uk/news is excellent for this), collected factual information on how the disasters occur, studied the ways of life of the people and examined how those places are promoted in tourist information and advertising.

Drawing conclusions from the processed data might be subdivided and in such a way help children begin to understand the complex nature of our world. Some conclusions may be quite factual: we can predict fairly accurately where a tsunami may occur and why it happens. Rather more challenging is the question of how are prediction systems going to be set up and who will do it. Even more open to discussion and interpretation could be trying to draw conclusions about whether local people should be allowed to live in possibly dangerous locations and if tourists should be allowed to visit.

The example hopefully shows that the structure of the enquiry allows pupils to begin to evaluate the issues they have researched and, most important of all, begin to refine their own understanding of the world based on their own personal ideas that they set out with.

The central idea in this section is to suggest to you that it is possible to cover the current requirements of the geography orders and develop pupils' progression in skills and understanding by using enquiry approaches. You do not need to be an expert on geographical information, but you do need to communicate a sense of real interest, awe and wonder about the world. Indeed, as you become more confident with your own understanding of geographical thinking, you may well increasingly enjoy working alongside your pupils as your collective understanding of the world develops.

Practical and reflective task

Music

Look back at the reflective task 'Is music always creative?' by Ashley Compton in Chapter 2 (page 15). In this task, there are three examples of music activities and you are asked to look at them and decide if they are creative. Look at them again to see if they involve aspects of enquiry.

Level 1

- Do any of the examples in the task fit the description of enquiry or investigative work as described above? If so, indicate how?
- How could you make a music activity, such as example 3, more investigative?

Level 2

- How can you extend / modify the examples in the reflective task in Chapter 2 to make them more investigative?
- Look at some music planning for your class and try to make it more investigative?

Level 3

- Look at the 3 examples in the task and see if you can modify / change / extend them to make them more investigative.
- Look at your music schemes of work and see how you can achieve the learning objectives through investigative activities.

Science

Science is an enquiry-based curriculum area and in the primary school all learning should incorporate an element of investigation. The scientific process (see Figure 10.1) which forms the major part of all scientific development in the primary school is incorporated in both explorations and investigations, in which the children take ownership of the direction of learning. Not all scientific enquiry involves investigations or follows the full pathway through the process. Most of what occurs in the primary school are explorations, which involve children in observing the world around them, asking their own questions, formulating hypotheses and developing some basic scientific skills. They include structured play activities to teacher-generated and self-generated explorations, which are the types of creative approach identified in Chapter 2, Planning for Creative Teaching (see also Figure 2.2, Creative teaching approaches). Provided these explorations involve ample opportunities to discuss and consolidate ideas, they can contain all the main features of enquiry. So children may explore a scientific phenomena and then move further down the process (see Figure 10.1) to interpret their explorations and communicate their findings to others.

Investigations can stem from children's exploration, observations or hypotheses and involve children taking increasingly more responsibility for their work, making decisions about:

- the focus of the investigation;
- the resources they will need;
- how they will conduct the investigation;
- how they will record the data collected;
- how they will communicate findings.

Investigative work helps children to clarify their ideas, make sense of the world around them and to develop basic and more advanced skills in science. True investigations are less common in primary schools as an investigation has specific characteristics (NCC 1990, 1991), which involve the systematic handling of variables, a skill which develops from a child's increasing ability to observe and classify but is not apparent in younger primary and Foundation Stage children.

Another type of scientific enquiry involves children solving problems, and this is a highly motivating way to develop scientific skills, understandings and attitudes, enabling children to make decisions for themselves in real situations. Good scientific explorations and investigations involve teachers in:

- providing opportunities and time for children;
- encouraging children in making their own decisions and raising their own questions;
- encouraging children in answering their questions through exploration or simple investigations;
- being a good role model;
- developing a motivational environment that encourages enquiry;
- allowing plenty of opportunities for discussion, debate and exchange of ideas.

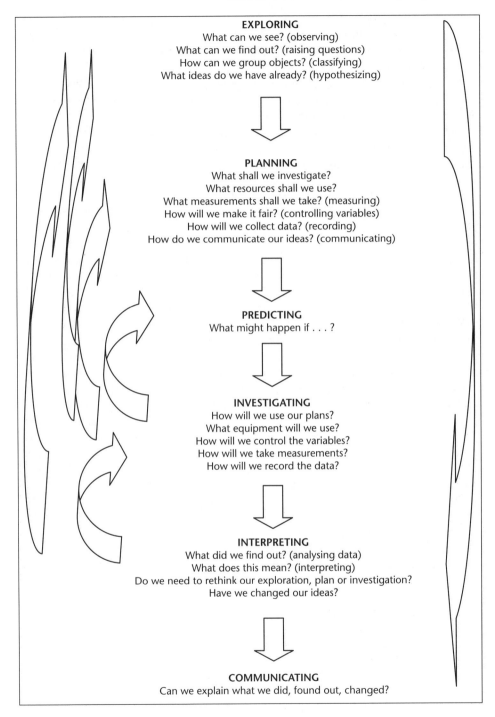

Figure 10.1   The scientific process (adapted from Johnston 2005: 32)

This type of approach will help children to construct their own meaning from their experiences (Scott 1987). The teacher's role in scientific enquiry changes as the exploration or investigation proceeds. It begins as a motivator, encouraging children in developing their ideas and focusing their plans and supporting the achievement of the learning objectives. It continues as a guide, interacting with the children and sometimes instructing them in the use of equipment, and finishes as a convenor, reflecting on experiences with the children and helping them to understand their own learning (metacognition). Metacognition, or reflection on your own thinking and problem-solving processes, is not only an important aspect of good enquiry, it is also an important aspect of cognitive acceleration programmes and materials (see, for example, Adey *et al.* 2003; Adey and Robertson 2004; Robertson 2006). Cognitive acceleration involves groups of children exploring the different ideas that others hold about a scientific phenomenon or different interpretations about the evidence from scientific enquiry. This can lead to cognitive conflict, or the conflict felt when ideas do not fit the evidence or ideas of others. As a result, ideas are reconstructed through social construction (making knowledge cooperatively) and children begin to understand their own thinking processes (metacognition) and the thinking processes of others (see Piaget 1950; Vygotsky 1978).

In one example, children were exploring a collection of objects (seeds, small stones, oak gall, pine cones, leaves) that they had found in the outside environment. They sorted all the seeds into one pile and there was a discussion among the children as to which ones were seeds. Some children included the pine cone and oak gall in the collection and one small stone was also mistaken for a seed. Through the social interaction, the children began to develop a group understanding of what a seed was and decided that in order to test out their ideas, they needed to plant their seeds and see what happened. This example contains elements of cognitive conflict (disagreements about the definition of a seed), social construction (an agreed definition), metacognition (understanding of why they and others hold particular definitions), decision making (deciding how to test out their ideas) and enquiry (practical exploration of seeds and investigation to test out ideas).

In another example, a class of Year 5 children were investigating a collection of paper towels. Each group of children decided what to investigate: One group decided to see how strong the towels were, another how absorbent, and another to investigate all the properties (strength, absorbency, softness, cost and so on). In order to do this, each group had to decide:

- what to investigate;
- what resources they needed;
- how they would control the variables;
- how they would measure the results;
- how they would record the results;
- how they would communicate to the rest of the class.

In doing this, they had to communicate as a group and discuss predictions as to what they thought would happen, hypotheses as to why they thought something had happened and interpretations as to what the result meant. In this way the

Picture 10.2 Discussing seeds

investigation had all the criteria for good enquiry and aided the development of both scientific skills and understandings.

Mathematics

Mathematics lends itself to some really good investigations and opportunities for decision making, metacognition and social construction (see Cognitive Acceleration in Mathematics Education 2006). The structure of the Numeracy strategy (DfEE 1999b) lends itself to social construction and metacognition, through group or whole-class interactions. Problem solving in mathematics enables children to understand mathematics as well as develop mathematical skills. Mathematical problem solving involves four steps (NZ Maths 2006):

1 Understanding and exploration of the problem.
2 Finding a strategy from a range available.
3 Using the strategy to solve the problem.
4 Looking back and reflecting on the solution.

Finding problem-solving strategies is an important part of the process. Strategies may range from guessing, using equipment, making lists, drawing diagrams, pictures, making tables or graphs, thinking and discussing. The advantages of problem solving in mathematics are that:

- It bases students' mathematical development on their current knowledge;
- It is an interesting and enjoyable way to learn mathematics;
- It is a way to learn new mathematics with greater understanding;
- It produces positive attitudes towards mathematics;
- It makes the student a junior mathematician;
- It teaches thinking, flexibility and creativity;
- It encourages co-operative skills;
- It is a useful way to practice mathematical skills learned by other means;
- It is similar to the approach used in other curriculum activities.

(NZ Maths 2006: 1)

One example of mathematical problem solving is the Towers of Hanoi problem (see Figure 10.2). In this problem, children have to move the discs from the left (base 1) to the right (base 3). However, they can only move one disc at a time and cannot place a larger disc on top of a smaller disc. Children should be encouraged to explore the problem, predict / guess how many moves it will take, and then try it out and count the moves. It can be made easier by using three discs and harder with seven discs, and children can try to predict how many moves it will take with more discs after they have solved the problem with fewer.

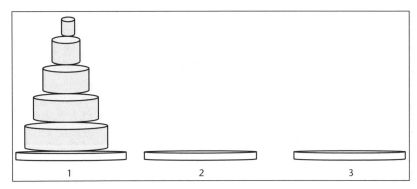

Figure 10.2 Towers of Hanoi problem

An example of a more relevant problem is for two children to have an 80 ml jug of water and be asked to share it equally. They also have two empty cups, one of which will hold 50 ml and the other 30 ml. How can they each measure exactly 40 ml of water and share the jug's contents.

Practical task

Investigative mathematics

Level 1

Look at some mathematics teaching you have previously taught or are planning to teach. Modify it to include some aspect of problem solving or mathematical investigation.

Level 2

Look at your planning for the next week or term and identify any mathematical problem solving or investigation. Modify your plans to include or strengthen problem solving or mathematical investigation. Review the activities after you have taught them and consider how well the learning objectives were achieved and what the advantages of mathematical enquiry are.

Level 3

Look at your school's scheme of work or medium-term planning in mathematics and consider how you can include more mathematical enquiry. Review the results at the end of the scheme and discuss as a staff what the advantages are of mathematical enquiry and how you can further include it in your teaching.

Conclusion

Throughout this chapter it has been accepted that you are working within a complex professional environment. There will be many factors that encourage you and prevent you in helping your pupils to develop their enquiry skills. Hopefully, the chapter has helped you to stand back a little in order to consider the type of child you hope will leave your primary school and how you may have, in some ways, prepared them for life in the world that we can only begin to comprehend and speculate on. Abbott (1999) argues that your success may best be judged not by the amount of knowledge that a child absorbs at school, but much more their desire to enquire and learn and an awareness of their own capacity for doing this. They will live in a world dominated by information: will it control them or will they have control over it through a personal desire to challenge and enquire?

References

Abbott, J. (1999) *Battery Hens or Free Range Chickens: What Kind of Education for What Kind of World?* Available at http://www. 21learn.org/publ/abbott-speech.html

Adey, P. and Robertson, A. (2004) *Let's Think through Science: A Programme for Developing Thinking in Year 4*. Windsor: NFER-Nelson.

Adey, P. and Shayer, M. (2002) Cognitive acceleration comes of age, in M. Shayer and P. Adey (eds) *Learning Intelligence: Cognitive Acceleration across the Curriculum from 5 to 15 Years*. Buckingham: Open University Press.

Adey, P., Nagy, F., Robertson, A., Serret, N. and Wadsworth, P. (2003) *Let's Think through Science: A Programme for Developing Thinking in Year 3*. Windsor: NFER-Nelson.

Cognitive Acceleration in Mathematics Education (2006) www.keele.ac.uk/depts /ed/cpdactivities/came-docs/Thinking

DES (1967) *Children and their Primary Schools. A Report for the Central Advisory Council for Education* (Plowden Report). London: HMSO.

DES (1975) *A Language for Life: Report of the Committee of Inquiry Appointed by the Secretary of State for Education and Science under the Chairmanship of Sir Alan Bullock* (Bullock Report) London: HMSO.

DfEE (1998) *The National Literacy Strategy*. London: DfEE.

DfEE (1999a) *The National Numeracy Strategy*. London: DfEE.

DfEE (1999b) *The National Curriculum: Handbook for Teachers in England*. London: DfEE / QCA.

DfES (2003) *Excellence and Enjoyment: A Strategy for Primary Schools*. London: DfES.

Dinkele, G. (2004) Geographical enquiries and investigations, in S. Scoffham (ed.) *Primary Geography Handbook*. Sheffield: Geographical Association.

Fisher, R. (2003) *Teaching Thinking*. London: Continuum.

Fisher, R. and Williams, M. (eds) (2004) *Unlocking Creativity: Teaching across the Curriculum*. London: David Fulton.

Hadow, W. (1931) *Report on the Consultative Committee on the Primary School*. London: HMSO.

Halocha, J. (2004) Student teachers' perceptions of geographical enquiry, in S. Catling and F. Martin (eds) *Researching Primary Geography*. London: Register of Research in Primary Geography.

Halocha, J. (2005) Developing a research tool to enable children to voice their experiences and learning through fieldwork, *Geographical and Environmental Education*, 14(4), 348–55.

Hardy, S. (2006) Wow! We built that!, *Primary Geographer*, 59: 30–2.

Higgins, S. and Baumfield, V. (2001) *Thinking through Primary Teaching*. Cambridge: Chris Kington Publishing.

Johnston, J. (2005) *Early Explorations in Science*, 2nd edn. Buckingham: Open University Press.

Kelly, G. A. (1955) *A Theory of Personality: The Psychology of Personal Constructs*. New York: Norton Library.

Lindfors, J. Wells (1999) *Children's Inquiry: Using Language to Make Sense of the World.* New York: Teachers College Press.

Lipman, M., Sharp, M. and Oscanyan, F. (1980) *Philosophy in the Classroom*, 2nd edn. Philadelphia: Temple University Press.

Moon, J. (2004) *A Handbook of Reflective and Experiential Learning: Theory and Practice.* London: RoutledgeFalmer.

NCC (National Curriculum Council) (1990) *Science Investigations: Working with Science AT1 in Key Stages 1 and 2. NCC Inset.* London: NCC.

NCC (National Curriculum Council) (1991) *Science Explorations. NCC Inset.* London: NCC.

NZ Maths (2006) Problem solving. Available at www.nzmaths.co.nz/PS/Info /Information.aspx

Ofsted (2003) *Expecting the Unexpected: Developing Creativity in Primary and Secondary Schools.* London: Ofsted.

Piaget, J. (1950) *The Psychology of Intelligence.* London: Routledge & Kegan Paul.

QCA (2000) *A Scheme of Work for Key Stages 1 and 2 – Art.* London: QCA.

Robertson, A. (2006) *Let's Think in the Early Years: A Programme for Developing Thinking in Reception.* Windsor: NFER-Nelson.

Scott, P. (1987) *A Constructivist View of Teaching and Learning Science.* Leeds: Leeds University.

Shayer, M. and Adey, P. (eds) (2002) *Learning Intelligence: Cognitive Acceleration across the Curriculum from 5 to 15 Years.* Buckingham: Open University Press.

Smith, G. (2004) Thinking skills: the question of generality, in E. C. Wragg (ed.) *The RoutledgeFalmer Reader in Teaching and Learning*, London: RoutledgeFalmer.

Storm, M. (1989) The five basic questions for primary geography, *Primary Geographer*, 2: 4.

Tan, I., Sharan, S. and Lee, C. (2005) Students' perceptions of learning geography through group investigation in Singapore, *Geographical and Environmental Education*, 14(4): 261–76.

Tanner, J. (2004) Geography and the emotions, in S. Scoffham (ed.) *Primary Geography Handbook.* Sheffield: Geographical Association.

Vygotsky, L. S. (1978) *Mind in Society: The Development of Higher Psychological Processes*, eds M Cole *et al.* Cambridge, MA: Harvard University Press.

Useful website

BBC News: www.bbc.co.uk/news

Part 3

Reviewing

11
Assessment for Learning

Mark Chater

> *Instruction touches the mind, assessment touches the heart.*
>
> (Weeden *et al.* 2002: 14)

Introduction

This chapter poses some important questions about the nature and purpose of assessment. It invites the reader to reflect critically on their own experiences, as a child and adult, of being assessed and fed back to. It describes the ways in which assessment policy and practice have developed in primary schools, and it focuses on the challenges and advantages of assessment for learning as a way forward.

Assessment, as a topic in education, is notoriously jargon ridden. It is necessary for professionals to know the jargon and, more importantly, to have an independent, thoughtful way of understanding what the words and phrases mean, and of evaluating their importance. Key terms are explained in the chapter, and readers are invited to engage with the tasks as a way of deepening their understanding of the terminology and of the educational issues behind the terms.

The purpose of assessment

What is the point of assessment? Is it to measure, motivate, inform, or some mixture of these? Many pupils and parents believe that the main purpose of assessment is to measure; to be able to say pupil x is performing at this level, pupil y at that level; that one of them is at the national average and the other is above it. In making this sort of assumption, pupils and parents are missing a crucial alternative purpose of assessment which is both ancient and recent, namely its power to inform teachers and pupils, parents and the state, and also to lead on to further improvement: in short, assessment *for* learning.

The Latin root of the word 'assess' is two words, *ad sedere* (*ad* = beside, *sedere* = to sit down). Literally, therefore, to assess is to sit down beside a pupil. The symbolism of 'sitting down beside' suggests dialogue, working together, help towards progress and mutual commitment. It does not suggest judgement, criticism or comparison with others.

Reflective task

Most teachers recognize that assessment yields information that can be put to many uses; that pupil progress is central to these, but is not the only purpose.

Level 1
Look at Table 11.1 and consider each *purpose* of assessment in the left-hand column. Match each of these to a *use* to which assessment information is put. The uses have been jumbled, so their order does not match the purposes. In practice, some purposes may match more than one use.

Level 2
Undertake the task above with colleagues and discuss your ideas.

Level 3
You can use the task above as part of a staff meeting or in-service session on assessment. Consider the different ideas among your staff and how you can move forward with any differences.

Table 11.1 Reflective task: match the purpose of assessment to the use to which it can be put

Purpose of assessment	Use to which assessment information could be put
To confirm or reinforce learning	League tables, value-added tables, Pandas and Ofsted reports
To provide information on pupils and needs	Teacher self-evaluation, appraisal and planning
To determine pupil needs at the start of a year, term or unit, or to discover the individual needs of a pupil at any time	Setting goals or targets with pupils
To inform teachers on their effectiveness	Pupil-teacher dialogue, targets and planning
To show pupils how they are doing and help them to take the next steps	Pupil profiling and contact with parents
To measure learning and achievement by national standards	Teacher planning, reporting to parents and learning support

Changes in assessment

Teaching and learning have changed considerably since the introduction of the national curriculum in 1989 and this has had a big effect on assessment, which has changed to match the curriculum. Before the introduction of the national curriculum, the primary curriculum focused on teaching basic skills and knowledge as a foundation for future learning. There was no common curriculum to follow and individual teachers or schools could plan the curriculum content as they saw fit. Teaching was often ad hoc, with little planned progression through the primary curriculum except where schools followed commercial schemes in some subjects (mainly mathematics). Teacher assessment was qualitative and formative and used to support the work the children were doing in class. External assessment was used to diagnose educational problems, with some subject associations producing assessment material to support their subject. During the early years of the national curriculum, that is during the early part of the 1990s, the national curriculum identified specific content to be taught within the relevant key stage. The Task Group on Assessment and Testing identified levels of attainment, and specific subject working groups identified criteria for assessment at each level (DES 1988). Assessment began by being practical, and the 1991 standard assessment tasks (SATs) at Key Stage 1 were highly practical. They involved children in taking messages to other classes (assessing speaking and listening skills) and in investigating floating and sinking (assess scientific skills and knowledge about the forces involved in floating and sinking). The tasks subsequently became more knowledge based after 1991 and less practical, with most SATs being focused around written responses. Recording of assessments was by ticking the large number of statements of attainment sheets.

In the mid-1990s the focus of the primary national curriculum became more knowledge based. Skills were still regarded as important, but because assessments focused on knowledge rather than skills, the emphasis on knowledge was reflected in the curriculum and in teaching and learning. However, educational research was more focused on learning, with many research projects focusing on the way children learn and the alternative conceptual understandings they constructed from teaching. When the national curriculum was remodelled in 1999 (DfEE 1999) there was an increasing dissatisfaction with the focus on knowledge so a move was made towards a combination approach: the development of skills and understanding. Assessment at Key Stage 1 was mainly by teacher assessment and still based on knowledge, although there was a move towards assessment which measures application. For younger children aged 3 to 5 years, the curriculum was skills based (DfES 2007) and assessed through teacher assessment (QCA 2003).

Difficulties in assessing

Assessment does come hand in hand with problems. Some of these are classroom-level problems or micro-level problems. These include children's misunderstandings which affect assessment. I once looked at an assessment task that a Year 3 child was asked to complete, which included the task of writing '10 odd numbers under 100'. Her response has been reproduced in Figure 11.1.

$$\frac{100}{1} \quad \frac{100}{3} \quad \frac{100}{5} \quad \frac{100}{7} \quad \frac{100}{9} \quad \frac{100}{11} \quad \frac{100}{13} \quad \frac{100}{15} \quad \frac{100}{17} \quad \frac{100}{19}$$

Figure 11.1 A Year 3 child's response to the assessment task 'Write 10 odd numbers under 100'

Some of these problems arise because of the way in which children develop their ideas. Because this is not linear, children often develop alternative conceptual frameworks which they modify as they become more experienced. For example, 10-year-old children have been found to hold alternative ideas about the way we see (Osborne *et al.* 1991). The most common of these alternative views is that of 'active vision', where the child believes there is some property of the eye which enables vision (see Figure 11.2a). This may be due to science fiction, such as Superman with his X-ray vision, or to do with our creative use of language. How often have you heard phrases such as 'she gave me a look like daggers' or 'her eyes were shining'? After teaching, children recognize the need for a light source in order to see something and they modify their idea to take this into consideration (see Figure 11.2b). Very few children actually identify the correct scientific version of the way we see (see Figure 11.2c).

Figure 11.2 Alternative views of the way we see (Osborne *et al.* 1991: 27)

Assessment problems originating outside the classroom or macro-level problems are numerous. Firstly and philosophically, the national curriculum can appear to be assessment driven, placing assessment before the curriculum and with the child trailing along behind. It does not consider Rousseau's belief that education should accommodate itself to the child (Rousseau 1911). Secondly and practically, assessment in the national curriculum can preclude the idea of formative development and long-term planning, as national tests are summative and therefore learning has to follow suit, and children at the end of a key stage need revision or booster lessons to revise learning completed earlier in their scheme of work. Thirdly, there can be problems because teachers do not always fully understand the requirements and criteria; hardly surprising when the latter change rapidly. For example, there have been things that children are expected to know at Key Stage 1 which, after modifications to the national curriculum (DfEE 1999), are moved to requirements at Key Stage 2, and vice versa. In another example, in the early days of the national curriculum there was a criterion in science at Key Stage 1 that children should recognize the apparent motion of the Sun across the sky. Some teachers thought that this meant that children should understand 'why', which is conceptually much too difficult for most Key Stage 1 children. Incidentally, this knowledge was one that was subsequently moved to Key Stage 2, but the requirement to know 'why' was not expected of primary children.

There has also not been consistent understanding about what to expect at different levels of assessment, with children at level 4 at Key Stage 4 being judged differently from children at level 4 at Key Stage 3. Although this problem has been overcome to some extent by changes to the national curriculum (DfEE 1999), it still exists in part, but even more concerning is the change from 'average' level at the end of a key stage to 'expected' level. This is not just a change of language but a change of expectations, as average level implies that approximately 50 per cent of children will reach this level, with 25 per cent at a higher level and 25 per cent at a lower level. 'Expected level' implies that 100 per cent of children should reach this level, a far cry from the intentions of the Task Group on Assessment and Testing (DES 1988).

The final macro-level problem relates to the jargon associated with assessment. Since the introduction of formal assessment in primary education, teachers have had to get to grips with associated assessment jargon. I once was discussing with an educationalist about assessment and he started to talk about 'dyna-rod'. For a moment I was confused and thought maybe it was a new assessment term, until I clarified it with him. Some of these assessment terms are difficult to understand, but it is necessary that we are clear about their meaning if we are to work effectively.

The rest of this chapter describes new approaches to assessment for learning and explains how they are different from some assessment priorities and procedures associated with testing and national standards. It argues for the advantages of assessment for learning, and shows examples of how it can work in the classroom.

The assessment and evaluation cycle

Teaching, learning and assessing are part of a complex, cyclic activity, which includes short-, medium- and long-term assessments (see Figure 11.3). These assessments can support future teaching and learning. In the short term, daily evaluation of teaching and assessment of individual children can be used to support planning to support learners in the achievement of your learning objectives at a level appropriate to their needs and abilities.

Practical task

Assessment jargon

Can you match these assessment terms and their definitions (1–9) below?

Norm referencing   Aggregation   Formative assessment
Teacher assessment   Agreement trials   Criterion referencing
Summative assessment   Moderation   Standard assessment tasks

1 An assessment which teachers can use in deciding how a pupil's learning should be taken forward, and in giving pupils feedback about their performance.
2 An assessment which provides overall evidence of the achievements of pupils and of what they know and understand and can do.
3 A system where a pupil's achievements are judged in relation to objectives irrespective of other pupils' performances.
4 A system in which pupils are placed in rank order, and (often) predetermined proportions are placed in various grades. It implies that grades are assigned by comparison to other pupils' performances rather than upon the absolute quality of the performance.
5 Classroom assessment of pupils by the teacher throughout the year.
6 An externally provided task for classroom assessment, which will incorporate a variety of assessment methods. It will be used nationally to cross-check the teacher assessments, thereby complementing teachers' own assessments.
7 Combining a learner's assessed scores, obtained over a variety of tasks, to give a single score for recording and reporting purposes.
8 Meetings and other activities which are designed to establish consistency of judgement and interpretation either between individual teachers or among groups of teachers.
9 The process of checking the comparability of different assessors' judgements to ensure a common standard. In the national curriculum this will take place within and across schools.

In the medium term, evaluative assessments of key lessons can help to record the class's progress towards your key learning objectives. To be really effective, the record should identify evidence, especially for individual pupils whose progress differs from the norm. This type of assessment enables teachers to identify how successful their differentiated expectations are.

In the medium / long term, assessments of individuals help to provide a profile of the child's understandings, skills and progress in science.

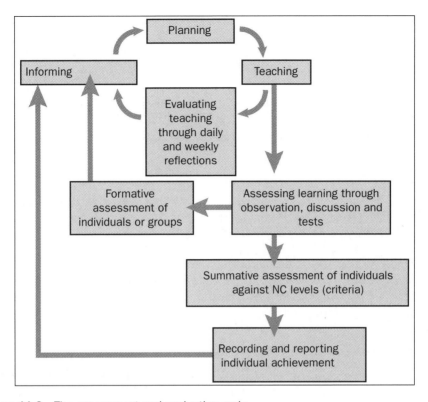

Figure 11.3 The assessment and evaluation cycle

How we record and report assessments

Record-keeping formats will differ depending on the type of assessment, but in all cases we need to remember why we are keeping assessments. and the main reason should always be because it will inform us as to how we can continue to support the child.

I have never been convinced as to the purpose or use of whole-class assessment records, especially where they use symbols to indicate if the children have completed a task or understood. My reasons for this are both pragmatic, as it takes a huge amount of time to keep such records, and also educational, as the records are not effective in providing formative and quality support for individual learners. A good record needs evidence to support an assessment and also to indicate how the child can be supported.

Assessments of individual children should contain some important features:

- Evidence to justify assessments made. Evidence can be provided through teacher assessment methods described above.
- Date and context of assessment.

- Comparability with other curriculum record-keeping systems.
- Comparability with other classes in school and with feeder schools.

Analysis of assessments should involve teachers in: deciding the criteria for assessment; comparing evidence with others (moderation) and coming to an agreement about what a level means; and considering national-curriculum-level descriptions and matching the assessments against them.

Assessments need to be reported to a number of different bodies:

- the child;
- the parents;
- the next class teacher / school (vertical move to next year group);
- the next class teacher (horizontal move within a year group);
- the local authority / moderator / outside agency.

Each report will need to be tailored for the specific audience. However, in this chapter we are more concerned with the child as not just an audience for reporting summative assessments but also as a partner in formative assessment: assessment for learning.

The case for assessment for learning

Imagine that you are due to be assessed on your understanding of this chapter. You are to be given a choice of assessment methods. How would you like this assessment to be carried out? Here is a list of possible ways:

- by submitting written answers to questions in your own time;
- by writing an essay in response to one set question;
- by writing a statement entirely made by you;
- by taking part in a group discussion;
- by answering oral questions in a tutorial;
- by responding to online questions in a time limit;
- by answering some (not all) questions in exam conditions;
- by answering all set questions in a standardized national test;
- by having your teaching and assessment practices observed on five occasions spread over a period of several weeks, and your teaching file scrutinized.

Your first choice should be the method that you feel will enable you to perform the best. Make a list of your three best methods, and your one least favourite method.

Now imagine how you would feel if your trainer, mentor or line manager, knowing your preferences, decided to apply the method that was your worst option – and did so in the name of raising standards.

The emergence of assessment *for* learning is based on the belief that assessment should not be separate from learning; it should not be the thing that happens at the end of learning, when learning has stopped; it should not be the antithesis of learning. Rather, the belief is that assessment and learning are mixed in with each other so much that they should become indistinguishable from each other.

Purposes of assessment can be interchangeable, and purposes are not the same as different kinds of assessment. In other words, a piece of assessment could be both formative and summative in purpose. Or, used for a different purpose, it could be one and not the other.

For this reason, the differences between assessment for learning and assessment of learning are not absolute, but are connected with the intention of the teacher, the extent to which the teacher plans to work with the children, and the purposes to which the teacher puts assessment information (Black 2003). The differences are not in type of assessment, but in assessment's purpose and use. Table 11.2 summarizes the distinction.

Table 11.2 Differences between assessment for learning and assessment of learning

	Assessment *of* learning	Assessment *for* learning
Timing	At the end of a stage of learning	Any time as part of the process of teaching and learning
Purpose	Summative; to measure	Formative; to shape learning
How it motivates pupils	Extrinsic (trading for grades)	Intrinsic (empowerment for learning)
Philosophy	Instrumentalist	Humanist
Assumptions	Standards are objective and can be measured Regular measurement improves standards	Standards are personal (ipsative) and improvement can be planned for Regular feedback improves understanding, thereby raising standards

The same test or task could be applied to a class as assessment of learning or as assessment for learning. The difference would depend on the teacher's actions and intentions. If the teacher:

- applied the test at the end of a unit of work;
- published the results to the class and to parents;
- used the grades (or perhaps the children's position compared with their classmates) as a measure;
- motivated them with grades and positions;
- advised them that top grades mean better job opportunities in future life;
- believed that this was a valid and reliable way to measure and to raise standards;

then this all suggests assessment *of* learning – a process relatively detached from learning itself. On the other hand, if the teacher:

- applied the test in mid-unit;
- published the results;
- advised each individual pupil on how to improve;
- motivated them with realistic and achievable targets;
- advised them that they had the power to do better and that fulfilment is its own reward;

and did so in the belief that assessment was designed mainly to provide feedback to pupils themselves, this would correspond to assessment *for* learning. It is a process firmly, regularly embedded in planning–teaching cycles. Advocates claim that it, too, raises standards, not through the test itself but through the effect of the feedback and negotiated targets for improvement (Black and Wiliam 1998). In addition, purposes can be evaluative (of the teacher, the resources or methods), and diagnostic (of a pupil's performance and needs).

To see the importance of assessment for learning (AfL), we have to recognize how radically different it is from its older counterpart, and how life and learning in some schools is severely limited. Weeden *et al.* (2002: 7) quote a parent on 'the ludicrousness of the test culture' and the 'boring and unadventurous' school. Their child reported pessimistically of the same school:

> It doesn't matter about understanding things in the juniors, just as long as we get them right. I mean there's no time to go into understanding stuff. That all takes ages and you have to have a go. In the juniors there's a lot less having a go and a lot more being told things.
>
> (Weeden *et al.* 2002: 7)

While there are some teachers who emphasize the importance of technical processes, end points and scientific accuracy in assessment, placing these as more important than motivational issues (Anderson 2003), most teachers see the importance of integrating assessment into teaching so that the data generated by assessment are put to some pedagogical use. Even those who favour strict summative assessment are aware of the dangers it brings in terms of the pressure to teach to the test, in other words to allow teaching to be distorted by the end result (Anderson 2003: 49). For some, the defence of summative assessment is connected with norm-referenced assessment, in the sense that it is felt necessary to administer tests at the end of learning stages and to use the information to create national scales and hierarchies, such comparisons being useful (Anderson 2003: 144).

Systems of assessment that interrupt learning, or impose tests that are seen as separate from learning, have been variously denounced by teachers with metaphorical sayings such as 'pigs don't get any fatter by being weighed' and 'you're just digging up the tree to see how it is growing'. These ironic remarks can be analysed. According to the pig-fattening metaphor, summative assessment is, in learning terms, futile; it is a displacement activity, yielding nothing useful. The second, more acerbic, remark implies that some forms of summative assessment are like destroying the tree while claiming to want to help it grow. According to this metaphor, summative assessment is not only futile but self-defeating too, because it interferes with learning to the point of destroying it.

The claims made for AfL include its capacity to help especially the lowest and weakest achievers (Weeden *et al.* 2002) because of its focus on feedback; and its tendency to improve motivation and behaviour, because of its focus on individual progress. AfL has the power to transform attitudes:

> A child who is curious, confident and engaged is a delight to teach. A child who is apathetic and afraid to try or one who protects their self-esteem through hostility to the learning process is a problem all too familiar to most teachers.
>
> (Weeden *et al.* 2002: 151)

And the answer, for such a child, lies not in enforcing an imposed, external and irrelevant regime of standards, but in taking slow steps and having enough interaction to lead the child on into the risks of learning.

Many teachers are concerned that if the external regime is rigidly imposed, there will be violence to the internal learning, self-esteem and sense of progress of individuals. There is a concern that 'the express train of students' capability [might be] running full tilt at the buffers of the assessment system' (Richardson 2003: 112).

How can AfL help in teaching and learning?

Any teacher who works on the assumption that assessment is integral to teaching will set out to help pupils know and understand the standards they are aiming for. This understanding helps pupils to own their learning, involves them in the shaping of goals for themselves and introduces a shared ownership between the teacher and learner. Such an approach requires a teacher to adjust their teaching in the light of assessment data. In particular, it means taking time to give effective feedback, to involve the pupil in self-assessment or self-evaluation, and to discuss ways to improve. It means identifying targets and negotiated ways of learning, and putting them back into the planning, so that the class moves on together, each pupil having made maximum use of the information yielded by the assessment (Weeden *et al.* 2002: 24–5; Black and Wiliam 2004).

All this requires the teacher to change not only actions but also underlying assumptions and philosophy. There needs to be a determined confidence that, given support, every pupil can improve; that pupils have an entitlement to be involved in the discussion of the progress; that when they are involved, their learning is more effective; that individual pupil progress by their own negotiated standards is intrinsically more important than the imposition of national standards.

For those teachers concerned that this form of assessment might lose its robustness or validity, it is clear that forms of AfL such as self-assessment can still work rigorously. Self-assessment, when implemented whole-heartedly, can be radical in giving pupils a look at themselves and their progress as if from outside: 'taking a step outside the learning process to look at it' (Weeden *et al.* 2002: 76). For pupils, to know a thing is one step; another, more exciting step is to know that they know, and to be able to show how it has changed them. This capacity is sometimes called metacognition, literally 'beyond knowing'.

Although pupils may take some time to accustom themselves to self-assessment, they can become more confident and accurate in using it if it is used regularly. It can include instruments such as review sheets, use of examples (as in 'what I'm looking for' and success criteria), discussion, interviews, journals or portfolios. A regular sequence of self-assessment questions helps pupils to get used to using self-assessment. Weedon *et al.* (2002: 90) suggest that pupils could ask:

- What have I learnt?
- What am I most pleased with about my work?
- What did I find difficult?
- How can I try to improve this?

Reflective task

Level 1
- How would you feel if someone told you what you had learnt, what you should be pleased with about your work, what you found difficult and what you needed to do to improve your work?
- How is your learning assessed and how are your learning targets identified?
- How could the assessment be improved?

Level 2
- What would happen if you told a pupil the answers to the questions above?
- How would it be different if a pupil answered the questions for themselves?
- What would be the extra 'yield'?
- How could you help your children towards self-assessment?

Level 3
- Do you operate a self-appraisal system with your staff?
- Do you support the children in your school to self-assess?
- What might be the advantages of self-appraisal and self-assessment?
- What might be the difficulties?
- How can you move towards improved self-assessment?

AfL, as practised in the classroom and at its best, is a whole-person approach. Instead of separating the person's self-hood from the task (in the name of objectivity), it can take into account the pupil's needs, preferences as to time of day or seating position or learning style; it can read and interpret body language; it can adapt the test to suit the needs of the learner, rather than forcing the learner to adapt to the requirements of the test. AfL can assess behaviour and effort as well as performance, and can engage a pupil in dialogue about improvement.

The positive effect of AfL on self-esteem is beginning to be known. Self-esteem, as measured at age 11, now seems a more important indicator of future success than intellectual ability measured at the same age (Weeden *et al.* 2002: 15). This is so because the emotional factor in learning is key to motivation, and it is precisely the motivational, personal element that is suppressed, or held at a distance, in standardized and summative assessments.

How can AfL help in marking and feedback?

It is in the attention to detail, and the connection between marking, feedback and future planning, that AfL makes a crucial difference (Black and Wiliam 2004). When marking is prompt and written feedback is focused on specific success criteria or progress points, where agreed targets are systematically recorded, the impact on pupils' development is maximized. It helps to overcome pupils' nervousness or vulnerability if the whole school staff agree to use a system of marking that is regular and consistent. For instance, whatever conventions and symbols are used in the margin should, if possible, be agreed and used regularly by staff. That way, pupils get used to them, and progression within and across years is facilitated (see also Chapter 12, Target Setting).

Once pupils have grown accustomed to feedback that is detailed, motivating and positive in its suggestions for improvement, they grow to rely on it and be guided by it. Teachers also have the satisfaction of working with pupils towards agreed goals. Compare these two pieces of feedback on the same piece of Year 5 written work. The first feedback is summative (assessment of learning) in style:

Good start. Development section weak, use of powerful adjectives very limited. Untidy at the end. Concentrate harder.

This second feedback looks at the same piece of work and offers formative assessment for learning:

Your opening section is exciting, and makes the reader interested. In the middle of the story, you could have used more powerful words, such as 'disgusting' instead of 'bad', or 'terrified' instead of 'scared'. Mostly your handwriting is fine, but it became less tidy towards the end, and you made some careless mistakes. Take more time over your work, because this will help you to use better words and avoid mistakes. Remember to check it carefully.

There are several points to note about the quality of the above two pieces of feedback. The first piece is brief to the point of terseness. It is written ungrammatically, setting a bad example. The term 'development section' may not be familiar to the pupil. The only advice is unhelpfully abstract. The pupil is reasonably likely to find this feedback unhelpful, even slightly rude, and to be less motivated as a result. The advice to concentrate harder is so vague that it would work only with a highly motivated pupil. In contrast, the second piece has many positive encouraging

Practical and reflective task

Level 1
- Make a note of the differences between the two pieces of feedback above.
- What would be the effect on the pupil in each case?
- Specifically, how would a pupil feel motivated, and how would a pupil feel guided, by each example?

Level 2
- Analyse some different written feedback you have given to children in your class.
- Do you tend to be formative or summative in your feedback?
- How do you think the children felt receiving your feedback? Ask the children and see how they felt on getting the feedback.
- How could you make your feedback more formative and motivating? Try out your ideas and see if they work.

Level 3
- Ask your staff to analyse some different examples of feedback that they give to children.
- Is the feedback formative or summative?
- How do you think the children felt receiving the feedback?
- How could you make the feedback more formative and motivating?

Plan to provide more formative and motivating feedback and monitor how the children respond.

---

statements, and sets a good example of written English. It is addressed personally to the pupil. It explains reasons for the advice, and offers concrete illustrations of ways to improve. These would be built on, and extended, in the one-to-one conversation and in setting goals.

While the acronym SMART (specific, measurable, achievable, realistic and time-related) has often been advocated as a model of good practice for feedback and goals, a more developed description of good goals in AfL would be that they should be 'realistic, specific, sensitive to pupils' goals, timely, descriptive, consciously non-judgemental, not comparing, diligent, direct, positive, aware' (Weeden *et al.* 2002: 118).

The use of grades in marking and feedback needs care. Many pupils, and their parents, become fixated on grades to the point that they may ignore other forms of feedback. Cartoon character Lisa Simpson, deprived of grades when her teachers go on strike, wails to her mother: 'Grade me, grade me!' Somewhat uncertainly, Marge picks a grade, whereupon Lisa lapses into a blissful state of certainty.

The disadvantages of grades are several. They encourage pupils to compare themselves with each other, rather than with their own performance or with national expectations. 'I got a B. What did you get?' Grades also give the impression of being

---

Practical and reflective task

Level 1

Try a similar exercise with this example. This time, it is a piece of Year 4 mathematics work being marked. Improve on the teacher's rather terse comments with about five lines of feedback supporting assessment for learning.

Better answers – more accurate. Workings not shown.

Level 2

Find a piece of summative feedback you have given to a child and try to make it more formative and motivating. Monitor the effect on the child.

Level 3

Monitor the effect on whole-school ethos of a more formative and motivating system of feedback to children.

---

solid, objective measures based upon an exact science, when in fact they are often rushed approximations. Grades can sometimes distract the learner from more nuanced comments and targets that follow. 'No point in reading the teacher's comments; I got a D and I'm useless.' These disadvantages become even more pronounced if teachers use national levels to assess specific pieces of work, a practice the level statements were never designed for. Occasionally, it is interesting and helpful for a teacher to abandon grades and rely solely on comments, focusing the pupils on the formative process and the goals rather than on the summative statements. In so far as grades end a conversation, they are unhelpful; in so far as they lead to a conversation about goals, they are useful.

In AfL, marking and feedback are contextualized, so that the teacher is able to tailor judgements, comments and goals to suit pupil needs. Comments and conversation have more capacity to do this than grades. An effective teacher, knowing the class well, is able to tell the difference between a pupil's characteristic or normal performance (called a trait) and the same pupil's actual or specific performance in a particular setting (a state) (Anderson 2003: 107). This personal knowledge of pupils, of what makes them tick and what is likely to cause them to perform better or worse, is a crucial ingredient of AfL.

What are the challenges of using AfL?

This section poses some of the frequently asked questions about AfL, exposing some of its disadvantages as well as discussing its potential.

What is the evidence that AfL raises national standards?

The drive to raise standards in primary schools has produced interesting side-effects. There is little doubt that teachers have responded to league-table pressure by 'teaching to the test' more frequently, and more effectively, than ever before. Inevitably, this means that teachers have tilted their strategy towards assessment of learning. To reverse this strategy, and assess in ways that are more embedded in teaching, might carry a danger that pupils are less well prepared for national tests, and that standards could therefore fall.

This begs the all-important question of what we mean by standards. If we care most of all about results in end of key stage tests, then undoubtedly we should prepare pupils to succeed in them, and tailor our teaching and learning cycles accordingly. We should get pupils used to this form of assessment by giving it to them frequently. On the other hand, if we wish to pay more attention to the inner process of learning that takes place between tests, we are more likely to unite assessment with teaching and learning. The principles and practice of AfL suggest that it produces pupils who not only know, but also know what they know (Black and Wiliam 2004); who can step back from their new-found knowledge, understanding or skill, show the way they came, and, with help, point to the next steps – in short, pupils with metacognition. There is some evidence that national testing has done little or nothing to improve this quality in pupils, and may even have diminished it (Weeden et al. 2002: 5). For pupils who do show metacognition independently, their ability is often more complex and less easily measurable, so it will not always translate into higher grades and levels. Even so, it is surely worth having.

AfL relies on a close relationship between teacher and pupils. How can a teacher use AfL and still administer professionally credible assessment?

In AfL, a teacher's involvement in pupil progress is intense. We have seen how it involves a radical transformation from external judgement to formative, personalized support. But any form of assessment that seeks credibility must be valid, reliable and manageable. Validity means that an assessment must measure only what it sets out to measure: for example, a geography test should not mark a pupil's drawing ability, and an RE test should not mark a pupil's writing ability. Reliability means that if the same piece of assessed work were marked by two teachers, it would gain the same result: this is achieved through having clear criteria that can be applied by any qualified person. Manageability means that the assessment can be conducted without disrupting the school's life, in particular teaching.

The challenge in AfL is for teachers to maintain their close dialogue with pupils while also being distant and objective enough to administer assessment that is valid, reliable and manageable. Manageability presents few problems for AfL, as it is designed to be integrated in teaching and learning. Likewise, validity is no more an issue in AfL than it is in other assessments. Reliability is more challenging: teachers will wish to personalize learning and assessment in order to give pupils their best opportunity. We saw in the section on marking and feedback that teachers could distinguish between trait and state; yet a reliable test must look only at state, ignoring background issues. Here there are tensions that teachers and schools must negotiate carefully and with professional integrity.

How can ICT be harnessed to support AfL?

For all sorts of reasons, to do with both professional change and financial constraints, the advance of ICT in education has been slower than predicted or hoped. AfL, while based on conversation, does offer new opportunities, and indeed creates new demands, for new applications of technology.

There is no technical reason why ICT cannot be used in the service of teacher–pupil conversation to support AfL. ICT can devise questions, log pupils' work, replay their steps and point out their progress or lapses. In doing this, it could reduce teacher workload (Richardson 2003). Among the many possibilities that ICT offers, simulated micro-worlds can give pupils problem-solving exercises that test their knowledge, understanding or skills in a new context. Data-based investigations and modelling, spreadsheet investigations and problem solving can test mathematical knowledge. Text annotation can test use of language or understanding and interpretation of sources. Multi-media authoring can be used as a basis for self- or peer assessment. These and many other examples show that there is no intrinsic contradiction between AfL and ICT applications.

There is, however, a potential tension between ICT and validity. Where ICT is used to test understanding that is not technical, the extent of mastery of the information technology itself can come between the pupil's true ability and their test performance. Pupils with greater ICT mastery have longer for the task, feel more confident and may produce a performance that looks more credible. In no other sphere is the danger of invalidity so great. This is a challenge for all forms of assessment.

Is the revolution over, or does AfL have further surprises for us?

AfL, especially when validly supported by information technology, offers further advances. It could liberate schools and the state from administering tests all at the same time. The possibility of testing a pupil when ready, rather than at a time set by the state, becomes more real. The prize would be a better balance between assessment that confirms and progresses learning, and assessment that guarantees external accountability (Richardson 2003).

In the longer term, AfL holds out the possibility of gains in pupil motivation, participation, self-esteem and capacity to work productively. These, when translated into the adult world, become gains in family life, social cohesion and economic success. A successful AfL strategy produces pupils and adults with deeper access to problem-solving strategies, better collaboration skills, and stronger resilience when confronted with failure or misfortune.

Conclusion

Assessment for learning does not change assessment solely. It transforms learning, and has the potential to shape a different future for society. It calls for a more interactive, democratic and shared treatment of knowledge, understanding and skills. It radically transforms the patterns of teaching and learning, giving shared ownership of feedback and goals. It requires teacher professionalism and pupil engagement in order to succeed. It carries with it some dangers and difficulties in relation to reliable assessment. Yet it also challenges some widely held assumptions about assessment and the standards agenda. It challenges teachers and pupils to think and act differently.

References

Anderson, L. (2003) *Classroom Assessment: Enhancing the Quality of Teacher Decision Making*. Hillsdale, NJ: Erlbaum Associates.

Black, P. (2003) *Assessment for Learning: Putting it into Practice*. Buckingham: Open University Press.

Black, P. and Wiliam, D. (1998) *Inside the Black Box: Raising Standards Through Classroom Assessment*. London: King's College.

Black, P. and Wiliam, D. (2004) *Working Inside the Black Box: Assessment for Learning in the Classroom*. London: Nelson.

DES (1988) *A Report: National Task Group on Assessment and Testing*. London: DES.

DfEE (1999) *The National Curriculum: Handbook for Teachers in England*. London: DfEE/QCA.

DfES (2007) Statutory Framework for the Early Years Foundation Stage; Setting the Standards for Learning, Development and Care children from birth to five. *Every Child Matters, Change for Children*. London: DfES.

Osborne, J., Black P., Smith, M. and Meadows, J. (1991) *Primary SPACE – Light*. Liverpool: Liverpool University Press.

QCA (2003) *Foundation Stage Profile*. London: QCA.

Richardson, C. (ed.) (2003) *Whither Assessment?* London: QCA.

Rousseau, J-J. (1911) *Emile*. London: J. M. Dent & Sons (first published 1762).

Weeden, P., Winter, J. and Broadfoot, P. (2002) *Assessment: What's in it for Schools?* London: Routledge.

12

Target Setting

Richard Woolley and Jane Johnston

Introduction

We are constantly setting ourselves targets for personal development and improvement. Target setting is not a new phenomenon, but it is one that has gained increasing prominence in education in recent times. This chapter begins by looking at what target setting in education is and who it is for. It will continue by considering how to develop and reflect on targets with individuals and groups of primary aged children.

What is target setting?

A target is an outcome that we commit ourselves to achieving, and target setting enables all concerned to continuously improve both teaching and learning for groups of professionals and children. Targets can be long, medium or short term. Long-term targets are statements of where we want to be in, say, three to five years' time. Medium-term targets indicate where we want to be in a term or a year. Short-term targets identify what we hope to achieve in the next week or two and they represent the steps we take to achieve both the medium-term and the long-term targets.

Target setting exists in all aspects of business and service and are part of good performance monitoring and management. Performance indicators – proxy measures to help us assess whether we are achieving our objectives – are an important element in performance management. National assessment and league tables provide national and local performance indicators and enable schools to set targets or specific goals to improve. Teacher appraisal and inspection can provide individual performance indicators to allow individual teachers to set personal targets. Assessment, marking and individual teaching can help children to set individual targets to support their learning. In this way, target setting is an integral part of planning teaching and assessing and should not be viewed as a statistical or administrative process carried out by managers and headteachers, the local authorities or the government.

Target setting is an important part of the process of learning and teaching. It can help members of staff to focus on the specific needs of individual children or small groups and to support children by helping them to understand the next steps they need to take. Teaching assistants, teachers and children can work in partnership to identify targets and to review them on a regular basis. Small-step targets, developed collaboratively, provide opportunities for children to be clear about teachers' expectations and what they need to work towards in order to take their own learning and development further. It is important that targets are SMART (DfEE 2001: 15), that is: specific, measurable, achievable, realistic and time-related.

Specific targets are those that are clear, understood by everyone involved and relate to an aspect of teaching and learning, improving the quality of teaching and learning for all involved. Good targets have a specific focus with an area for 'development, improvement and enhancement' (Primary National Strategy 2005: 14). They should be measurable, so that input, output and outcome can be seen and success is obvious. The measurement does not need to be quantitative, but it does need to contain a means of measurement or it will be difficult to assess how well you are doing in achieving the target. Targets need to stretch, but they should be achievable or they will frustrate and contribute nothing. SMART targets are realistic and achievable in a timescale that is identified and are not too numerous or set in stone.

Practical task

Identifying SMART targets

Level 1

Identify which of the following targets are SMART.
- To improve reading.
- To sit quietly during story time for the rest of the week.
- To be able to catch a ball six times out of ten.
- To stop shouting out in class this year.
- To use a capital letter at the start of each sentence in a piece of writing.
- To learn how to save work in Word on the computer by the end of term.
- To be able to use the index of a book.
- To learn how to read.

How can you make them all SMART?

Level 2

Identify SMART targets for specific children in your class. Get a colleague to help you check that they are all SMART.

Level 3

Identify SMART targets for your school. These may be taken from your school improvement plan. Share them with your colleagues and check that they are SMART. Discuss with your colleagues how you can put these targets into practice.

Who is target setting for?

Who do you think target setting is for? Is it for individuals, groups, classes or schools?

Practical and reflective task

Level 1
Identify reasons why target setting is important for individuals.

Level 2
Identify reasons why target setting is important for groups of children or your class.

Level 3
Identify why target setting is important for your school.

Individual targets are important to help teachers identify their personal and professional aims and to help children identify and work towards their personal and educational development. The identification and development of individual targets help individuals take ownership and control of their development. It does not mean that the individual does not need support in order to develop the targets, but it does mean that the target is more likely to be successful if both the individual and those who work and support them are clear on what the target is and how it can be developed. Professionals identify targets through appraisal, and these may focus on an aspect of their work with children (teaching or support of learning) or professionalism or management of behaviour and so on. These targets are usually negotiated during appraisal and so the individual professional takes ownership of the target and is supported by the appraiser to identify steps to achieve the target, a timescale for achievement and any support needed to enable the target to be achieved. Individual targets for children should similarly be negotiated with the child, with clear, achievable steps, a timescale for achievement as well as identification of support needed.

In one class of primary children, each child had an individual target related to the construction of sentences. Some children had to be able to write a sentence beginning with a capital letter and ending with a full stop. Other children had to write sentences using commas or other punctuation marks. Others had to ensure that their sentence had a verb and noun. The targets were decided as a result of self- and teacher assessment of their written work, identifying the next stage in the development of their written work. Each child had their target written on a piece of card, and at the start of each writing activity they were reminded of their target and they placed the card above their books so it was visible while they were writing. The teacher and teaching assistant focused on the target when looking at the writing with the child and the child was encouraged to look at their writing with their personal target in mind. Differentiated target setting is also described in Chapter 7, Differentiation.

Group targets can be useful where groups of individuals have the same or similar targets and can support each other in working towards their achievement. Groups may also have a common or shared target, so a team of teachers in one year group or key stage may share a target to teach in a more cross-curricular way or to incorporate ICT into their teaching. Of course, these targets would have to be SMARTer than this in that they would have to be more specific and have clear ways in which achievement can be evidenced within a time frame. Children may also have group targets. These may be social or behavioural, where a group or class needs to focus on an aspect of behaviour, such as cooperation with peers or respect for others in the playground. An example of group behavioural target setting is described later in this chapter.

Group targets may also be educational. In the example described above of targets relating to the construction of sentences, children may be grouped according to ability, with the same targets set for children working beside each other in one ability group. Children at this table can help each other to focus on the target for their group, by reminding each other, especially if the group is working independently. If the group is working under the guidance of an adult, then the adult and other children in the group can remind the group of the target at appropriate times during the activity. Group targets can be written on card and placed in the centre of a table where children are working. The cards might be held in individual card or picture holders which can be obtained from gift shops or department stores. Some of these come in the shape of animals or flowers and in different colours and so each table can have a different target holder in the middle of the table. If these holders are used then the card probably needs laminating and the target written on each side, so all the children can see it. If a dry wipe pen is used, then the target can be renewed at regular intervals.

School targets may emerge from the School Improvement Plan (SIP) and be identified through inspection. These may be curricular targets based on learning objectives from the relevant curriculum, identified by analysis of children's work, discussions with children, teacher assessment information and test performance. The Primary National Strategy into the birth to five phase has identified how staff in the early years can support curricular target setting in ISP (Intensifying Support Programme) schools (Primary National Strategy 2005). An ISP is a school improvement programme targeted schools performing below average and emphasizes a whole-school approach to raising standards, improving teaching and learning, improving the conditions for learning and developing the school as a learning community. Whole-school curricular targets are used to these ends, raising standards, improving the pace of developments, and focusing on a whole-school approach to, and responsibility for, improvement. The process involves a layering of targets that begin with whole-school curricular targets which are translated into year group targets; age-related targets that inform teaching, learning and assessing. Curricular year group targets can also be translated into targets for classes, groups and even individuals, based on personal achievements. School target setting is not new and may involve scrutiny of test data and analysis of the school's strengths and weaknesses in core subject areas and the targeting of groups and individuals in order to raise performance and standards. Clearly, there does need to be coherence between the different levels of target setting, so that:

- the targets have clear relevance to the school's improvement plan (SIP);
- the targets have appropriate theoretical underpinning and knowledge relevant for the educational stage and how children learn;
- the targets provide opportunities for children to take ownership of their own development.

The Primary National Strategy (2005) provides an example from the Foundation Stage of a setting's curricular target to improve personal interpretation and response to literature, which the Foundation Stage professionals decided to develop through the use of talk and role-play in response to a shared story (see Figure 12.1).

Whole-School Focus
Interpretation and response to literary text

↓

Layered Year 2 Group Targets
Begin to understand the effects of different words and phrases,
e.g. to create humour, images and atmosphere
Consider which of the scale points of the *Foundation Stage Profile*
(QCA 2003) these targets might relate most closely to. In this case,
the practitioner might choose the following:

↓

- Use imagination to recreate roles and experiences
- Use talk to organize, sequence and clarify thinking, ideas,
feeling and events
At this point, many other choices could be made on the basis
of the learning needs of the children

Figure 12.1 Informed target setting in language development – developing success criteria for children's end of key stage achievement to improve teaching (Primary National Strategy 2005: 10)

Developing targets with children

Targets can be cognitive, physical (skill-based) or social / behavioural. A cognitive target could be to know or understand something, such as to know and recount five facts. A physical target could be to be able to catch a ball five times out of ten; whereas a skill-based target could be to form the letter 'p' correctly in a piece of writing. A social or behavioural target would focus on the development of social skills and interaction with others, and so it may be that a child's target is to wait patiently for their turn to speak to the class. It is most important that social and behavioural targets are positive in that they should focus on positive behaviours and not negative ones. The target to 'wait patiently turn to speak to the class' is positive; 'not to speak out of turn' is negative. Targets can also be subject specific or generic, so a child may have a target to be able to use books to collect facts or to be able to recount five facts about the Romans. Targets may also be individual or group or even be targets for the whole class, year group or school. Individual and small-group targets are more likely to be cognitive and subject specific or skill based, whereas class and school targets are more likely to be social and behavioural and generic. For example, a target of walking in the school may be set for a individual, a specific class, year group or even the whole school, whereas to know how to use the index of a book is more likely to be set for an individual, group or class, and to be able to skip five times is more likely to be set for an individual or group.

When starting the target-setting process it is important to support children and to help them to develop the skills necessary for identifying realistic small steps. In many cases a child will be aware of their particular need; however, their knowledge and understanding of the process necessary to address that need may be limited.

Reflective task

Individual targets; giving Matthew choices
by Richard Woolley

Matthew was aware that sometimes he responded angrily to other children. He was among the most able in his numeracy class, but felt that the other children in his group 'wound him up'. We discussed his behaviour and it appeared that members of his group were well aware that they could subtly provoke him to the point where he used inappropriate language and became aggressive. It was difficult to monitor the situation, as my proximity to the group affected the actions of the children. Matthew and I agreed that when he felt uncomfortable with the other children he would move away to a quiet area in the classroom and work on his own. He had permission to move at a time of his own choosing, and we agreed a target: 'To move to a quiet place when I feel I will work best on my own.' The target did not work immediately. In the early stages I needed to give reminders to move to the quiet place. Sometimes he would lose his temper, pick up his work and stamp across to his individual table. However, over time he began to react to the situation earlier and his outbursts became less frequent. Ultimately the result of Matthew learning to make the choice to walk away from trouble was that the group tried to trigger his anger less frequently: without the desired outcome there was less point in taunting him.

This target addressed several important areas. Firstly, it provided the opportunity to speak with Matthew about the situation and to assure him that I wanted to support him. Secondly, it provided him with an additional choice: to become aggressive, to lose his temper, or to walk away at a time of his choosing. Thirdly, it provided me with an indication of the situation with the group, and with an opportunity to praise Matthew for his mature approach to the situation. Most importantly, it acknowledged

cont.

that I believed that Matthew had the potential to cope with the situation, and provided him with a strategy to do this.

Level 1

Choose one social or behavioural target. This may involve an issue you have experienced in the past. Identify how you can ensure the target is SMART.

Level 2

Set a target for a child you teach who has an individual social or behavioural need.
- How have you ensured the target is SMART?
- How can you involve the child in setting the target?
- How will you monitor the success of the target?

Level 3

Set a social or behavioural target for your school.
- How have you ensured the target is SMART?
- How will you involve all teachers and children in setting the target?
- How will you monitor the success of the target?

Developing group support

Six boys in upper Key Stage 2 were identified as having particular behaviour difficulties which were affecting both their own learning and that of others in their classes. It was decided that the group should meet with a member of staff for half an hour at the end of each week to review progress and to set targets for the coming week. The children were not a part of each other's friendship groups; however, after a couple of weeks they began to comment on each other's targets and the progress (or otherwise) that they had observed during the week. An important aspect of this process was that the boys did not compare themselves with one another, but focused on reviewing their own achievements, and those of others, in their own right (MacGrath 2000).

I (RW) was surprised by the targets that the boys set for themselves and for each other; they were greater in number than I would have desired. The targets were recorded on a personal sheet decorated with graphics of their choosing, with a grid to indicate whether they had been met in each lesson. The children had to decide how many times they would meet their targets during each week in order to receive a reward with the group. The boys chose their own rewards, usually involving food, for example baking buns or icing biscuits. They set high expectations for themselves, and initially I was concerned that they were setting themselves up to fail. While success is a tremendous motivator, as are praise and recognition, choice is an important factor that must not be overlooked. It allows the development of independence and personal freedom (MacGrath 2000) and helps the children to take ownership of the process. By choosing their reward the children had a vested interest in achieving the targets that they had also chosen.

An example of one chart included the following targets:

- If I have something to say I will put up my hand and wait quietly for my teacher to deal with me.
- I will listen to what my teacher says to me and I will follow instructions at the first time of asking.
- I will stay in my seat unless I am given permission to leave it.
- I will treat others in a kindly way.

Each target was phrased carefully and in a positive manner (Rogers 2001). The focus was on success rather than avoidance. The first three targets seemed ambitious but did address directly the elements of behaviour that caused disruption to lessons. The final target seemed, to me, to be too general, but again addressed verbal and physical behaviours that distracted other children. I was able to share my responses to the targets with the child, but he decided that he would proceed with the targets and work towards them. In the early stages of target setting it was important that my discussions with the children provided an opportunity to model effective and achievable targets and allowed the children to explain why the targets they chose were appropriate and realistic (MacGrath 2000). Bassey (1989) maintains that children should always know what they are expected to do, where and when the teacher wants it to be done and what it is that they should do next. Developing a small range of clearly focused targets provided the children with the scaffolding to support these outcomes.

The project relied on the goodwill of teachers to complete the target grids after each lesson and to support the idea of rewarding the boys for improved good behaviour. The impact was startling. Despite setting ambitious targets, and expecting themselves to achieve the targets with a high degree of regularity, the boys managed to achieve their aims nearly every week. Generally, they enjoyed the attention received at the end of each lesson. The fact that if they failed to meet a target in one lesson then there was a fresh start in the next worked well. Both teachers and children were aware of the goals and this made it possible for staff to offer gentle reminders during lessons to focus on the targets and to work towards achieving them. This was particularly important in the early stages of the project. In all this, fairness was fundamental. By agreeing expectations in advance, some of the emotion was taken out of later situations (Rogers 2001: 47). The children were aware of the consequence if they failed to meet a target in one particular lesson. They also understood that it would be unfair on the rest of the group if the teacher ignored their inappropriate behaviour and indicated that the target had been achieved. By making expectations explicit, all involved in the process understood the ground rules and worked towards similar goals. Although the language used is always open to interpretation because 'there is always a qualitative change between what we mean and the words we choose to express it' (Jacques and Hyland 2003: 109–10), the targets provided a clear framework to help the children to work towards restructuring their behaviour. Members of staff were also given a clear set of criteria by which to measure success.

The boys kept the grids on their tables as a point of reference. While each child did not always achieve his reward each week, the review of targets and the discussion about why this was the case provided a supportive setting in which to aim for progress in the next week. Indeed, it was important that those who failed to achieve their goal did not receive the reward and understood the reasons for this. This maintained a sense of fairness that the children appreciated. A sense of fairness throughout the whole process was key to its success.

A key issue that arose from the project was the need to reward children whose behaviour was always good. Members of staff felt this to be important in order to maintain a sense of fairness. While the improvement in the learning environment gained from targeting a key group of children was positive, it was important to acknowledge that other children consistently approached their learning and relationships in positive and constructive ways and they deserved acknowledgement for this. It was also important to ensure that all the members of staff involved were willing to work with the system. 'Incentives need to be discussed within the school's philosophy about rewards as balanced with encouragement. Some teachers have strong philosophical objections to rewards or incentives and this needs to be taken into account if school-wide incentive programs are used' (Rogers 2001: 41). In this case the project was small scale and did not impinge on the whole school. However, it was important to ensure that it complemented whole-school policies for behaviour management, praise and rewards. Barrow *et al.* (2001) provide an interesting discussion of the nature of such agreements and the ways in which they need to fit within the overall ethos and structures of a school. It is important to ensure that the structures developed to support disaffected or 'difficult' pupils do not alienate other children or cause tensions among members of staff and thus create further issues.

Reflective task

The following questions relate to the group target setting example above.

Level 1
- What factors may lead to the success or failure of the process?
- How do you think the majority of children who consistently behave appropriately would feel during the process?
- What could you do to reward their good behaviour?

Level 2
Identify the problems you might experience in adopting this approach in your class.
- How would you overcome the problems in your class?
- What strategies could you adopt to reward the majority of children who consistently behave appropriately and often remain unacknowledged?

cont.

Level 3

Identify the problems you might experience in adopting this approach in your school / setting.

- How might a range of staff and children respond to this approach with a targeted group of children?
- How might children and staff share their views on the fairness of the process?
- How else could you monitor the process?

Targets and personal learning

If the focus of the learning process is to be on the development of children's skills, the children need to become active participants in identifying what successful learning entails. Involving children in identifying success criteria for an activity is an important part of this process and provides opportunities to make clear expectations, to review and to reinforce key skills.

Working on a non-fiction text over the period of a week, children developed a summary of the life of a famous person from the Victorian era, in the style of an autobiography. Laura chose to research the life of Elizabeth Fry. Having worked in this genre before, and having noted its main features as a part of whole-class text-level work, she was able to draft her own success criteria for the writing task:

- To write in the first person.
- To include the character's feelings.
- To include three facts.
- To use paragraphs.
- To include direct speech.

The use of paragraphs did not relate specifically to the focus of the task, but did reflect a comment that I (RW) had made on a previous piece of Laura's work. I was able to review the success criteria before they were used: Laura thus set her own targets for the work, they were reviewed and agreed by her teacher, and they provided focused support during the process of writing up her research. The earlier discussion of a text provided support and ideas to help with the identification of the targets.

At the conclusion of the process, Laura used her checklist to comment on her own work. She ticked each target to indicate that she felt that she had achieved her goals and wrote a brief overall comment. Others in the class undertook the same process, with many having chosen similar areas on which to focus. Laura was thus able to explain what she felt that she had achieved using a format that did not take a great deal of time to complete. When marking her work I noted that although she thought she had used direct speech she had in fact used indirect speech to report a conversation. I was able to comment on this and to target support in a following lesson. The marking process was transparent: Laura and I had agreed the criteria that we were to work to, and I was able to concur with her judgements for the most part.

A strength of this approach is the introduction of regular target setting that focuses on a specific piece of work or project. It provides the opportunity for all children in a class to have specific targets to work towards, and the processes of reflection, review and marking involve both child and teacher in commenting on what is intended and what has been achieved. As the children and members of staff become familiar with the process and develop their skills, the novelty of the activity is replaced by an appreciation of its importance – even to the point of the children reminding the teacher that targets need to be set before drafting can commence.

Taking on a key role in the target-setting process enables children to become intrinsically motivated learners: they identify their own aims and work towards them; they can evaluate their own progress and gain pleasure from experiencing success; and they become able to sustain effort and try out alternative approaches even when experiencing difficulties (DfES 2004: 46).

Practical and reflective tasks
Setting individual targets

Level 1
Examine the work in Figure 12.2 and identify what the child's target would be. What small steps would help them to reach that target. How could you support them through your teaching?

Level 2
Examine a piece of work completed by a child in a recent lesson. Consider what questions you could share with the child to help them to identify next steps and to help them to agree targets. Try this out and monitor how you support the child.

Level 3
Discuss with your staff how you might encourage children in your school to work collaboratively to review each other's targets and to give constructive feedback? How might this develop their learning? Try out some of your ideas and monitor their progress.

Reflection and review

Target setting and review is one part of the assessment process, whether this be an assessment of learning or of behaviour. If it is addressed in a cooperative manner with staff and children working together, with parents / carers as appropriate, then it can foster greater independence and help the children to set realistic expectations for themselves (MacGrath 2000). Indeed,

At its best, target setting can give a sense of purpose and direction, for individual pupils as well as for whole groups, especially if both pupils and teachers are party to the process, rather than the victims of it. At its worst, however, a sense of desperation to meet targets will override professional judgement about what needs to be done and will distort, rather than enhance, the educational process.

(Wragg 2001: 84)

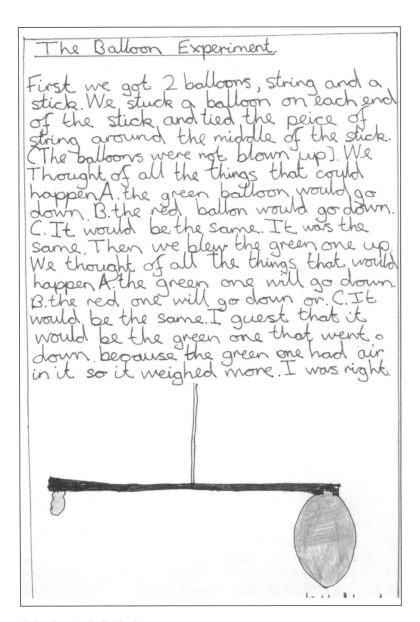

Figure 12.2 Setting individual targets

Setting targets will not make a positive impact upon children's development unless it is supported by a collaborative process. Children need to feel that their targets are realistic, achievable and fair. They also need to develop respect for the integrity of their teacher during discussions about their achievement of, or failure to achieve, their targets. If they feel that the process is unfair, that decisions are too lenient or that they are inconsistent, the whole process will be undermined and the process will compound the difficulties that it was intended to resolve. If teachers do not make success criteria overt by developing targets, they are denying the children the opportunity to succeed; it is demoralizing to be assessed against hidden criteria, like trying to win a game without being told the rules.

At best, the teacher will also identify personal targets to work towards in the classroom, thus modelling the process so that the children can support them and offer praise at appropriate moments. Agreeing clear expectations is an effective way of motivating children and of providing small steps to facilitate their learning: they are aware of what is needed for them to succeed and can work towards this success with greater confidence and independence (Jacques and Hyland 2003). Teachers can model this process and can ensure that it becomes an accepted part of classroom routines. At its best, target setting provides a clear indication to all parties of what is to be achieved, and the reflection that follows helps to identify the next small steps in the continuum of learning.

Reflective questions

- How can the process of setting and reviewing targets be made manageable?
- How can children be enabled to take ownership of the targets?
- How might others react to the target-setting process (including other children, staff, parents/carers)
- What role should rewards play, and how can new behaviours or achievements be maintained in the medium and long term?
- How can targets be developed and reviewed in a positive atmosphere which focuses on opportunities for learning rather than on disappointment and negative stress.

References

Barrow, G., Bradshaw, E. and Newton, T. (2001) *Improving Behaviour and Raising Self-esteem in the Classroom*. London: David Fulton.

Bassey, M. (1989) *Teaching Practice in the Primary School*. East Grinstead: Ward Lock Educational.

DfEE (2001) *Supporting the Target Setting Process*. Nottingham: DfEE.

DfES (2004) *Excellence and Enjoyment: Learning and Teaching in the Primary Years – Learning to Learn: Progression in Key Aspects of Learning*. Norwich: HMSO.

Jacques, K. and Hyland, R. (2003) *Professional Studies: Primary Phase*. Exeter: Learning Matters.

MacGrath, M. (2000) *The Art of Peaceful Teaching in the Primary School*. London: David Fulton.

Primary National Strategy (2005) *Developing the Foundations for Curricular Target Setting in ISP Schools: Birth to Five* London: DfES / Sure Start.

Rogers, B. (2001) *Behaviour Management*. London: Paul Chapman.

Wragg, E. C. (2001) *Assessment and Learning in the Primary School*. London: RoutledgeFalmer.

13

Professional
Communication

Jane Johnston

Introduction

Communication is a skill unique to social animals. Many animals communicate through pheromones, gesture, noise and expression, but only humans communicate through complex social speech, combined with body language, emphasis and gesture. In teaching, communication is of vital importance, so that professionals, carers, children and all connected with teaching and learning can work effectively together. This chapter considers what learning partnerships are and how professionals can develop their communication skills to benefit their teaching and the children's learning.

Learning partnerships

In education, there are many individuals and groups that need to work together in an effective partnership. A learning partnership (Figure 13.1; see also Johnston 2002), consists of two levels:

1 the everyday partnership that occurs in the classroom;
2 the wider partnership that influences teaching and learning.

Bronfenbrenner, in his ecological systems theory (Bronfenbrenner 1995; Bronfenbrenner and Evans 2000) identifies four levels, which together form a complex social system affected by relationships and the surrounding environments. The microsystem involves relationships with those most close to the child – family, teachers, classroom assistants, peers in the class – as well as the wider school and community in which they live, work and play. The microsystem has an effect on the child's behaviour, although not their innate characteristics (physical attributes, personality, abilities). The next level is the mesosystem. This involves professional communication and interactions between the different aspects of the microsystem – home, school, childcare and so on. These interactions can affect the child's social,

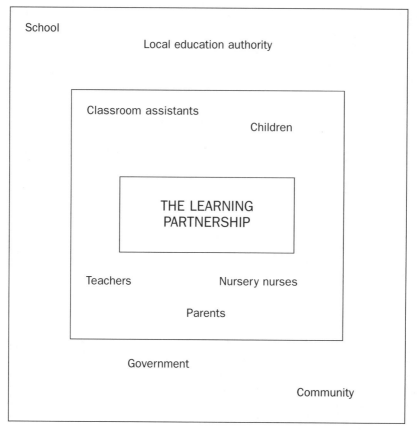

Figure 13.1   The learning partnership (from Johnston 2002: 31)

psychological and cognitive development, in other words they can greatly influence learning. The third level is the exosystem, which includes indirect interactions and informal support for the child from extended family, friends, neighbours, workplace, church and community ties as well as more formal support such as community and welfare services. While their influence is indirect and does not affect social and psychological development, it is felt that poor relationships in the exosystem are likely to be linked to increased conflict and child abuse (Emery and Laumann-Billings 1998). The final level and the one furthest removed from the child, is the macrosystem. This involves the cultural values, laws, customs and resources which affect the support children receive in the microsystem. Changes in curricular demands, social changes and financial changes within the government are examples of influences in the macrosystem.

Reflective task
Professional partnerships

Level 1

List the different types of partnerships in your life. How do your role and responsibilities change in each partnership? Map out the professional partnerships you have experienced in an educational context and identify if they belong to Brofennbrenner's (1995) microsystem, mesosystem, exosystem or macrosystem. Which professional partnership do you need to develop most? How can you do this?

Level 2

List the different partnerships you have in your professional life. Do these partnerships belong to Brofennbrenner's (1995) microsystem, mesosystem, exosystem or macrosystem? How do your role and responsibilities change in each partnership? What partnerships do you feel you need to develop and why? How could you develop these partnerships?

Level 3

Consider Brofennbrenner's (1995) systems and decide which one poses the most challenges in your setting / school. Analyse your role in the partnerships in this system and the factors that make the partnership challenging. How can you develop this partnership to make it less stressful / more effective / more supportive of school development and teaching and learning?

Communicating with other professionals

Effective teaching and learning involves effective day-to-day partnerships in the classroom and effective communication between professionals. The importance of professional communication is clearly identified in the professional standards for higher-level teaching assistants (TDA 2006a), qualified teacher status (TDA 2006b) and early years professionals (CWDC 2006). However there are many other professionals indirectly involved in the education and care of children, albeit on a more occasional as well as indirect basis. These include subject and special educational needs coordinators (SENCOs), health visitors, educational psychologists, speech therapists, physiotherapists, educational welfare officers, student teachers and teaching assistants, and tutors in further education and higher education. The partnership between these professionals is often quite complex, with changing roles and responsibilities for individual professionals depending on the context and reason for communication. However, the main purpose of the communication and partnership should remain the same, that is, to support development and learning in children.

An effective professional partnership is one that is built on trust in the abilities and expertise of other professionals and trust in their desire to further children's learning and development. In an early years setting, children are often unaware of the different expertise, experience, role and responsibilities of teachers, teaching assistants, students and other adult helpers, although these may be significantly different. Teachers will know about the early years curriculum (DfEE 1999b; DfES 2007; DfES 2006b) and how children learn; learning and teaching assistants often have in-depth knowledge of childcare and child development; together they can provide quality and effective support for children's educational, social, emotional and physical development.

Research and reflection on professional communication
by Claire Taylor, Bishop Grosseteste University College Lincoln

Cajkler *et al.* (2006) have conducted an extensive literature review focusing on the perceptions of ways in which support staff work to support pupils' social and academic engagement in primary classrooms. The 17 studies analysed in depth focused on primary schools in the European Union. The studies confirm that teaching assistants have an important pedagogical role, but that this is dependent upon the guidance of teachers and senior managers in schools. Therefore, the implications for good lines of communication in the classroom are clear, particularly as teaching assistants believe that they are 'acting as a bridge between teacher and pupil' (Cajkler *et al.* 2006: 4). In this respect, teachers are responsible for planning for the inclusion of the teaching assistant and need to ensure that the 'bridging' contribution of the teaching assistant facilitates pupil learning. This implies close partnership working and sound communication between teacher and teaching assistant, with shared understandings of curriculum planning and expectations for pupil achievement.

Working with support staff and volunteers
What's in a name?
The job titles of those who support teachers in schools are many and various. For example, you may have come across the following: classroom assistant, learning support assistant, 1:1 support assistant, teaching assistant, child support assistant, special needs assistant, non-teaching assistant, general assistant, specialist teaching assistant, ancillary, welfare assistant. All of these titles are now generally covered by the umbrella term 'teaching assistant' (TA) but the role of the TA is still a wide and varied one, covering the following:
- support for pupil, teacher, curriculum, school;
- enabling pupils to participate academically and socially, and with more independence;
- helping to raise standards of achievement.

In addition, a TA may find themself working with a particular pupil, with a small group, with a whole class, or a combination of these over a 'typical' week in school. Therefore, it is important that you know who is supporting you within the classroom and what their role is.

cont.

A step-by-step guide to working with teaching assistants
- Find out who may be supporting your class. When are they timetabled to be with you? Are they supporting 1:1 special educational needs (SEN) work, or small groups, or could they cover your planning, preparation and assessment (PPA) time?
- Talk to your TA. What experience do they have? What qualifications do they hold? Do they have particular areas of expertise?
- Consider how your TA could be used to enhance teaching and learning. Think about before, during and after each lesson. Do they have a role in assessment of pupils? Do individuals, groups or the whole class need support?
- How will you communicate effectively with your TA? What systems are currently used? Do they work?

Reflecting upon professional communication
'The effectiveness of the team is bound, to a degree, to depend on personalities, but the way the relationship is managed will also determine the degree of success. Discussions with colleagues who work in a variety of settings, reveal wide variations in the degree of communication within the Learning Support team. However, those TAs who play an active part in planning, discussing the children's barriers to learning and contribute to the assessment of pupils, not only feel more able to support the children's learning and to contribute to future planning, but feel more valued themselves'.
Glenys (ex-teaching assistant and now qualified teacher, Nottingham)

The importance of professional communication between teaching and non-teaching staff is identified in a case study (NCSL 2006) where a third party adviser facilitated professional dialogue as part of the workforce remodelling and the introduction of 10 per cent PPA time. The use of a 'critical friend', mentor or adviser can facilitate effective professional communication and solve professional challenges, bringing professional partners closer in understanding and purpose. Workforce remodelling created some challenges to professional communication, as teachers were concerned about teaching assistants undertaking traditional teaching roles, and teaching assistants felt that they were undervalued by some teaching colleagues. With effective communication, these misunderstandings can be remedied and all professionals work together more effectively. For example, as well as undertaking PPA time, teaching assistants are ideally placed to observe pupil performance when children are working as a whole class, group and individually. Trained teaching assistants can work with teachers to assess children's achievements, although there are some important communications involved:

- Teachers need to communicate the intended learning outcomes / success criteria with teaching assistants.
- Both teachers and assistants need to communicate to identify quality time to prepare and plan time effectively in order to ensure meaningful assessments.

- Assessment opportunities, the types of assessment and strategies to be used, and the role of the teacher and teaching assistant in these assessments needs to be well communicated.
- After the assessments, teachers and assistants need to agree assessment decisions.

There are a number of assessment activities that teaching assistants use to make assessments, such as using puppets as talking partners (Keogh *et al.* 2006; see also Chapter 9, Supporting Children in Recording Work), analysing concepts and observing children interacting (see also Chapter 11, Assessment for Learning).

Picture 13.1 Teachers practising using puppets as an assessment tool

Reflective task

Level 1
Reflect on some teaching you have been involved in as a student teacher, classroom assistant or adult helper.
- How well were the learning objectives / success criteria communicated to you?
- Were you clear about your role in the classroom?
- How could communication in the classroom have been improved?
- What will you do on your next school placement to improve professional communication in the classroom? *cont.*

Level 2

Reflect on your current teaching in the classroom.

- How have you communicated the learning objectives / success criteria to other professionals and adults in the classroom?
- How could you improve professional communication?

Take one future lesson plan and identify how you can work effectively with other professionals to support children's learning and development. Share and discuss your ideas with other professionals in your classroom.

Level 3

Identify how the different professionals in your setting / school communicate with each other.

- How effective is the communication between professionals? (Find out by asking them and observing some interaction);
- How do you think you can improve communication in your setting / school?

Discuss with professionals in your setting / school and decide how to improve communication. Try out some of your ideas and reflect on their success.

Research into effective professional learning communities (EPLCs) (Bolam *et al.* 2005) identifies eight key features which professional communication can develop:

- shared values and vision;
- collective responsibility for pupils' learning;
- collaboration focused on learning;
- individual and collective professional learning;
- reflective professional enquiry;
- openness, networks and partnerships;
- inclusive membership;
- mutual trust, respect and support.

This was facilitated not only by professional dialogue and the use of outside parties or 'critical friends', but also by individual staff commitment and motivation, links with other schools, focused continuing professional development (CPD) coordination and site facilities that helped collaborative work. Factors adversely affecting the development of a professional learning community included resistance by staff to change, resource and budgeting policies, and staff changes particularly at senior level.

Research into professional communications between teachers and trainee teachers

by Denise Gudgin, Bishop Grosseteste University College Lincoln

My research was concerned with some of the issues surrounding trainee teachers working in challenging classrooms and how teaching, learning and professional communication were affected by these circumstances (Gudgin 2006). I studied an opportunity sample of 24 trainees from four training routes, some in the early stages of training and working in collaboration with other trainees, others more experienced, and others about to enter the profession. Three were newly qualified teachers reflecting on incidents from their training.

My primary data were obtained from narrative accounts. I sought the trainees' interpretation of events, and my own enlightenment through their perspectives (Collay 1998: 245). Careful probing of the narratives enabled me to identify the underlying motivations, experiences, tensions, responses and emotions contained within.

It became evident that in the context of a challenging classroom, there is increased potential for professional communication to become compromised: between pupil and trainee, trainee and school, and trainee and mentor. In adverse circumstances a trainee's immediate response is governed by the primitive protective instincts of the brain. The brain is designed for survival. The wiring of the brain favours emotion over cognition, giving supremacy to unconscious emotions over thought systems. In adverse circumstances it acts to override what it sees as prejudicial decision making such as re-engagement with a challenging pupil (LeDoux 2003: 2). Instead, self-protection informs the trainee's classroom relationships.

I observed how in class some trainees abandoned notions of teacher presence. They sought to remove themselves from the spotlight of attention and merge in with the children. The engagement of the pupils with learning tended to be minimal and superficial; trainees appeared only to require that 'something' be done – to get the lesson over and done with. A number of trainees revealed that they did not feel they 'had permission' to manage challenging behaviour. Others felt uncomfortable about managing pupil behaviour, and were inconsistent when they attempted to do so. Some attempted to bring about beneficial change in pupil behaviour by using appeasement strategies such as overfriendliness, and their uncertain body language conveyed their insecurity to the pupils. They were not conscious of doing these things at the time, but looking back after a gap of two years one participant was able to reflect: 'Do I think my reptilian brain had taken over? Yes. Did I engage in appeasement? Yes. We did have some very useful lectures on managing behaviour, and I've got some excellent notes; but the trouble is, reptiles don't go looking through their filing system.'

The testimonies of trainees contained many examples of the potentially devastating effect of a trainee's perceived competence being called into question. Challenging pupil behaviour aroused feelings of personal or professional failure: 'I felt inadequate, responsible, paranoid, an enormous amount of self-blame. I nearly gave

cont.

up teaching.' Many wished to conceal their perceived inadequacy from the school: 'When children are so badly behaved, you feel you've let yourself down. I didn't like to use the sanction "send to another teacher" or, "send to the Head". I preferred to deal with it in class. Contain it if you can.' Other trainees revealed their desire for self-protection through denial: 'There's only so much I can do. They're not used to listening.

Once powerful evolutionary mechanisms have taken hold, trainees appear to become resistant to intervention. In some instances trainees were so adversely affected by pupil behaviour, so deeply affected by self-protection and impervious to help and advice, that satisfactory classroom interactions eluded them on the placement. However, trainees who are prepared with prior understanding of the underlying predilections which proceed from the brain's programme for survival, its protective instinct, and its influence on thoughts and actions, may be in a good position to recognize and resist them.

Communicating with children

Professional communication is also an important aspect of interaction with children, and skilled adults can support children's cognitive development through social and cultural interaction. This is an important aspect of Vygotsky's cognitive theory (Vygotsky 1978) in that Vygotsky identified that there was a difference between tested levels of cognitive development and potential development, achieved through interaction with adults. This difference is known as the zone of proximal development (zpd). Vygotsky has shown the need for sensitive interaction between the professional and child, with the professional ensuring that the child is active and that they (the adult) do not dominate interactions. In other words, professionals give children the space they need to develop independently and support when required.

There are two main forms of communication between children and professionals: non-verbal and verbal communication. Non-verbal communication occurs when a professional models behaviours for the children and shows them by example learning behaviours and attitudes appropriate to support future development. By interacting with the children while they are involved in learning and by learning with them, children come to see adults as learners, rather than all-knowledgeable. Verbal communication focuses children on learning and development by questioning and discussing issues with them and can aid cognitive development, forming part of the whole-class interactive introduction in literacy and numeracy hours (DfEE 1998, 1999a) and creative argumentation in science (Johnston 2005).

While interacting with children, it is important that we understand the subliminal messages we are communicating about learning. For example, the current practice of working with a focus group for most, if not all, of a lesson, sends messages to children about the importance of certain types of activities. This can be seen in the case studies described in the reflective task below.

Reflective task

In one Key Stage 1 classroom a teacher had a number of play activities linked to her literacy theme of rhyming words and children could freely play with these while she and her classroom assistant sat with groups of children who were writing poems using rhyming words. The classroom appeared to be very productive, with children engaged in a variety of activities, and the teacher and assistant did not need to direct attention away from the groups they were working with to manage the behaviour of other children. However, on closer inspection the children playing with words were not focused on the learning objectives but playing in alternative ways. For example, the sand in the sand tray was wet and there were laminated cards with rhyming words that the children were to stand up in the sand in pairs. The children, however, were making marks in the sand and building structures using the laminated cards.

In another Key Stage 1 classroom, a teacher was undertaking numeracy activities linked to number. She began with a focus group, who were drawing picnic items on a picture of a picnic basket to prepare for a picnic with a set number of people. She explained the activity and set the children off. She then left them for a while and motivated the children playing and interacted with them to encourage them to think about number. One child asked her for another cup to set up tea in the play corner for three teddies. The teacher's questions included:

- How many cups do you need altogether?
- How many cups do you have?
- How many more do you need?

Level 1

- What messages were the two teachers communicating about the play activities?
- How can you ensure that you focus on the learning objectives and give quality interactions to both the focus group and others in the class?
- What could you do in your next work with children to ensure you are sending positive messages about all activities?

Level 2

- Does your teaching best fit the first or second example?
- How can you ensure that you focus on the learning objectives and give quality interactions to both the focus group and others in the class?
- How could you develop your teaching approaches to send positive messages to children about all types of activities?

Level 3

- What messages does the teaching in your setting / school send about different types of activities?
- How can you support your staff to ensure that they focus on the learning objectives and give quality interactions to both the focus group and others in each activity?
- How can you support your staff in the development of teaching approaches to send positive messages to children about all types of activities?

Communicating with the home

The importance of parents, carers and effective home–school communication is well recognized (for example, Bastiani and Wolfendale 1996; QCA 2007; DfES 2003a; Abbott and Langston 2004; Sage and Wilkie 2004), although the practice of providing effective communication between home and school is much harder in practice. For example, I have found that newly qualified teachers find this a difficult aspect of their professional practice and would prefer to avoid or limit professional communication (Johnston 2002).

Children spend considerably more time at home than in schools, and their parents and carers have knowledge of their children which, if shared, can help professionals attempting to support children's learning and development. Home–school communication can take a number of formats: parental information sessions, family learning workshops, and newsletters. However, it is important to see communication as a two-way process with parents and carers providing information,

- about their children;
- in areas where they have particular expertise;
- about their preferences for their children's care and education.

The Education Act 2002 identified that schools must consult with parents and more widely regarding the provision of extended services, that is, a 'range of services and activities, often beyond the school day, to help meet the needs of children, their families and the wider community' (TDA 2006a: 1). These services might include extended childcare, activities such as homework, sport and creative arts clubs. The DfES (2006a) identifies the benefits of extended and integrated services as including opportunities for professional communication between professionals and parents, although a challenge is how to communicate with and include a range of carers and the whole school community. It is hoped that, through effective communication and partnership, the key objectives of the *Every Child Matters* (DfES 2003b, 2004) agenda (that children stay safe, are healthy, enjoy and achieve, make a positive contribution and achieve economic well-being) can be met and that core extended services will be available to all children through schools by 2010 (TDA 2006a). It is also expected that extended services will build on and develop links between schools, professionals within a cluster of schools, outside agencies and local authorities.

Practical and reflective tasks

Level 1

Identify a five-point action plan to identify how you can improve home–school communication in your future practice?

Look at the professional standards for an early years professional (EYP) which can be found on the CWDC website (www.cwdcouncil.org.uk), or qualified teacher status (QTS), which can be found on the TDA website (www.tda.gov.uk). Reflect on whether the standards can be achieved through your action plan. *cont.*

Level 2

Reflect on your own communication with parents and carers of children in your class. Identify what you currently do well in home–school communication and what you could develop in the short, medium and long term to achieve better communication.

Level 3

Conduct an audit of your professional home–school communication. Identify areas for development and produce a development plan to improve home–school communication. Identify what you can do in the short, medium and long term.

Communicating with the wider community

Integrated and extended services are recognizing the school's place in the wider community. The community is affected by the social, moral and educational development of its children and so has a vested interest in communicating with schools. Local shops, bus companies, leisure centres and industries are all affected by anti-social behaviour and all have expertise that they can share with schools. Generally, communities are very supportive of education and not only influence provision but can also be useful in extending learning. Local industry will often allow children to visit and experience their work; businesses may work with children on simple products, extending understandings and developing skills; individuals may visit schools and share their experiences and expertise. One school worked with a local waste disposal company in a project to learn about decomposition of waste and to extend understandings of the practicalities and issues surrounding recycling. Another school used individuals with particular expertise, such as a weaver or an electrician and from different cultures, such as an Asian chef, to work with the children to give them wider and deeper experiences than the school or teacher could provide. Community projects involving children, for example to create a garden or plant trees and bushes in the local community, can have the effect of teaching about the growth of plants and ensure the life of the trees and plants by giving the children a sense of pride in their community.

Sure Start, a government programme in England to deliver the best start in life for every child, is a good example of professional communication. Sure Start programmes rely on effective communication between professionals in education, childcare, health and family support and between professionals and the wider community, through consultation and community-led provision. Examples of this professional communication are the partnerships between the Sure Start Extended Schools and Childcare Group and Jobcentre Plus, local training providers, and further and higher education institutions in an effort to reduce the number of workless households (see, for example, Sure Start 2004).

Communicating with professional associations

There are a large number of subject and professional associations and institutions designed to support teachers. Many subject associations provide help for teachers via their websites, journals and meetings (both local and national). Some subject associations have worked together to provide cross-curricular support. For example, the Curriculum Partnership, comprising members of many subject associations, joined together to produce a cross-curricular publication to support teachers in the foundation stage for learning (de Bóo 2004). DfES-initiated centres and networks of centres, such as the National College of School Leadership and the Science Learning Centres network, provide advice and continuing professional development (CPD). Web addresses for some associations can be found at the end of this chapter.

Support for planning, teaching and assessing can be found on DfES and QCA websites (see the end of the chapter for addresses) and on Teachers' TV, a digital TV channel for teachers, and there are many published and web-based schemes of work and ideas to support teachers. In fact there are so many places to go for support that it is sometimes difficult to know where best to go. Teachers attending CPD courses have often been unaware of the support available by communicating with other professionals through professional associations and networks. They also identify that their main needs are:

- to develop their current ideas for practice;
- to provide hands-on activities, rather than worksheets;
- for courses to support practical activities.

Communicating between key stages and settings

Transitions are scary whatever age you are. During our lives we make large numbers of transitions such as moving house, leaving home, starting school, university or work, changing jobs, as well as those between different aspects of education, from one key stage to the next, for example, or between different year groups. These are all anxious times in our lives. Research into transition from the Foundation Stage to Key Stage 1 (Sanders *et al.* 2005; Primary National Strategy 2006) has identified that communication between professionals, children and parents is an essential ingredient in effective transitions. Although this research involves younger transitions, the principles and recommendations are the same as for older transitions.

Transition in schools should be viewed as a process rather than an event and involves excellent communication between professionals, from both the feeder and the recipient school, key stage or class. This communication should include information about the individual children's main achievements and targets for the future (see also Chapter 12, Target Setting). There are some professionals who prefer not to prejudge children on the basis of their previous teacher's assessments, but this is not supportive of children who need progression in their learning journey and it also devalues the work of the previous professional, implying that their assessments and targets are not correct.

In Belgium, bridging modules of work ease the transition from primary to secondary education, and these and other examples can be found on the QCA website (see end of the chapter). Many local authorities are also producing bridging units to ease transitions from the Foundation Stage to Key Stage 1, from Key Stage 1 to Key Stage 2, as well as from Key Stage 2 to Key Stage 3. These units can facilitate the adoption of similar routines and good practice at each stage and provide staff development, enabling teachers to see where children have come from and where they are going to. Within Lincolnshire there is a network of schools that use a skills-based curriculum from Foundation Stage through to the end of Key Stage 2. This curriculum uses the six key areas of the Foundation Stage (personal development, communication, language and literacy, mathematical development, knowledge and understanding of the world, physical development and creative development) and identified the generic and specific learning skills that children at different ages and stages need to develop (Watson 2006).

Parents identify that within transitions they want their children to be happy, supported by professionals who know them, encourage them, but do not pressurize them (Primary National Strategy 2006). They also identify the importance of quality relationships with staff who care for and teach their children and of sessions where they can be involved in the life of the school or setting and meet other parents. Schools that have liaised well with parents, consulted with them, welcomed them, shared with them and involved them fully in the life of the school are more likely to have smooth transitions and fewer problems educationally, emotionally or socially.

Case study

Transitions in the early years

by Bia Sena, Foundation Stage Coordinator, The British School, Rio de Janeiro

The Foundation Stage at the British School of Rio de Janeiro is organized into six Nursery classes with 12 children in each class. We have one teacher and one assistant teacher for each class. The Nursery is an independent unit where the children can move around safely and independently. In the Reception year we have five classes with 20 children, one teacher and one assistant for each class. As a result, children need to be regrouped when moving from Nursery to Reception and are mixed and placed in five new classes. Reception is a bigger unit placed next to Key Stage 1 classes. The classrooms are also laid out differently: Nursery has a play / learn-based area; Reception has a 'teaching approach', tables and chairs. There is a clear need to provide a smooth transition to help the Nursery children to feel secure, relaxed and comfortable in their new environment. Teachers should create a more balanced classroom taking into account the children's perspective, interest and needs.

Another barrier to ensure smooth transitions is the different pedagogical approach. The curriculum has two different foci. The Nursery curriculum is more skills-based, learning through play. The Reception curriculum is based more in competence than in

cont.

skills, with fewer playing opportunities. It is important to have a balance between adult-led and child-led activities. This is crucial for the children's development and learning process. It is also important to focus on the readiness of the child. What kinds of knowledge, skills and behaviour are expected from the children? The curriculum should have continuity and progression. However, there are some important points that can be considered in relation to pressure for a more formal approach in Reception, at the end of the Foundation Stage. As the classrooms are in the same Key Stage 1 unit and both year groups' teachers are in contact, the tendency is to prepare the children for Infant 1. Children should not be 'school ready' but teachers need to provide a curriculum that is 'child ready'. Perhaps a change in assessment practices could help to maintain a focus on children's learning throughout this transition period. At Foundation Stage, learning should be free and playful.

Another aspect is that teachers accuse parents of valuing a more formal approach. In this case what is valued as appropriate learning in early childhood is not explained clearly to parents. The school curriculum needs to be a rich daily life which includes learning and development as essential ingredients, along with other children and adults, interacting and engaging, and meaningful opportunities. Lately, relationships between teachers and parents have become more uncertain. Parents have become questioning and more critical about issues of curriculum, the quality of teaching, and practices used to assess and evaluate their children.

After a month of studying transition through visiting schools in the UK, discussing with other professionals and reading, an action plan was drawn up to support my work in facilitating transition in my school.

Short term
- Discuss and compare my findings with Nursery and Reception staff and the head of the lower primary school.
- Find out what is going well and what is not functioning.
- Share my UK experience with the Nursery and Reception staff and the head of the lower primary school.

Medium term
- Create a transition team.
- Implement transitions ideas.

Long term
- Build on findings to improve transitions from Foundation Stage to Key Stage 1.

In order to be successful the programme developed in school needs to:
- provide activities to bridge the gap and create links between Nursery and Reception;
- provide communication and collaboration between all people involved in the process;
- be evaluated.

Within one school, smooth transitions between classes can be facilitated by improved continuity. This is achieved where professionals have a shared educational philosophy, aims, values and expectations. This sharing relies on professional communication, which may include a teamwork approach to policy, planning, teaching and learning. In larger schools it could involve shared planning for one year, and in smaller schools, planning for a key stage or school.

Reflective task
Professional communication audit

Level 1
How do you communicate with the following individuals or groups of individuals?
- Class teachers
- Teaching assistants
- Tutors
- Learning mentors
- Parents
- Children

How could you develop your professional communication with individuals or groups of individuals? Identify a five-point action plan for your next professional practice.

Level 2
Consider how you currently communicate with other professionals and individuals and groups of individuals in your learning partnership.
- Teaching assistants
- Parents
- Other teachers in your setting
- Teachers in other settings
- Senior management in your school
- Children in your class and other children in the school
- Professional associations or subject experts
- Students
- Tutors

Place the groups in order of how effective your communication with them is. How could you develop your professional communication with these professionals, individuals and groups of individuals? Start at the bottom of your list and produce a bullet-point action plan to develop your professional communication.

Level 3
What policies are in place in your setting that identify professional communication with the following professionals, individuals and groups of individuals?
- Parents
- Teachers in other years groups and key stages

cont.

- Teachers in other schools
- The community in which your school is situated
- The local authority
- Inspectors and advisers
- Outside visitors (students, tutors, outside experts etc.).

What areas of professional communication do you need to develop? Produce a development plan for one area of professional communication. Identify the short-, medium- and long-term actions you can make to develop this area of professional communication.

References

Abbott, L. and Langston, A. (eds) (2004) *Birth to Three Matters: Supporting the Framework of Effective Practice.* Buckingham: Open University Press.

Bastiani, J. and Wolfendale, S. (1996) *Home-School Work in Britain: Review, Reflection and Development.* London: David Fulton.

Bolam, R., McMohan, A., Stoll, L., Thomas, S. and Wallace, M. with Greenwood, A., Hawkey, K., Ingram, M., Atkinson, A. and Smith, M. (2005) *Creating and Sustaining Effective Professional Learning Communities.* London: DfES. Available at www.dfes.gov.uk

Bronfenbrenner, U. (1995) The bioecological model from a life course perspective: reflections of a participant observer, in P. Moen, G. H. Elder, Jr and K. Lüscher (eds) *Examining Lives in Context.* Washington, DC: American Psychological Association, pp. 599–618.

Bronfenbrenner, U. and Evans, G. W. (2000) Developmental science in the 21st century: emerging theoretical models, research designs and empirical findings, *Social Development,* 9: 115–25.

Cajkler, W., Tennant, G., Cooper, P. W., Sage, R., Tansey, R., Taylor, C., Tucker, S. A. and Tiknaz, Y. (2006) A systematic literature review on the perceptions of ways in which support staff work to support pupils' social and academic engagement in primary classrooms (1988–2003). *Research Evidence Education Library.* EPPI-Centre, Social Science Research Unit, Institute of Education, University of London.

Collay, M. (1998) Recherche: teaching our life histories, *Teacher and Teacher Education.* 14(3): 245–55.

CWDC (Children's Workforce and Development Council) (2006) *Early Years Professional Standards.* Available at www.cwdc.org.uk

de Bóo, M. (ed.) (2004) *Early Years Handbook: Support for Practitioners in the Foundation Stage.* Sheffield: Curriculum Partnership / Geography Association.

DfEE (1998) *The National Literacy Strategy.* London: DfEE.

DfEE (1999a) *The National Numeracy Strategy.* London: DfEE.

DfEE (1999b) *The National Curriculum: Handbook for Primary Teachers in England.* London: DfEE / QCA.

DfES (2003a) *Excellence and Enjoyment: A Strategy for Primary Schools.* London: DfES.

DfES (2003b) *Every Child Matters.* London: DfES.

DfES (2004) *Choice for Parents, the Best Start for Children: A Ten Year Strategy for Children.* London: DfES.

DfES (2006) *About Integrated Services.* Available at www.dfes.gov.uk (accessed February 2006).

DfES (2006b) *The Early Years Foundation Stage, Every Child Matters, Change for Children.* London: DfES.

DfES (2007) Statutory Framework for the Early Years Foundation Stage; Setting the Standards for Learning, Development and Care for children from birth to five. *Every Child Matters, Change for Children.* London: DfES.

Emery, R. E. and Laumann-Billings, L. (1998) An overview of the nature, causes and consequences of abusive family relationships: toward differentiating maltreatment and violence, *American Psychologist.* 53: 121–35.

Gudgin, D. M. (2006) An exploration of issues surrounding trainee teachers in challenging classrooms. Unpublished dissertation, Sibthorpe Library, Bishop Grosseteste University College Lincoln.

Johnston, J. (2002) Teaching and learning in the early years, in J. Johnston, M. Chater and D. Bell (eds) *Teaching the Primary Curriculum.* Buckingham: Open University Press.

Johnston, J. (2005) What is creativity in science education, in A. Wilson (ed.) *Creativity in Primary Education.* Exeter: Learning Matters, pp. 88–101.

Keogh, B., Naylor, S., Downing, B., Maloney, J. and Simon, S. (2006) Puppets bringing stories to life in science, *Primary Science Review*, 92: 26–8.

LeDoux, J. E. (2003) Management wisdom from a neuroscientist, *Gallup Management Journal*. Available at http://gmj.gallup.com/content/default.asp?ci=9844

NCSL (National College for School Leadership) (2006) www.ncsl. org.uk/media/9FF/CF/changing-times-changing-roles.pdf

QCA (2007)

Sage, R. and Wilkie, M. (2004) *Supporting Learning in Primary Schools*, 2nd edn. Exeter: Learning Matters.

Sanders, D., White, G., Burge, B., Sharp, C., Eames, A., McEune, R. and Grayson, H. (2005) *A Study of the Transition from the Foundation Stage to Key Stage 1.* London: DfES / Sure Start.

Primary National Strategy (2006) *Seamless Transitions: Supporting Continuity in Young Children's Learning.* Norwich: DfES / Sure Start.

Sure Start (2004) *Working Together: A Sure Start Guide to the Childcare and Early Education Field.* Annesley, Notts: DfES.

TDA (Training and Development Agency for Schools) (2006a) *Professional Standards for Higher Level Teaching Assistants.* Available at www.tda.gov.uk

TDA (Training and Development Agency for Schools) (2006b) *Revised Standards for Classroom Teachers.* Available at www.tda.gov.uk

Vygotsky, L. (1978) *Mind in Society, The Development of Higher Psychological Processes*, eds M. Cole *et al.* Cambridge, MA: Harvard University Press.

Watson, M. (2006) Skills-based learning framework. Unpublished curriculum materials from St Lawrence CE Primary School, Skellingthorpe, Lincolnshire.

Useful websites

Association for Science Education (ASE): www.ase.org.uk

Birth to Three Matters: http://www.surestart.gov.uk/resources/childcareworkers/birthtothreematters

British Educational Communications and Technology Association (Becta): www.becta.org.uk

Children's Workforce Development Council: www.cwdcouncil.org.uk

Department for Education and Skills (DfES): www.dfes.gov.uk

Every Child Matters: Change for Children: www.everychildmatters.gov.uk

Foundation Stage for Learning: www.surestart.gov.uk/improvingquality/ensuringquality/foundationstage

Geographical Association: www.geography.org.uk

Historical Association: www.history.org.uk

Mathematical Association: www.m-a.org.uk

National Association for Special Educational Needs (NASEN): www.sen-forschools.co.uk

National Association for Teachers of English (NATE): www.nate.org.uk

National College for School Leadership (NCSL): www.ncsl.org.uk

Qualifications and Curriculum Authority (QCA): www.qca.org.uk

Sure Start: http://www.surestart.gov.uk

Teachers' TV: www.teachernet.gov.uk/professionaldevelopment/teacherstv

Training and Development Agency for Schools (TDA): www.tda.gov.uk

14

Developing as a Reflective Practitioner

Mark Chater

One of the most astonishing features of most work organisations in this country is the contempt extended to those who stop to think. It is not that thinking is wrong but that we must not be seen to be doing it, because it looks as if we are doing nothing.

Whitaker (1997: 152)

Introduction

This chapter considers what a reflective practitioner in education is and does, and how important such a person is to improving pupils' performance and life chances. Some characteristics of the reflective practitioner are suggested. The characteristics are categorized into those that function at classroom level and have an impact in the corridor, playground, assembly and school (the micro level); those that function at school level and can impact other schools in a consortium, community or region (the meso level); and those that operate at regional and national levels, where they influence schools and classrooms (the macro level). Finally, it is argued that in the nature of reflective practice the context, as defined by the learning needs of teachers, other professionals, pupils and their families must be taken into account as the governing factor in shaping reflective practice.

What does a reflective practitioner do?

Being a practitioner in education who is critically reflective, and who allows his / her practice to change, may be a matter of following certain habits which, if repeated, develop into a virtuous professional circle. Some of these habits are listed in the reflective task below.

Reflective task
Investigate the habits of a reflective practitioner

Rank the following professional 'habits' in order of their importance, in your view; then share your choices with a more experienced colleague.

A reflective practitioner . . .
- self-evaluates frequently and thoughtfully;
- has a balanced mix of pragmatism and idealism, and avoids falling into cynical or passive attitudes of mind;
- remembers what it was like to be a child and strives to see the curriculum and pedagogy from the learner's point of view;
- enters into coaching or mentoring relationships that enable the mutual sharing of critical perspectives on practice, based on mutual collaboration and challenge, not on competition;
- has not stopped engaging in learning and enjoying it;
- is proactive in seeking out appropriate continuing professional development (CPD) experiences and insights, discussing needs and opportunities with the line manager and team colleagues;
- pays due attention to educational research and changes classroom practice accordingly;
- reaches out to, and collaborates with, members of other children's service professions;
- responds maturely to new initiatives and political developments in education.

Level 1
Select five qualities which are 'must-have' items for:
- a successful trainee;
- a mentor of trainees and those entering the profession.

Level 2
To what extent are the above nine qualities visible in:
- the way you work with your colleagues?
- the ethos of your school?

Level 3
Imagine that you are a headteacher considering how to lead your school staff as a community of reflective practitioners. Arrange the nine qualities as a 'diamond nine' (that is, rows of one, two, three, two and one – see Figure 14.1) to symbolize their relative importance.

cont.

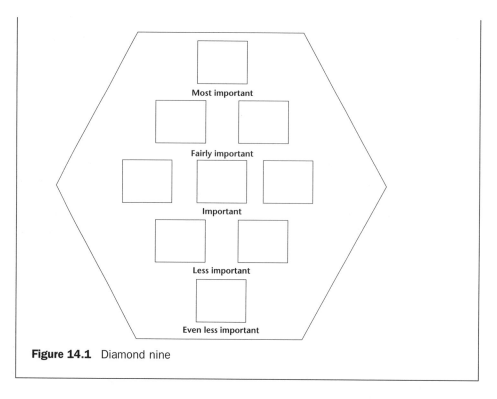

Figure 14.1 Diamond nine

There is no blueprint for being a reflective practitioner, just as there is none for being an effective or good human being. However, this does not mean that teachers must learn and grow in isolation, nor does it imply that personal and professional development take place in a relativist vacuum. It simply means that the journey of development as a reflective practitioner has no motorways, but several paths and signposts. There is the framework of legal requirements and guidance which determine, in minimum terms, what the state requires of teachers; there is the community of support, advice and wisdom provided by the profession at all levels from school through local authority to national and international sources such as university-based research; and, perhaps most important, there is the individual's own disposition to ask questions and learn from experience, including negative and positive episodes.

Negative learning points could be mistakes in planning or content, losses of credibility, failures of pedagogy, misjudgements in professional relations or unsuccessful applications for jobs. Such episodes may be painful, but when reflected on they can yield types of personal and professional learning which have the potential to strengthen us as human beings in a workplace, to make us more wise and effective as educators and to render us more perceptive, challenging and compassionate as managers or mentors of other teachers.

Positive learning points may seem, on the surface, to be both more easy to identify and more fruitful and pleasant to think about. After all, a lesson that goes well, a training experience that satisfies and excites us, or a pastoral situation with a good outcome may all be easy to remember and may teach us something good about our performance. But many positive professional experiences lie beneath the surface, are less easy to identify and require harder work to interpret. One individual teacher may never know that her compassionate and authentic style of communication has deeply impressed a 10-year-old; another teacher may discover, years later through an accidental meeting with an ex-pupil, that his leadership of an assembly and his management of sporting occasions were powerful role models. These lost learning points can be retrieved if school information systems are working well and if teachers are taking care to notice the reactions on the faces of individual pupils. But there is certainly much more to positive learning points than recalling things which made a teacher feel good at the end of each day.

For both negative and positive experiences, there is a need for teachers to be systematic in gathering the information and reflecting on it thoughtfully. Journal keeping, counselling, mentoring and coaching are all widely in use as receptacles for collecting the wisdom from negative and positive experiences and distilling it into messages and action points for individual professionals and for teams.

The most immediate level at which teachers can reflect and gain insights is that of their most important forum for work: their own mind. The teacher's thinking affects everyday environments such as the classroom, corridor, playground, assembly hall, dining hall, grounds and whole school. As the subsequent discussion of meso and macro levels shows, teachers should not satisfy themselves with reflecting solely on this immediate level, but it is a natural and logical place to start building the habits of a reflective practitioner.

The micro level: reflective practice in the teacher's mind as it affects classrooms and schools

How should a reflective practitioner think and feel about their everyday work? There are no set answers to this, but some characteristics of reflectiveness that set the tone for critical reflection are suggested here.

- **A reflective practitioner self-evaluates frequently and thoughtfully**

Thoughtful and systematic evaluation of lessons is important; so is the evaluation of whole units, years and programmes of work for key stages. Evaluation needs to embrace a good deal more than describing what went well or badly. Also, evaluation is not always a solitary activity. In a collaborative, critical-friend model of evaluation, Campbell *et al.* (2004) advise that peers can challenge and support each other through listening, asking questions, articulating each other's beliefs and aspirations about teaching, and giving feedback. This type of relationship is neither an aggressive investigation of a colleague's competence nor a passive mutual validation: it offers a model midway between these two extremes. Outlining a possible model for collaborative evaluations, Smyth (1991: 113) suggests using four questions:

- Describe: what do I do?

- Inform: what does this description mean?
- Confront: how did I come to be like this?
- Reconstruct: how might I do things differently?

Reflective task

Level 1

Consider your last piece of teaching and your evaluation of the lesson. How does Smyth's model (above) compare with your evaluation?

Level 2

Focus on your current teaching and consider how your current evaluation compares with Smyth's model (above). How might you improve your evaluation using Smyth's four questions?

Level 3

Consider how Smyth's model (above) compares with your present practice of evaluating programmes of study or long-term planning.
- What are the current strengths of your evaluations?
- How might you improve your current evaluation?

The concept of 'critical incidents' is also a useful ingredient of reflective evaluation processes. A critical incident is not an extreme case, an unusual episode or an emergency; it is any professional experience which offers significant meaning. It can be an encounter with a parent, a conversation with a pupil, an observation of two or more pupils talking, playing or working, an appraisal conversation, a decision on resources, or a piece of inspired teaching. It can be positive or negative. The reason it carries significant meaning is that it captures and delivers, to the professional, an understanding of the working context that goes beyond the one incident and is somehow applicable to the context more generally. The light of knowledge, filtered through the prism of one critical incident, becomes a full spectrum of understanding. Usually, professionals recognize critical incidents after they have happened, rather than going looking for them. Nevertheless, it is useful for professionals who wish to reflect critically on their work and their context to be aware of critical incidents and to have a mental attitude that is ready to receive and interpret them when they happen.

As a fictional example, let us take a teacher who works with a mixed Year 4–5 class in a high-achieving primary school. She is a confident and sophisticated user of assessment for learning techniques, and organizes her teaching to allow for detailed feedback conversations with individual pupils, followed by target setting. Although she is skilful in her use of this approach, she is not aware of her own gaps in understanding: specifically, she is vague about why the approach works. She has implemented it not so much because she believes in it, as because it is school policy. After a conversation with another teacher, she decides to 'track' attitudes to learning in some of the less mature Year 4 pupils after feedback. She observes some improvements in motivation and commitment, and in time these changes are translated into better academic performance in the weakest areas for those pupils. The critical incident for the teacher has been a professional conversation which led to a decision to use the aftermath of target setting in a different way. The incident led to learning for the teacher and to improvement for the pupils.

Critical incidents can feed into reflective evaluation from any number of sources: critical friend conversations, mentors / coaches, discussion groups, diary writing, a skilled helper (Campbell *et al.* 2004), as well as more formal appraisal processes, CPD or interviews for jobs (successful or not).

A critical incident approach to the curriculum and pedagogy enables a teacher to evaluate much more accurately and to discover answers to the only question that matters: what are the children learning? Viewed from the stance of this question, many of the normal evaluation 'checklist' items take on a different significance (Darling 1994) and may be developed into more searching questions, as set out in Table 14.1. While some conventional or traditionalist teachers may find such questions too intrusive, progressive teachers also need to be aware that these questions must constantly shift according to the context.

In addition to penetrating more deeply into an understanding of the learning achieved by pupils, these evaluative processes should trigger questions on the wider support structure of the school. While evaluation of lessons is a high-frequency activity, evaluative consideration of issues such as reporting, information systems, assessment or pastoral care should normally happen on a lower frequency, perhaps after a term's or a year's work.

Table 14.1 Reflective evaluation checklist

Normal evaluation questions	Possible pupil significance
How were the desks laid out?	Can pupils see? Are they comfortable?
Were the lesson objectives met?	Do pupils know what they learnt?
Was behaviour acceptable?	Are pupils taking pride in their positive engagement?
In what manner did the teacher address the class?	Is there an absence of fear? Are there good interpersonal relations?
Was pupil work displayed on the walls?	Can pupils see, and respond effectively and cognitively to, their own work?

Evaluations will take different forms, and while some will be informed by pupil progress or by critical incidents, others may be shaped by specific, limited elements of insight from research. Reflective practitioners usually aspire to a praxis of complexity in which no single theory or model is elevated above criticism (Sharp and Murphy 2006). They prefer to avoid what has become known as the 'tick box' approach, in which the focus is on the teacher's actions in conformity with a received model of good practice which is rarely actively interpreted, let alone questioned. Nevertheless, some have advocated a 'science of teaching' approach, which argues that we do know the main ingredients of good teaching, recognize that these ingredients can be straightforwardly itemized and adopted, and even claim that the ethos or climate of a classroom can be correctly created (Gipps *et al.* 2000: 159). Yet even in these teachers' minds, diversity of approaches remains at high premium, as this Year 2 teacher clearly believes:

> I think I may have a way that I think works but I will always find a child that it doesn't work with, so I have to go back to the drawing board.
>
> (Gipps *et al.* 2000: 115)

Teachers should not feel compelled to evaluate everything they do every time they do it. A sense of proportion, and an effective and economic use of limited time and energy are highly necessary. Lesson evaluations done when tired may be of little use; whole-unit evaluations accomplished at leisure and when wide awake could yield more professional wisdom and pointers for improvement. Discussions of an assessment system, if rushed and forced into an already packed agenda, might merely pluck at the issues instead of examining them carefully, and could even lead to some poorly considered decisions.

- **A reflective practitioner has a balanced mix of idealism and pragmatism, and realizes that personal health and attitude are important**

The pace of change in schools over the past 20 years, the impact of specific initiatives such as the Primary National Strategy, and the reforms to the structure of schooling and assessment have generated much comment on how teachers deal with change. There is a wide consensus that the most important resource in schools is the staff, that schools are unique climates for managing, that the attitude of the staff is likely to be the key decider between good and poor quality, and perhaps most importantly that the element of personal attitude, rather than any technical skill or structure, is the central and indispensable characteristic of an improving school (Middlewood and Cardno 2001). As the popular adage goes, attitude changes everything.

While most teachers would accept this adage as true, there are many who fall into regular attitude traps that can have consequences for their reflectiveness about their work. Two such attitude traps are extreme idealism and extreme pragmatism. Teachers who are excessively idealistic may wish to have the entire scope of their work, and their immediate environment, made perfect immediately; they may therefore come across as angry, rigid or inflexible, because their idealism generates a dissatisfaction with the imperfect present. This constantly drives them to criticism and to greater improvement efforts. Often they will be their own harshest critics, but they will also seem critical of everyone and everything else. To some extent, this frame of mind is needed in a reflective and improving school. Yet it needs to be tempered by a pragmatism that accepts that the pace of change will sometimes be slow, that the school may not be perfect, that some priorities must wait, and that there may be more than one 'right' way of doing things. But this pragmatic attitude, if taken too far, has dangers of complacency or a lack of direction in the improvement efforts of a school or team. In developing as reflective practitioners, teachers need to strike a balance, in their personal make-up, between a radical dissatisfaction leading to an energy for change, and an equally radical patience leading to an energy for making the best out of circumstances. Not only in individuals, but also in teams, there will be a need for this balance. Those who tend towards perfectionist idealism, and their colleagues who incline towards relaxed pragmatism, need to respect each other's starting points in order to find ways of engaging each other's energies creatively.

Two related attitude traps exist for some teachers: hyperactivity and passivity. Whereas some colleagues may energetically pursue every new initiative, volunteer for every project and be positive about every new idea, others may decline to volunteer for anything and see the downside of everything. It is as if their default positions are set at positive and negative. Teachers in the first trap are likely to say, 'That's a really good idea and I'd like to pilot it this week', whereas those in the second trap are more likely to be heard saying, 'We tried that eight years ago and it didn't work'.

Although we may be more sympathetic towards one or other of these remarks, both represent traps for a reflective practitioner. Hyperactivity in teachers can bring in the danger of wastefulness of effort. Teachers do not have limitless reserves of time and energy, and are unwise if they squander it on ill-considered whims or half-prepared ideas. In our discussion of research (below) we consider how research can help teachers to make a sober assessment of the value of a development, and to plan their improvements on something more solid than a whim or a personal tendency to experiment.

Equally, passivity in teachers can bring in the danger of spoiling a staff room atmosphere with cynicism or pessimism. Any reflective practitioner who has tried to instigate an improvement plan, only to be met with remarks that it is hopeless, will make no difference, should have had a longer consultation, should have been implemented years ago or does not get at the main problem, will find that their sense of hope and energy for improvement may begin to erode. Such is the damage of self-indulgent cynicism in staff rooms that, sometimes, the cynical remark becomes a self-fulfilling prophecy: a good idea can die for lack of constructive support.

Reflective practitioners take care to steer a delicate middle course between these attitude traps. If the staff room may be imagined as a large greenhouse in which beautiful plants (good ideas) grow to maturity, the climate of the greenhouse must be kept in balance and protected from excessive degrees of heat (idealism), moisture (pragmatism), waste (hyperactivity) and pollution (passive cynicism). In schools that have prioritized emotional literacy, there is a recognition that healthy attitudes among teachers make a difference to their work and to the pupils' outlook (Weare 2004). Individual teachers will also try to protect their own inner balance in the same way if they wish to succeed and enjoy their professional life. They will wish to protect themselves from excess or imbalances in colleagues, to ensure that their personal health of mind and body, their relaxation habits and work / life balance, all contribute to nurturing a good balance between idealism and pragmatism, and an avoidance of hyperactivity or cynicism.

Work pressures can have an effect on the mental attitude of teaching staff. In a climate of growing awareness of, and concern about teachers and overworking, more is now known than ever before on the intimate connections between healthy teachers and healthy schools (Weare 2004). At the same time, humanist management thinking is critical of the stimulated climate of overwork and presenteeism, seeing these phenomena as a widescale problem in several other professions in the public and private sectors of the western world. Work becomes a pressurized 'cage' demanding unreasonable levels of commitment, and fatigue becomes virtually a badge of honour (Handy 1995: 189).

Our main interest here is not in itemizing the reasons why some teachers become tired, fall ill, become cynical or burn out, but in advocating an approach to reflectiveness that encourages a teacher to take account of their own physical and mental health needs. A tired teacher is one who will probably still be able to perform the basic minimum functions of planning, teaching, keeping order, assessing, reporting and attending meetings. That is not to say that all is well. A tired teacher is more likely to go through the motions, and less likely to listen generously, assess accurately, feed back thoroughly, collaborate imaginatively and, above all, to learn effectively. Because a tired teacher is not flying an aeroplane, no fatalities occur and the cost of the fatigue is hidden, but the cost is still there in personal unhappiness and professional underperformance.

- **A reflective practitioner remembers what it was like to be a child and strives to see the curriculum and pedagogy from the learner's point of view**

Emotional literacy has established itself as a key indicator of health and success in schools. The potential exists to improve education by having teachers skilled in understanding their own emotions and in engaging creatively and appropriately with the emotional life-world of pupils. This happens when teachers shift their focus from purely cognitive attainment to addressing the whole person (Matthews 2005). This priority achieves two 'wins' for the reflective practitioner: firstly, it succeeds in engaging pupils more positively and fully, thus making it more likely that behaviour and standards will improve; and secondly, it engages the teacher more thoughtfully and satisfyingly, and at a deeper level, with the planning and teaching processes, thus making it more likely that the teacher's own motivation will improve. It is important to acknowledge that these improvements, important and achievable though they are, cannot be had without paying attention to other school policy issues such as equality of opportunity (Matthews 2005).

To see the curriculum and pedagogy from the child's point of view does not mean taking the child's 'side' or subscribing uncritically to what are perceived as children's views. It means that a teacher will frequently remind themselves, and perhaps their colleagues, that what happens in a primary school is seen, by the pupil, in more unitary terms, because it is the adult's tendency to compartmentalize that distorts our understanding of the child's experience. For instance, the curriculum is not to be understood as the written Orders issued by government and implemented in school; it is not to be understood as divided into subjects; it is not to be limited to what is taught between 8.50am and 3.00pm. In the pupil's experience, it is more meaningful to speak of the curriculum as the entire learning experience of the child. This sort of definition has now entered official thinking (QCA 2006a: 6). Teachers, in focusing (as they must) on the technical aspects of their performance, may run the risk of losing sight of what the child actually experiences. If a child listens to an Assembly on how we should respect and accept each other, and is then belittled, ostracized or bullied in the corridor going to class, he / she has learnt something about hypocrisy and injustice. If a child acquires skills in accessing information from literacy hour, and applies them in a geography project, he / she has learnt something about the nature of knowledge, about how to learn and about the reliability of rules in life. Metaphorically speaking, the reflective practitioner is the one who positions him / herself – in corridor, classroom or playground – in the spot where these pupil experiences can be seen and understood.

The meso level: reflective practice in schools, consortia, communities and regions

Not only teachers but schools too can be reflective, or can fail to be reflective by neglecting to learn from their own information and experience (Senge *et al.* 2000). A non-reflective school frustrates the individual teacher's efforts to be reflective. A reflective school allows the fora, and provides the equipment, for teachers to support and challenge each other in critical dialogue about their work.

- **A reflective practitioner enters into coaching or mentoring relationships that enable the mutual sharing of critical perspectives on practice, based on mutual collaboration and challenge, not on competition**

The many forms of mentoring relationship that now exist have capacity to offer teachers a variety of ways to think critically about their own teaching skills and to plan their own development. The mentoring relationship has changed considerably and broken away from the paternalistic master craftsman / apprentice model that used to be dominant (Stammers 1992). Now, mentoring is used by trainees as a means to meet the standards for qualified teacher status, by newly qualified teachers to pass fully into the profession, and by experienced teachers who wish to commit themselves to further improvement. Of the many divergent models of mentoring and coaching now on offer, the following are particularly relevant to the needs of the reflective practitioner:

- Mentoring relationships for professionals newly appointed into a school: an arrangement designed to help a colleague settle in, gain knowledge of a school's ways of proceeding, and to ask questions without feeling too exposed. This can often be mentoring for a more junior colleague by a more senior colleague.
- Group mentoring relationships: a small group of professionals at the same level who opt into membership of a group in which professional challenges are

honestly discussed, and in which there are no line manager or appraisal relationships.

- Coaching relationships designed to teach a specific set of skills (refereeing, or use of interactive whiteboard, or first aid): once the skills are taught, the relationship is no longer needed. It is, in effect, a temporary contract.
- Co-coaching relationships: two professionals of equal status, perhaps in neighbouring schools, contract to meet and offer each other professional challenges such as observation and feedback, as well as professional support. This relationship works best when the two colleagues are very clear, open, consistent, committed and confidential with each other's professional development.
- Coaching triad relationships: this is similar to co-coaching but involves three colleagues who share and rotate the roles of coach, coachee and observer. The role of observer is there to guarantee that the coach / coachee interaction is fair and to offer an objective commentary on the quality of the relationship. The fact that all three partners will act in all three roles gives an equal balance of power to the relationships. Triadic coaching, at its best, can produce deep, strong bonding between professionals and can yield tough, challenging feedback as well as profound affirmation.

Success in all the above models of relationship depends on openness, clear communication, transparency about the aims, product and duration of the relationship, and as equal as possible a power relationship between the members. It is perfectly legitimate for two professionals to enter, say, a co-coaching relationship, to agree its 'rules' between them, and to say that they will have this arrangement for one year, review it and then either end or continue with it. While it would be wise for them to inform their respective line managers that this relationship exists, they are under no obligation to gain permission for it or to report on its progress. They have total shared ownership of the relationship; its separateness from appraisal processes is what gives it power, freedom and fertility.

Reflective task

Review the forms of mentoring or coaching relationship listed above.

Level 1

- Which models have you received as a mentee or coachee?
- How did you feel in that role?
- How do you view the relationship between you and your mentor or coach?

Level 2

- In which models have you been a mentor or coach?
- Which model(s) currently best fit your professional development needs?
- How can you set about acquiring this relationship?

cont.

Level 3
- Which model(s) are used in your setting?
- Which model(s) fit the short- and medium-term professional development needs of your setting and your School Improvement Plan?
- How can you set up and / or develop these relationships?

- **A reflective practitioner has not stopped engaging in learning and enjoying it**

In addition to engaging in everyday evaluation and school-based CPD, teachers need to develop their autonomous professional sense of self through systematic study, leading to the questioning and testing of ideas. This discipline saves teachers from slavish adherence to modish models of learning on the one hand, and from going it alone on the other (Stenhouse 1975). The recent emergence of measures to judge the impact of research and CPD on learning and standards, and the development of evidence-based practice, have vastly advanced the profession's ability to convert research insights into pedagogical practice effectively (Yates 2004). Yet there is more to be done. Teachers need to be aware that educational research, unlike research in some aspects of medicine or technology, produces ambivalent results that can suggest divergent forms of practice in different cultural or values contexts. Therefore the *sine qua non* of professional learning is the capacity to think critically about any new learning and how it should or should not be applied. Examples of new theoretical material entering the profession without being properly understood or critically assessed by teachers ought certainly to include some aspects of brain theory and learning styles (Sharp and Murphy 2006). Critical thinking is normally seen as a worthwhile aim of education, related to autonomy and the development of identity and of key skills. While it may be difficult to define, it is central to most liberal western professional models (Barrow and Milburn 1990) and applies as much to teachers as to children.

The critical thinking of the reflective practitioner is sometimes held to be in conflict with the need to meet certain standards to enter the profession or successfully pass the induction year. Yet these values need not be in competition, in so far as the values that need to be shown in the induction process serve to draw out the implications of being a reflective practitioner (Arthur *et al.* 2005). There is a clear recognition that teacher education appropriately goes beyond inculcating skills or meeting standards of competence, that it should foster the beyond-cognitive virtues associated with reflective practice and that, when it does so, teacher performance, and therefore also pupil and school performance, are enhanced (Brookfield 1996; Bolton 2005).

As part of teacher learning, teachers need to be able to say, just as pupils can, what helps them to learn, what does not, and how they can best contribute to planning in their school or consortium (Whitaker 1997). If it is true that children progress better when they are able to take risks, this is also true of teachers in their professional learning.

- A reflective practitioner is proactive in seeking out appropriate CPD experiences and insights, discussing needs and opportunities with line manager and team colleagues

Professional development opportunities, whether stand-alone, sequential or credit bearing, are more accessible and better supported now than at many times in the recent past of the profession. It is common for local authorities to collaborate with local higher education institutes, and with the Teacher Learning Academy established by the General Teaching Council, to encourage structured, challenging opportunities in CPD, and to work together to offer these with both a professional recognition and an academic reward. While a few staff rooms may still harbour a lingering suspicion that CPD experience distracts from the day-to-day tasks of teaching, this view is increasingly rare, and has been replaced by a determination to have all teaching staff update their skills and awareness.

A key to success in establishing a staff room of reflective practitioners is to have CPD programmes that are focused on the school's developmental goals, that are delivered by people with established expertise, that do not leave key improvement issues to chance, and that involve the staff in doing as well as listening (Campbell *et al.* 2004).

Potentially, any experience can bring CPD. Several schools and higher education centres apply a portfolio approach in which any experience, whether chance (such as a critical incident, or a mentoring or coaching episode) or planned (such as a staff development day or briefing on a new data system), can count as having impact on the renewal of skills and awareness in a professional.

- A reflective practitioner pays due attention to educational research and changes classroom practice accordingly

The word 'research' tends to alarm or alienate many classroom teachers, perhaps because it carries connotations of elitism, irrelevance or extreme difficulty. Yet growing numbers of teachers are also researchers, placing their own or other people's findings alongside their daily practice in order to determine how to change and improve.

Reflective task

Look at the following list of statements about educational research:
- Educational research is out of touch with real primary classrooms.
- Educational research means using statistical data.
- Educational research is highly subjective.
- Educational research happens when a teacher keeps a journal for a term.
- Educational research 'proves' what we all knew as obvious. It makes no difference.
- Educational research can suggest good practice but needs careful interpretation.

cont.

Level 1

Sort the statements into two categories – true or false, in your opinion.

Level 2

Discuss the statements with colleagues (both teaching and non-teaching).

Level 3

Discuss the statements with staff and governors in your setting.

In responding to the above task, you engaged in a small piece of research. It involved you in reflecting on your experience, questioning assumptions and, perhaps, seeing new possibilities.

Educational research can employ many techniques. These include statistics, but also questionnaires, surveys, observations, interviews and the subjective thinking, reading or discussions of a teacher. The best possible combination of techniques is used in order to get an accurate and usable answer to a precise question.

If a reflective practitioner wishes to integrate research into their professional life, the first thing to think about must be: why. Sometimes a teacher will be genuinely engaged with a recurring puzzle and will want to test some answers; for instance, why does a gender group underperform and what can be done about it? A teacher may have a hunch or preliminary insight that the answer may lie in a specific factor, such as teaching approaches or resources. After refining the question and the hunch, the teacher may then begin on a course of action that tests the insight and provides evidence that is, or is not, valid. The course of action may be long or it may be brief, but it should always be ethically justifiable, so that, for instance, a particular group of pupils will not be ill-served or placed at risk. When this type of research is pursued in the context of practice, with an intention to disseminate the learning, it is sometimes known as practitioner research. In theory, any question relevant to teaching could become the subject of educational research.

The personal beliefs of teachers (political, religious, moral, educational or other) can and should be put to the test by research. Personal beliefs should not be outlawed in the profession – that would make robots of us all – but they should be placed into a disciplined perspective. To run smoothly, the education system needs its employees to refrain sometimes from following their personal beliefs and to appeal to reason rather than conviction (Brighouse 2006). Any educational belief, or habit, that claims to place itself above reason should be automatically suspected – including this one.

As well as being willing to engage in their own research, reflective practitioners are competent in using and interpreting other people's. A salient dimension of school improvement is getting schools to be more confident in their use of their own and others' data, more self-critical, and more skilled in the use of research and evaluation tools. This should include finding relevant research literature in books and journals and on the internet (Campbell *et al.* 2004). A reflective practitioner, aware of research findings, has the capacity to augment a team's knowledge, understanding and values nexus as it approaches challenges (Whitaker 1997).

For teachers, taking research seriously is not only an academic and professional commitment but also a matter of personal openness to their own learning and transformation. Here we can note parallels between the learning expected of pupils and the openness to change expected of teachers. The deepest learning, in which pupils gain new knowledge, understanding or skills and are aware of the difference it makes to them, is sometimes referred to as metacognition. Payne (1996) argues that, for metacognition to be real, learners must change the way they think and learn, to become increasingly reflective and autonomous, and decreasingly inclined to rote learning and dependency. Importantly, this argument, and the process it promises, must apply as directly to teachers in their own change and learning as it does to their pupils.

To achieve this, teachers need to demonstrate much more than a knowledge of the subject matter in hand. Reflective teachers also aspire to a complex understanding of how they and the pupil know what they know (Hartmann 2001; Fox 2004), and of what else can be gleaned from this in terms of personal self-development.

Reflective teachers, whether engaging in research for themselves or reading and interpreting other people's, are guided by conventions on research design and methodology. This guidance helps them to choose between methods – for example, questionnaires, surveys, case histories, life history approaches, observation, structured or semi-structured interviews – and to judge the appropriateness of other researchers' choice of methods. This guidance also helps them to interpret data and to build analysis from raw information. Above all, they will wish to use such advice to ensure that their research is ethically defensible (Cohen *et al.* 2000).

Research can shed light on specific issues of teaching and learning, assessment, behaviour management, school leadership, diet, family background, equal opportunities and many others. It cannot deliver a holy grail of simple truth: education does not work in that way. The parameters that set a debate, and the factors that can change, are all too diverse and too fluid for there to be much hope of simple solutions (Yates 2004). For example, it may seem straightforward to 'prove' that changing the diet at school lunches from highly processed foods to fresh salads has a direct effect on learning and behaviour in the afternoons. One might begin by monitoring the amount of off-task behaviour before and after the change in diet. If the number of off-task incidents goes down, one might feel one has proved a causal link. But how can the school ensure that diet, and diet alone, is responsible for the change? Has this one factor been isolated and all other possible factors removed? Might the change have happened anyway for other reasons? Can family, housing, socio-economic well-being, curriculum subject, teacher, teaching assistant and even day of the week all be isolated so that there is certain knowledge of a causal link? This is just one example of how research can be more complex and interesting than it sometimes appears – and how rewarding it can be both for those who engage in it and for those who use it to develop policy.

- A reflective practitioner reaches out to, and works with, members of other children's service professions

Looked at from the child's point of view, there is a right to certain forms of protection and an entitlement to levels of service (Smith 2005), and these rights are more important than any profession which supports them. The distinctive ethos, language and culture of any profession – be it nursing, social care, child psychology, police work or teaching – can operate rather like a club, in other words it can unite those who belong and exclude those who do not. A professional club should not be more important, as a shaping force, than the needs of the child. Yet schools sometimes behave as if it were the other way round. The rules and restrictions placed around access of different professionals, the language difficulties, the incompatibilities of information systems, the misunderstandings of role and preoccupations with professional status are all obstructing progress towards a dynamic, coherent alliance of professionals working in support of children as whole people.

In local authorities where multi-agency work has been piloted in support of children's emotional needs, sometimes under the aegis of the Healthy Schools Initiative (Weare 2004), the best successes were achieved where local authorities pulled the work together to ensure that teachers and other professionals could navigate their way through an excessively complex landscape of initiatives, and where school leaders espoused and supported a project.

Individual teachers who wish to respond to this reflective challenge will therefore need to make alliances with fellow professionals in other branches of the children's services and also to engage in advocacy to ensure local authority and school leadership support for forms of collaboration.

The macro level: reflective practice in regions, nations, policy contexts

The pedagogue has long been insisting that everyone should recognise the profound importance of his art. . . . Pretensions such as those . . . as the critic of legislation, the adviser of Department, . . . must be checked and crushed without mercy.
Government report of 1879, quoted in Darling (1994: 110)

- A reflective practitioner responds maturely to new initiatives and political developments in education

We now come to a major difficulty with reflective practice, perhaps the greatest tension residing in the concept. It is that reflective practice and policy will often be in contention with each other in ways that do not facilitate, or may actually impede, the evolution of a coherent practice on the ground. All teachers in state schools are aware that, as public servants, they come under legal, regulatory, inspectorial or supervisory pressures to adopt initiatives, whether or not the new idea accords with their core values, their evaluative wisdom or their interpretation of research.

Political directions in education, and the specific policy developments that flow from the directions, are subject to changes of government or, to a lesser extent, changes of personnel or values in a continuing government. For instance, the previous Conservative government began a radical set of moves against aspects of child-centred learning:

> Over the last few decades the progress of primary pupils has been hampered by the influence of highly questionable dogmas which have led to excessively complex practices and devalued the place of subjects in the curriculum.
>
> (Alexander *et al.* 1992: 1)

In the wake of the above-quoted report, much theme-based learning and child-centred pedagogy was swept away and much critical experimentation by teachers was ended. Any research that suggested merit in the older, child-centred approach was dismissed as fashionable. New models of pedagogy were imposed through a punitive inspection system. These developments undermined teachers' sense of professional autonomy.

A second illustration of political direction is taken from the 1997 change from Conservative to a Labour government, which was followed by a more interventionist approach based on a determination to implement a model from the centre and to see results coming out as early as possible. Labour's tendency to impatience with education, and the public sector in general, could be explained by its desire to raise standards for the poorest:

> We need to act in a new way because fatalism . . . is the problem we face, the dead weight of low expectations, the crushing belief that things cannot get better.
>
> (Tony Blair, quoted in Hyman 2005: 354)

In order to take on what it saw as a fatalistic public sector bureaucracy that consistently let down the poorest, the Labour government was determined to move fast to impose good practice. While educational researchers might be hesitant in defining good practice because (as we have seen) educational research is never simplistic, policy makers were impatient with such hesitation, interpreting it as professional weakness or academic dilettantism. The problem, in the government's eyes, was not about identifying answers; the answers were, or should be, known already. The challenge was about delivering the known answers and getting the results:

> Why can't we do whatever it takes to get rid of bad headteachers? . . . Why can't we target the persistent criminals? . . . How do we drive our will down through the system, monitor progress and then achieve delivery? A stronger centre would give more direction and keep on the job until we are sure people are moving in the way we want.
>
> (Hyman 2005: 174)

Whether or not we sympathize with the aims and methods of the Labour government, we notice in their thinking a natural impatience with the teaching profession and other public sector professions which at times appeared slow to change and satisfied with mediocrity. What became known as the Primary National Strategy was born of this impatient desire to see rapid improvement. The 'handbags' of good practice entered every primary classroom in the land, encouraging uniformity. The use of this educational *force majeure* could be said to have changed the teaching profession into one less inclined to be reflective because it had been conditioned to be obedient.

It is believed by many teachers that reflective practice, as a value, is implicitly threatened by bureaucratic imposition (Whitaker 1997). This clash of values is not new; it is 'a tension that teachers have to live with' (Darling 1994).

In another dimension, that of school leadership, a similar clash is observed. The government-sponsored National College of School Leadership (NCSL) is criticized by some researchers for allowing its thinking to become captured and dominated by officially approved ideas (Thrupp and Wilmott 2003). The NCSL's detractors claim that instead of demonstrating a proper objectivity in its search for good practice, it limits its links to official organizations, acts as a conduit of Labour policy, campaigns for approved policies with missionary fervour and uses a closed system of thought.

The relationship between the state and the education profession needs to be understood more as a partnership (Smith 2005) if the concept of reflective practice is to be a reality. Many aspects of education have become more centrally controlled in recent years, to the detriment of the teacher's experience of partnership or autonomy. There must be consequences to this process, and for some educationalists they are severe:

> Constant and relentless attacks on professional integrity and performance, accompanied by massive changes ... have driven teachers into a crisis of confidence and effectiveness, lowering morale and increasing stress.
>
> (Whitaker 1997: 108–9)

Policy makers, if they wish to be truly effective, need to proceed more collegially, by taking the thinking of the profession into account, and also more thoughtfully, by engaging seriously with research. Some believe that policy makers are not drawing deeply enough, or carefully and subtly enough, on the considerable well of school effectiveness and improvement research (MacBeath and Mortimore 2001). There is evidence of an intention to change this in curriculum terms by ushering in an era of less prescription and encouraging localized diversity (QCA 2006a).

When policy making and research work with, instead of against, each other, results can be creative and liberating for teachers. Teachers are more free to reconceptualize aspects of their work, including curriculum design, in the light of contemporary priorities. For instance, when some Norwegian teachers were engaged in curriculum innovation, including new alliances between subjects, they were able to identify curriculum outcomes in terms of:

- personal meaning
- creativity
- work effectiveness

- enlightenment
- cooperation
- environmental responsibility.
        (Whitaker 1997)

Practical and reflective task

Level 1

This task is designed to open up one practical example of an interface between policy and reflective practice. It requires you to map the subjects of the present English national curriculum (plus RE) onto the above list of priorities identified by Norwegian teachers. In doing this, you will have opportunities to reflect on what each curriculum subject contributes to the priorities, and this will help you to see the subjects, and their comparative importance, in a new way.

Level 2

Undertake the task above in Level 1 with a colleague. Reflect on, and share with a colleague, which subjects service the six priorities well, and which ones struggle to be represented.

Level 3

Undertake the task above in Level 1 with your staff. Try the same mapping exercise using the five outcomes of *Every Child Matters* (listed below) and again reflect on the results.

- Be safe
- Keep healthy
- Enjoy and achieve
- Participate
- Economic well-being

A second example of reflective practice at the interface of policy and classroom implementation is in the development of child protection processes that run across professions to produce a sense of united and integrated policy as expressed in *Every Child Matters*. At the time of writing, *Every Child Matters* is a new policy development. For Key Stages 1 and 2, 67 per cent of schools think the initiative has had a positive effect, but just over 25 per cent think it is too early to tell (QCA 2006b: 8–9). This presents reflective practitioners with the challenge of absorbing, quite rapidly, the reasons for the policy development, and the implications for school structure and professional communication. Teachers find that they are afforded little room for debate about these priorities. In that sense, their autonomy is limited. However, teachers are given wide powers and responsibilities to implement the policy's priorities through the curriculum and pedagogy; in this realm, professional autonomy remains high. There is little point in a reflective practitioner expending time or effort on questioning the original set of values or procedures, but there is a great deal of point in a reflective practitioner carefully deliberating on how their implementation might meet the overall aims and rationale of the policy. In this sense, and when the focus is in the right area, policy and classroom practice can work together.

An example of where policy and research can fruitfully work with, rather than against each other, is in the field of implementing ICT in schools. The generating of some principles for use of ICT discovered that ICT is, in the main, best applied to give concrete representation to abstract ideas, rather than as an abstract alternative to tangible, real-life experience where this is appropriate and readily available. This has major implications for the kinds of subjects, and the cognitive processes, in which ICT is best applied. ICT alone does not provide the range of learning experiences that amounts to a broad and balanced curriculum. A variety of ICT-based and non-ICT-based resources should be employed in the effective delivery of a curriculum (Becta 2006: 5).

Reflective task

Level 1

Use the research insights gained on ICT (above) to generate a quick list of curriculum subjects and learning experiences in which ICT would be most usefully applied.

Level 2

Take one specific subject, say mathematics or PE, and break it down into learning experiences which do lend themselves to ICT and those which do not.

Level 3

Consider how this research–policy interaction could be used in your setting.

Conclusion: the grind and the grand

The reflective practitioner may be portrayed as someone who successfully combines the visionary and the practical in a changing, improving dynamic; someone who pays attention to the grand narrative of education, including its ideological direction, without stinting on the daily effort to make the vision happen where it counts, in classrooms and in pupils' lives.

> Real 'delivery' is about the grind, not just the grand. It's about the combination of often small things that build over time, through individual relationships and genuine expertise and hard work.
>
> (Hyman 2005: 385)

By combining vision and daily attention to detail in their own working context, teachers make their practice stronger and their work more meaningful. They will be more likely to succeed in terms of pupils' academic achievement and personal flourishing. The combination of vision and daily detail – of 'grand' and 'grind' – is not always easy, as we have seen. Indeed, certain features of the educational system, including the speed of political priorities and the processes of some accountability structures, may make the balance harder to keep. In the end, the reward for the teacher is the sense of integrity that arises from a professional life spent thinking about the work, rather than going through the motions of it. And the reward for the pupil is to have a teacher who has the humility and determination to keep learning and improving.

References

Alexander, R., Rose, J. and Woodhead, C. (1992) *Curriculum Organisation and Classroom Practice in Primary Schools*. London: DfES.

Arthur, J., Davidson, J. and Lewis, M. (2005) *Professional Values in Teaching and Learning*. London: Routledge.

Barrow, R. and Milburn, G. (1990) *A Critical Dictionary of Educational Concepts*. Hemel Hempstead: Harvester Wheatsheaf.

Becta (British Educational Communications and Technology Agency) (2006) *ICT Amenability and the BBC Digital Online Curriculum Service in England: Becta's Report to the DCMS*. London: DCMS.

Bolton, G. (2005) *Reflective Practice: Writing and Professional Development*. London: Sage.

Brighouse, H. (2006) *On Education: Thinking in Action*. London: Routledge.

Brookfield, S. (1996) *Becoming a Critically Reflective Teacher*. San Francisco: Jossey-Bass / Wiley.

Campbell, A., McNamara, O. and Gilroy, P. (2004) *Practitioner Research and Professional Development in Education*. London: Paul Chapman.

Cohen, L., Manion, L. and Morrison, K. (2000) *Research Methods in Education*. London: Routledge.

Darling, J. (1994) *Child-centred Education and its Critics*. London: Paul Chapman.

Fox, R. (2004) *Teaching and Learning*. Oxford: Blackwell.

Gipps, C., McCallum, B. and Hargreaves, E. (2000) *What Makes a Good Primary School Teacher? Expert Classroom Strategies*. London: Routledge.

Handy, C. (1995) *The Empty Raincoat: Making Sense of the Future*. London: Arrow.

Hartman, H. (ed.) (2001) *Metacognition in Learning and Instruction: Theory, Research and Practice*. Norwell, MA: Kluwer Academic Publishers.

Hyman, P. (2005) *One Out of Ten: From Downing Street Vision to Classroom Reality*. London: Vintage.

MacBeath, J. and Mortimore, P. (2001) *Improving School Effectiveness*. Buckingham: Open University Press.

Matthews, B. (2005) *Engaging Education: Developing Emotional Literacy, Equity and Co-education*. Maidenhead: Open University Press.

Middlewood, D. and Cardno, C. (2001) *Managing Teacher Appraisal and Performance*. London: RoutledgeFalmer.

Payne, M. (1996) *Self-talk for Students and Teachers: Metacognitive Strategies for Personal and Classroom Use*. Boston, MA: Allyn & Bacon.